THE
DAN BROWN
ENIGMA

THE
DAN BROWN
ENIGMA

THE BIOGRAPHY OF THE WORLD'S
GREATEST THRILLER WRITER

GRAHAM A. THOMAS

JB

JOHN BLAKE

Published by John Blake Publishing Ltd,
3 Bramber Court, 2 Bramber Road,
London W14 9PB, England

www.johnblakepublishing.co.uk

www.facebook.com/Johnblakepub   facebook

twitter.com/johnblakepub   twitter

First published in hardback in 2011

ISBN: 978 1 84358 302 8

British Library Cataloguing-in-Publication Data:

A catalogue record for this book is available from the British Library.

Design by www.envydesign.co.uk

Printed in Great Britain by CPI Mackays, Chatham, ME5 8TD

1 3 5 7 9 10 8 6 4 2

Papers used by John Blake Publishing are natural, recyclable products made from
wood grown in sustainable forests. The manufacturing processes conform to the
environmental regulations of the country of origin.

Every attempt has been made to contact the relevant copyright-holders, but some were
unobtainable. We would be grateful if the appropriate people could contact us.

To my family and friends and especially my colleague Craig Cabell for giving me the support to write this book

ACKNOWLEDGEMENTS

I'd like to thank my good friend and colleague, Craig Cabell, who provided the introduction for this book but more importantly the inspiration to write it.

I'd also like to thank all the people who take the time to write reviews on the various book websites across the internet. Their views and opinions have been instrumental in shaping this look at Dan Brown.

And I'd like to thank Dan Brown for writing the great novels that have had such an impact on our culture.

CONTENTS

AUTHOR'S NOTE

Thrillers are part of the modern psyche. The genre is a relatively new one dating back to 1915 with the publication of John Buchan's *The Thirty-Nine Steps*. The story has all the essential elements of a modern thriller: an ordinary man thrown into an extraordinary situation full of tension, danger and intrigue. The hero overcomes physical danger, fear and many other obstacles in his path as he races to complete his quest and unravel the mystery that surrounds him.

Dan Brown's books have these same elements, which is what drew me into his stories. My thriller hero has always been Alistair MacLean, who wrote such masterpieces as *Night Without End, Fear is the Key* and *When Eight Bells Toll*. When I first came to Brown I didn't want to read him, but his blend of fact and fiction in a modern style at rocket pace caught my attention.

What intrigued me was his ability to blur the boundaries so well that the reader ends up believing everything on the page. It is how he takes myths that are buried deep in our collective subconscious and explodes it onto his pages that I find so interesting.

Everyone was going crazy about *The Da Vinci Code* so I steadfastly refused to pick up the book. But one day I did and never looked back. The more I started researching this book, the more involved I became in Brown and his characters, plots and ideas.

Whether the information Brown uses in his books is correct or not is not as important as the man's story. The facts he uses can be debated time and time again and they have been. There are dozens of books claiming to decode the mysteries in Brown's books. Are these mysteries and strange facts true? Who knows? But that's not the point. Brown is a master storyteller who has managed to tap into our collective psyche, draw us in and blend it all together with staggering effect.

I wanted to write this book to get to grips with the effect that his books have had on organisations like the Catholic Church and the Freemasons. That effect has been profound. The Church has gone to great lengths to refute everything that Brown claimed was a fact in *The Da Vinci Code*. Why did they do this?

It is the writer's choice to wind fact into his fiction and in some cases to dress up fiction as fact to push the story forwards. If Brown hadn't put a Fact page at the very beginning of *The Da Vinci Code*, it's likely there would have been no outcry, no debate, as there has been since its publication.

The Dan Brown Enigma tries to unlock Brown's methods of creating his mysteries, how he builds intricate puzzles while weaving in ancient texts, myths and legends into the stories. In a way he reminds me of Number Six from the cult Sixties TV series *The Prisoner*. We never really know who he is but we are hooked by his quest to escape the village and above all to find out who is really behind it.

Brown's quest to find information and research that forms the basis of his novels is just as addictive. How does he do it? Why does he do it? Who is he?

Read on and enjoy the ride.

'We want information.'
'You won't get it.'
'By hook or by crook, we will.'

Graham A. Thomas
Warminster, March 2011

A ROBERT LANGDON OMNIBUS

DAN BROWN

ANGELS AND DEMONS

THE INTERNATIONAL BESTSELLERS

THE DA VINCI CODE

Only
£12.99

THE NUMBER ONE *NEW YORK TIMES* BESTSELLER

DAN BROWN

THE DA VINCI CODE

'Enthralling and absorbing ...
A great, riveting read. I loved this book.'
HARLAN COBEN

Bestselling author of *THE DA VINCI CODE*

DAN BROWN

The Lost SYMBOL

Signed by
the Author
at Waterstone's

The Lost SYMBOL

DAN BROWN

www.rbooks.co.uk

WORKS OF FICTION

It was a chilly, dry morning in 2009 that I found myself at Waterstone's the booksellers in London's Piccadilly to attend the official UK launch of Dan Brown's *The Lost Symbol*.

Although the great man wasn't there, there was still a strong media presence as devoted fans queued to get their hands on one of only 150 signed, book-plated copies of the first edition UK hardback. Each special copy had a colour flaming key pictorial plate with bold black signature – gold dust to the true fan and restricted to one copy per person.

I spoke to *The Times* and did some radio sound bites, answering such questions as: why is Dan Brown so popular? What sort of person reads Dan Brown? Do you think the new novel will live up to the notoriety of *The Da Vinci Code*?

I answered the questions while the fans looked on expectantly. Some smiled; others nodded their heads in staunch seriousness. At least they agreed with me, but the thing I learned from this experience was that Brown fans took his work very seriously. They believed in the threat of a *Digital Fortress* code, they believed in the Holy Blood line, they believed in ancient societies enduring from the Dark Ages to the present day.

Did I?

There is a difference between what one wishes for and what one suspects is true. And that's where – for me and many Brown fans – Dan Brown exists. He is a storyteller of great power and works on the minds of enquiring people with his fervent imagination. When all is said and done, Dan Brown writes stories. There may be some hard facts there but there will also be some supposition, so one doesn't really know what is the fact and what is the fiction. The resulting 'faction' is not a new concept. The creator of such work in modern times is Frederick Forsyth, with such key books as *The Day of the Jackal* and *The Fourth Protocol*.

When I left Piccadilly – still before most commuters' breakfasts – I glanced at the queue of people eager to purchase their special copy of Dan Brown's latest novel. For them, the latest book didn't have to be *The Da Vinci Code*. It did, however, have to have Robert Langdon in it, and that's where Dan Brown will endure: through his most popular character. He had waited long enough for the hype of *The Da Vinci Code* to calm down before releasing the next Langdon book. The book wouldn't be as controversial, but then Brown didn't set out to make *The Da Vinci Code* controversial in the first place. The media did that. He simply told his intricate chase novel and thrilled his audience.

With *The Lost Symbol* it was the Freemasons who were now under scrutiny, not the Catholic Church; but unlike the Catholic Church, the Masons didn't respond negatively to the book, so there was no media circus and over-analysis of the text.

In short, Brown had created a new type of faction, which initially shocked certain people but as Tony Robinson found with his excellent programmes about *The Da Vinci Code* and *The Lost Symbol*, there's little to get uptight about – just enjoy the story!

This book continues to break down the mystery surrounding Dan Brown and his works. It outlines the writer's life and works and becomes an essential companion to the half-dozen books by the American author. It has not been released during the hype of *The Da Vinci Code* nor on the back of the *The Lost Symbol*. It sits in a space where we can soberly analyse the life and work of one of the world's most successful writers, and I for one applaud its companionship.

Craig Cabell
London, March 2010

PART ONE

THE EARLY YEARS

CHAPTER ONE

JUST THE FACTS

Failure was not an option. For the longest time he stared at the blank screen in front of him; around him lay the books and papers he was using for his research. He and his wife had been through them all. Now was the moment of truth: the time to start writing.

He'd written three books so far, all well received but flops at the booksellers. Yet in his heart and his soul he knew they were good. This was what he was meant to do, wasn't it? He'd even had his eureka moment which had showed him writing was his true calling. But they hadn't sold. His music career in L.A. hadn't worked out either, so now his fourth novel just had to work. The pressure was on. If this book didn't sell then he'd be back teaching again. He knew he couldn't face that.

He felt the pressure keenly and he felt the failure deeply as well. It was now or never. He and his wife had travelled to Europe twice and investigated the Louvre museum in Paris as thoroughly as they could. He'd read countless books on religion and the Sacred Feminine. He stared at the keys knowing that they would not move by themselves. He looked at the headset that he used for dictating and which freed him to move around his little cottage. Now was not the time for that technology. Now he had to start typing.

The cursor blinked. He touched a key on the keyboard and the letter appeared on the screen. What was his big idea for this book? Though it wasn't yet completely clear he knew it would come to him. This one just had to work.

And indeed it did. The book in question was *The Da Vinci Code* and the man behind it was Daniel Gerhard Brown – Dan Brown.

Brown has said he is a very private person, so to know the man we need to look at how he writes, because there must be something special about a man who has probably sold more books than any other writer.

How does he do it? Is it the fact that he hangs upside down in his anti-gravity boots two or three times a day? 'You're hanging upside down and you're seeing the world through a different lens and I think you think differently,' Brown said. 'I may be crazy but I've solved a bunch of good problems upside down.'

To spend as much time as Brown does on researching his books – *The Lost Symbol* took six years – he must have an abiding passion in what he is researching. 'If you are researching secret societies, abstruse science or all things ancient, it could take a lot of extra time,' Brown remarked. 'All things arcane interest me.'

But before we delve deeper let's look at some basic facts about the man. He was born on 22 June 1964, in Exeter, New Hampshire in the United States. He is the eldest of three children and his father, Richard G. Brown, taught mathematics until he retired in 1982. Both his mother and father are musicians and singers, having served as church choirmasters and his mother as a church organist in the Episcopalian faith in which he grew up.

As a child, his home life was filled with puzzles, mysteries and secrets where codes and ciphers, created by his parents, were used to set up intricate challenges. As a boy he would spend many happy hours working out anagrams and completing difficult crossword puzzles. On family holidays he and his two younger siblings would go on treasure hunts devised by his father. At Christmas, instead of finding gifts under the tree, the children would take part in a treasure hunt for gifts throughout the house and sometimes through the town. Indeed, Chapter 23 of *The Da Vinci Code* was inspired by one of these childhood treasure hunts.

Brown's high school years were spent at Phillips Exeter Academy, which gave him a real grounding for his life. To show how much this school meant to him, Brown made his main character, Robert Langdon, a graduate of Phillips Exeter.

After high school Brown went to Amherst College, where he studied art history and writing among other subjects. Here he was a student of visiting novelist Alan Lelchuk, sang in the Amherst Glee Club and was a member of the Psi Upsilon fraternity. In 1985 he attended the University of Seville in Spain, where he was enrolled as an art history student. The following year he graduated from Amherst.

Once he'd left college Brown attempted a career in music. Using synthesisers he first recorded and produced a children's cassette, *SynthAnimals,* that featured synthesised animal noises. It sold a few hundred copies.

Deciding to move on to the adult market, he formed his own record company and produced his first album, *Perspective*, but that too sold only a few hundred copies. Undaunted, Brown moved to Los Angeles in 1987 to pursue a career in music. His goal was to be a singer-songwriter and he taught classes at Beverly Hills Preparatory School to support himself while he did so.

His life changed when he joined the National Academy of Songwriters. He attended many different events held by the Academy and at one of them he met Blythe Newlon. Twelve years older than Brown, she was the Director of Artist Development for the Academy at the time.

The two quickly formed a bond and she helped to promote Brown's musical projects. Although it was not officially part of her job, she set up promotional events, wrote and sent out press releases and put him in contact with key people who could help him in his musical career. While this was going on the pair formed a relationship they kept quiet from their friends and associates. It only came to light when Brown moved back to New Hampshire and Blythe went with him.

The aspiring singer-songwriter released his first CD, *Dan Brown,* in 1993 and followed that up with *Angels & Demons* the following year. Now his wife, Blythe was thanked in the liner notes for being his co-producer, co-writer 'significant other and therapist'.

Back home in New Hampshire, Brown took up teaching English at his alma mater, Phillips Exeter, and also taught Spanish at Lincoln Akerman School to sixth, seventh and eighth graders.

But all this time Dan Brown had been writing. 'In school I read all the classics through high school and university, and as a kid it was the Hardy Boys, but I never read any adult thrillers,' he says. 'I assumed adults read classics. But when I went on holiday to Tahiti I found a copy of Sydney Sheldon's *Doomsday Conspiracy* and thought, "Wow, this is fast-paced and fun and interesting, and maybe I can do something like that.'"

Thus inspired, Brown began work on *Digital Fortress,* a thriller set in Spain and Maryland. The book was published in 1998 but before that he and his wife co-wrote the humour book *187 Men to Avoid: A Guide for the Romantically Frustrated Woman.* It was under the pseudonym Danielle Brown but the copyright is attributed to Dan Brown.

In 1996 Brown gave up teaching to become a full-time writer. He wrote two more thrillers, *Deception Point* and *Angels & Demons,* before hitting the big time with *The Da Vinci Code.*

These are the basic facts. Now let's dig a little deeper.

CHAPTER TWO

WHO IS DAN BROWN?

Some of us find our miracles in the pages of Holy Scripture and some of us find our miracles in the pages of Scientific American.

DAN BROWN

Dan Brown is an enigma, a very private man. Little is known about him and what makes him tick, other than what he himself has revealed. He is fascinated by puzzles, treasure hunts and all things arcane, which is apt since piecing together the facts of his life is like going on a treasure hunt for clues that reveal a little bit more about him.

Brown's father, Richard G. Brown, taught mathematics at Phillips Exeter Academy and wrote a bestselling series of textbooks – the first was entitled *Advanced Mathematics: Precalculus with Discrete Mathematics and Data Analysis*, which is still considered an important tool for teaching advanced mathematics. Indeed, he was honoured by President George H. W. Bush in 1989 when he received a Presidential Award for Excellence in Science and Mathematics Teaching.

Both Brown's parents were creative. Both have been church choirmasters and members of a Symphony Chorus that toured the US and Europe. His mother, Connie, has a master's degree in sacred music and was a professional church organist, while his father sings and acts in musical theatre. 'This love of music, like many things my parents loved, was inherited by me. When I was at Amherst I was very interested in music composition and creative writing. I also loved languages.'

The Brown family lived on campus and young Dan – the eldest of three children, with brother Gregory and sister Valerie – grew up in an atmosphere of academia. Brown, however, had a very interesting childhood because he did not spend his time staring at the TV. The family didn't have one. 'I had a dog and we lived up in the White Mountains in the summer and I had no friends up there and I would go and play hide-and-seek with my dog and probably had some imaginary friends. They have since left and I spend my life now with a lot of other imaginary friends.'[1]

His life was also filled with secrets, puzzles and treasure hunts. Codes and ciphers were the order of the day as they tied into the mathematics, music and languages that were part of the work of his parents. He would spend hours working on crosswords or trying to devise anagrams. On holidays, the three children would go on treasure hunts created by their father to keep them occupied. As already stated, at Christmas, rather than just ripping open their presents in the usual way, the Brown kids would be foraging throughout the house and outside, following treasure maps drawn up by their father to find out where their gifts were hidden. The clues would include limericks or mathematical puzzles leading the kids to the next clue. 'And so, for me, at a young age, treasure hunts were always exciting,' Brown said.

Clearly this was something that has stayed with him,

because at their core each of his novels is a treasure hunt: the protagonist is following a series of clues to figure out the mystery and save the day.

Writing came early to Brown. He was just five years old when he wrote his first book, *The Giraffe, The Pig and the Pants On Fire*. 'I dictated it to my mum and I did all the illustrations,' he recalled.

When Brown was nine years old he went to Washington D.C. with his parents and was fascinated by its museums. What he saw there also stuck with him and as he grew up his interest in art and architecture also grew. This fascination for the country's capital would later show itself in the backdrop for *The Lost Symbol*.

Science and religion were bedfellows in the Brown household and as he grew up young Dan was torn between the two. 'I was lost from day one,' he said. 'Where science offered exciting proofs of its claims, religion was a lot more demanding, constantly wanting me to accept everything on faith. Faith takes a fair amount of effort, especially for a young child in an imperfect world. So as a boy I graduated towards the solid foundations of science but the further I progressed, the mushier the ground started to get.'

Brown, who was raised Episcopalian, was very religious as a child but around the ninth grade he began to look beyond religion, studying astronomy, cosmology and the origins of the universe. When he tackled a church minister about the contradiction between science saying there was an explosion known as the Big Bang and the Bible saying God made the earth in seven days, and asked which was right, the response was a letdown: 'Nice boys don't ask that question.' That was the point when a light bulb went on in Brown's head and he decided the Bible was not logical. He gravitated away from religion to science, which made far more sense to him. [2]

Except it didn't. The more he studied science, the more he saw that: 'Physics becomes metaphysics and numbers become imaginary numbers. You start to say, "Oh, there is an order and a spiritual aspect to science."'[3] This interplay fascinated Brown and drew him to Leonardo da Vinci, a man who also believed that science and religion complemented each other. It was an interest that would eventually play a big part in *The Da Vinci Code*.

As a child the Brown family lived on the campus of Phillips Exeter Academy but by the time Brown attended the school there the family was living off campus on Nelson Drive in Exeter and Brown was a day student studying English and Spanish among other things. 'While at Phillips Exeter and [later] Amherst College, I pursued advanced writing courses and was published in school literary magazines,' he explained. 'At Exeter, I chose creative writing as my senior project. At Amherst, I applied for and was accepted to a special writing course with visiting novelist Alan Lelchuk.'

Brown also managed to get on to two exchange programmes, both for Spain. The first time was a two-month world tour with the Amherst College Glee Club in the summer of 1983 that brought him face to face with some of the great architecture and cultures of Europe. He fell in love with Spain when he first arrived and managed to get back again a few years later. After graduating from Amherst College, he decided that Spain was the place he wanted to be, so in 1987 he left New Hampshire for the sunny climes of Seville, where he spent the summer studying an art history course at that city's university.[4]

'This art course covered the entire history of World Art, from the Egyptians to Jackson Pollock,' Brown recalled. 'The professor's slide presentations included images ranging from the pyramids, religious icons, renaissance painting and sculpture, all the way through to the pop artists of modem times.'

These studies opened Brown's eyes to the idea of art as communication between the artist and the beholder, and he discovered a new language of symbols and metaphor. He could suddenly see the hidden meanings in Picasso's Guernica and its violent images have stayed with him ever since. 'The course covered many other works that resonated with me as a young man, including the horror of Goya's *Saturn Devouring His Son* and the bizarre anamorphic sexual nightmares of Bosch's *Garden of Earthly Delights*.'[5]

Brown discovered, too, that there were dark qualities to Da Vinci's *The Last Supper,* which inspired him to find out about that painting and Da Vinci himself. He recalled: 'I remember the professor pointing out things I hadn't seen before, including a disembodied hand clutching a dagger and a disciple making a threatening gesture across the throat of another.'

It was not just the art course that influenced Brown greatly but the country of Spain as well. Years after taking that course, the architecture and streets of Spain became the backdrop for much of the action in his first novel, *Digital Fortress.*

CHAPTER THREE

ROCK MUSICIAN

Over the course of the ten years after college, I wrote and produced four albums of original music. I met my wife, Blythe, through the National Academy of Songwriters, where she was the Director of Artist Development. Blythe, like me, loved art. She also was a very talented painter. Despite the Academy's best efforts to promote me, my music career never really took off.

DAN BROWN

Although Brown had been writing since he was a child, it was music that beckoned when he graduated from Amherst College in May 1986. He'd been taking piano lessons since he was 10 and now he wanted a shot at writing music. 'I had two loves,' he said, 'writing fiction and writing music.'

Singing with the Amherst College Glee Club enabled him to sign up for a world tour which took a few months and covered more than a dozen countries. 'I would never have seen those countries otherwise,' he said. 'It was amazing.' Indeed, this exposure to new cultures was the most important part of the trip for him.

Brown doesn't do anything by halves. When he graduated

from Amherst College he decided to make his mark on the world of pop music, and stayed in Exeter to teach himself the basics of composing and recording music. He could have gone totally unprepared to the West Coast with a dream, as many people do. But he didn't. His education had prepared him to be confident enough to try all kinds of things and to be a well-rounded individual who could be competent at almost anything. So Brown purchased some recording gear, bought a synthesiser and set out to become a singer-songwriter.

He toiled away for several months, learning everything he could about recording and all things related to making electronic music. Experimenting with the synthesiser, he discovered that if he played the keyboard using a certain combination of settings, he could make a noise that sounded like a frog croaking. Using this idea, he composed a piece that sounded like a whole pond filled with frogs and called it 'Happy Frogs'. The floodgates had opened and he began experimenting with other animal sounds, coming up with such pieces as 'Suzuki Elephants', 'Swans in the Mist' and 'Rats'. From this he created an entire cassette for children called *SynthAnimals*. [6]

Through dogged determination Brown went round to all the local music and record shops in Exeter and got them to take copies of his work. Some of the local papers did short pieces on it but sales were in the low hundreds.

Yet for Brown this was a success. It was a good exercise in recording, producing and distributing his own material. Now it was time to step up to the plate and make music for adults. Using a backup band of two of his friends who played keyboards, guitar and bass, as well as adding backing vocals, he recorded his first album, *Perspective*, and released it via his own record company, Dalliance, in 1990.

Although the CD sold only a few hundred copies locally, Brown was happy with the result. He categorised it as being Top 40 but with a twist: the music was lyrical and the songs tried to tell a story. *Perspective* was good enough to show the producers and distributors in Hollywood what he could do.

So in the spring of 1991, like so many aspiring musicians over the years, Brown moved to L.A. He knew his music was good but it needed to be improved; he also knew that meeting people who could kick-start his career was even more important.

Once in Hollywood, he took an apartment at the Franklin Regency, a low-rent apartment complex 'whose hallways overflowed with unusual individuals – aspiring rock stars, male models, drama queens and stand-up comics.' Some of these characters would later be found in his first published novel. [7]

Brown knew he couldn't just walk in the door and expect a million-selling album – he had to work hard at it. He also had to make ends meet while he spent every available moment on his music, so he got a job teaching Spanish at the Beverly Hills Preparatory School. Juggling his day job and his evening/weekend job of working on music would become a routine that lasted for several years.

Once he was settled in, Brown contacted an organisation that distributed material from independent artists through a catalogue that went nationwide. This organisation was called the Creative Musicians Coalition and Brown sent in a copy of *SynthAnimals* to see what reaction it might get. To his surprise the owner, Ron Wallace, put it into the catalogue.

While this was a positive step, Brown knew it was just a tiny one on a very large ladder. He had to get his foot in the door of the influential crowd and then behave as if he was a bona fide member of it. This was one of the many lessons he'd learned in his private-school education: to believe in himself enough to fit into any environment and thrive by making friends and building business relationships. He felt that once he was in that crowd, the natural instinct of the established members to protect or nurture a new person would kick in and he would be accepted.

So he looked around and joined the National Academy of Songwriters, that boasted famous members such as Prince and Billy Joel. The Academy's purpose was teaching songwriters the ins and outs of the music business as well as providing guidance in musical technique. Keen to get on, Brown attended many courses and workshops and spent much of his time at the Academy as he felt increasingly comfortable there. He struck up friendships with some of the students and the staff, one of whom was Blythe Newlon.

In her book *The Man Behind the Da Vinci Code: An Unauthorized Biography*, Lisa Rogak tells us that as Director of Artistic Development at the Academy, it was Blythe's job to provide him with advice and guidance on how the business worked. Blythe helped him hone his musical style and also showed him the technology involved in making modern soft rock music, which was his style. [8]

Suddenly, however, Blythe stepped outside of her day-to-day role and took Brown on as his manager, something she had not done with any of the other songwriters who were members. The staff at the Academy were supposed to be impartial and Blythe's direct involvement on Brown's career was frowned on by her colleagues, but that didn't stop her.

As Brown's manager, she began arranging bookings as well as setting up meetings and auditions with the great and the good of the music industry.

The first thing she did for her new protégé was book him into the Acoustic Underground, the talent showcase run by the Academy at the club At My Place in Santa Monica (and later at The Troubadour in West Hollywood). Most people had to audition for this, but Brown didn't, as Blythe was his manager and co-producer of the event.

Blythe's co-producer was Paul Zollo, who also hosted the event. The editor of the Academy's magazine *SongTalk*, which was published and distributed to the membership, he was also the author of two books, *Conversations with Tom Petty* and *Songwriters on Songwriting*. The latter was a compilation of interviews that had originally appeared in *SongTalk* and had received a lot of attention from the press when it was published in 1991. Zollo worked in the office next to Blythe and was used to seeing Brown come and go. When Zollo came in to tell people about the press coverage for *Songwriters on Songwriting*, Brown's ears pricked up. So that was it. Now he understood that getting a lot of positive attention in the press was key to getting ahead in the music business.

With Blythe working hard to get his career off the ground, Brown soon got a chance to record his second CD, using some of the best musicians in Hollywood. Blythe paired him with one of Hollywood's top producers, Barry Fasman, who had won the British Record Producer of the Year back in 1982. Fasman did not come cheap, nor did the studio musicians hired to back Blythe's friend. [9]

Brown did everything he could to raise the money. According to Rogak, he went into 'overdrive' to ensure he could meet the bills needed to get the CD done and distributed. He begged and borrowed from everyone he knew, working as many hours as he could tutoring students outside of his teaching.

But Ron Wallace thought the Academy were supporting Brown directly and couldn't understand why they would when they represented so many other members. 'Why would they put the money into him?' Wallace wondered. 'I guessed that maybe somewhere, sometime, there was a sugar daddy involved.' Instead it was Brown working like a man possessed that raised the cash for the CD. [10]

Throughout this period Blythe had become more to Brown than a friend who was helping him with his musical career. Love had found its way into their hearts and they were a couple, but they kept their passion for each other as quiet as they could. Blythe held an important position at the Academy and as she was guiding Brown's musical career, she could have been open to accusations of misuse of her influence and position.

Then there was the age difference. She is 12 years older than Brown and even today, when an older woman gets involved with a much younger man, it doesn't seem right to many people. When Dan and Blythe got together in the early 1990s there were many disapproving stares, so this could have been their main concern. [11]

As the final mix and mastering of the album took place Blythe fired out press releases to all the magazines and newspapers interested in new talent. She set up interviews with reporters, got articles in the trade press and did her best to get him an agent. 'Brown was being moulded and promoted as a brainy but sensitive young singer who had a bit of the tortured soul about him.' [12]

In due course the CD, *Dan Brown*, was released on his own label, DGB Music. In a press release to the trade Blythe wrote that the National Academy for Songwriters had decided to take a hands-on approach to managing Brown's career. One has to wonder how much of the Academy was actually involved in this production, or if this was just Blythe working through the Academy.

Dan Brown has elements of smooth dinner jazz, lush arrangements and professional instrumentation. The songs are full of intelligent lyrics and romantic and spiritual imagery. Already he was experimenting with themes that would appear in his novels. 'Birth of a King', for example, could be Brown's first attempts at writing something around the search for the Holy Grail. The lyrics are full of mystical symbolism and talk about a traveller arriving from a distant land to give the listener power and majesty.

Despite all this effort the album didn't sell. The main reason, according to Rogak, was because Brown didn't want to be up on stage. He was content to be making the music but didn't want to perform for people. He didn't want to be in an industry where his image had to be created or moulded so he could be classified and indexed in a specific genre. 'The problem was,' Rogak states, 'that his music was pop, and it put him in a position where he had to be a Barry Manilow in order for his music to be heard.'

Could it be that he resented people less intelligent or educated than he was telling him how he should behave and look, and what was best for his music career?

Before the CD was out, Brown was already working on the next one but he was growing tired of Hollywood. His educational background and the values instilled in him by Phillips Exeter and his parents meant he behaved differently than most people trying to make it big in the music industry. He wore a shirt, tie and jacket to meetings with producers and agents, making him stand out like a sore thumb. Most of the successful people he needed to talk to were self-made and many had dropped out of high school. Long hair, jeans, drugs, alcohol abuse, poor education – they were the embodiment of everything that Phillips Exeter was not. The only way for him to deal with such a gulf was to spend as much time teaching as he could. 'With all the Hollywood hype, classrooms have a way of keeping you grounded in reality,' Brown said. 'Everything I've accomplished in my life I owe to my education.' [13]

But he did one thing in Hollywood – he learned to speak the language of the music business by making everything positive and by exaggerating or spinning the various realities to suit the occasion. This talent for exaggeration and for putting his own unique interpretation on facts would become a trademark of his fiction. Perhaps the core of the mystery of Brown's writing can be seen in a statement by Lisa Rogak: 'His propensity for stretching the facts while steadfastly maintaining he spoke nothing but the truth would later provide significant fuel for his most rabid critics.'

In 1993 Brown suddenly announced to his friends that he would be moving back to New Hampshire because he'd secured a publishing deal in New York and he'd be going back for a year to write. In truth, the deal was for a very small humour book, but Brown headed back to Exeter. Once there, he began teaching English and creative writing to students at Phillips Exeter Academy, supplementing his income by teaching Spanish to sixth, seventh and eighth grade pupils at the Lincoln Akerman School, a bicycle ride away in Hampton Falls. Blythe went with him. Four years later, at Pea Porridge Pond near Conway, New Hampshire, the couple were married.

CHAPTER FOUR

ONE DOOR CLOSES, ANOTHER OPENS

And so Brown came full circle. The couple arrived back in Exeter where Brown immediately felt at home. His memories of growing up here were good ones. He was home again in the bosom of his family and friends.

Living in the Franklin in Hollywood, Brown had been exposed to many different characters right on his doorstep, from rock stars who still hadn't made it to stand-up comics and everything in between. These were people he would never have met back home in the conservative society of Exeter. From this natural source of material Brown decided to put together a list of some of the most bizarre people he'd seen.

This manuscript was called *187 Men to Avoid: A Guide for the Romantically Frustrated Woman*, and included such perceptive observations to steer clear of as 'men with their initials shaved into their sideburns' and 'men who consider Cream of Wheat a home-cooked meal'. 'Blythe thought the list was hilarious,' Brown said. 'She quickly wrote to several literary agents and included a portion of the list. To my astonishment, I immediately got calls from a number of agents, including George Wieser, who told me he had already spoken to Putnam Books and could get me $12,500 for the manuscript.' [14]

This new success surprised Brown. He'd been plugging away at the music with little success and now, suddenly, here was what he'd been looking for. The book was written by Brown but under a female pseudonym, Danielle Brown – the author profile on the jacket sleeve reads, 'Danielle Brown currently lives in New England: teaching school, writing books, and avoiding men' – but the copyright is listed as Dan Brown's.

As with Brown's music it was Blythe who made all the moves to get it sold. Using the skills she'd honed at the National Academy for Songwriters, she fired off the necessary notices and letters, only this time the letters were going to book publishers. [15]

Lisa Rogak states that it was Elizabeth Beier who picked up *187 Men to Avoid* for Berkley Publishing Group. It was published in 1995 but sold only a few thousand copies, despite the press releases sent out by the publishers. Brown put it down to experience and looked forward to his next publishing venture. The book then went out of print.

But before the book's publication Brown had a eureka moment – one that would set his life on the path to becoming the bestselling thriller writer of all time. Shortly before returning to New Hampshire in April 1993, he and Blythe had gone on holiday to Tahiti. Mooching around on the beach, Brown found a tattered copy of Sidney Sheldon's *Doomsday Conspiracy*. It was the first time he'd read any commercial fiction since reading the Hardy Boys (children's adventure books) as a child. 'Up until this point, almost all of my reading had been dictated by my schooling (primarily classics like Faulkner, Steinbeck, Dostoyevsky, Shakespeare, etc.),' he said. 'The Sheldon book was unlike anything I'd read as an adult. It held my attention, kept me turning pages, and reminded me how much fun it could be to read.'

Brown was inspired by its simple prose and efficient storyline. This was very different from the complicated and intense novels he'd read throughout his schooling. 'I read the first page... and then the next... and then the next. Several hours later, I finished the book and thought, "Hey, I can do that." [16] I began to suspect that maybe I could write a thriller of this type one day.' And so the seed was planted.

Around the time that *187 Men to Avoid* was published, Brown had lunch with his new literary agent, George Wieser, who had come across an article Brown had written for the school magazine at Phillips Exeter. It was entitled *Goodness and Knowledge on the Sunset Strip* and was about what it was like for Brown, describing himself as a preppie-geeky-nerdy kid, to live in the heart of the music industry, a fish completely out of water. 'I wrote it just for kicks,' he recalled, 'and I got a call from a literary agent in New York.' Wieser told Brown he thought his writing style was unique and that he loved his powerful use of observation. 'I've been in the business a long time and I know a novelist when I see one,' Wieser had told Brown. The budding novelist explained: 'We talked about an hour, and I told him stories. He said, "You should write a novel." I basically said, "I can't imagine what I would ever write about." This guy looked across the table and said, "You're a storyteller. I can tell. There will come a day when you know what you want to write about, and then you will write a novel." I sort of said, "OK, sure, nice to meet you... crazy old man." And went home.' [17]

Brown had not yet entirely given up music. Since his

return to New Hampshire in 1993 he had been working on the second CD but this time he had none of the professional people who had been part of his debut album to help him. He was, essentially, on his own.

The new CD, *Angels & Demons,* was in stark contrast to his debut. It was almost entirely Brown himself, using synthesisers with friends backing him up on a variety of different instruments to fill out the sound. The only musical credit was Brown himself as writer, producer and arranger. Acknowledgements went to John Langdon, Macintosh Computers and a software company called Digidesign that produces ProTools, an advanced music sequencing software. Blythe, who added backing vocals, got a double acknowledgement.

On the first album the majority of songs had been love songs. On *Angels & Demons* the love songs were gone. Instead, the darker feel to the album reflected his disillusionment with Hollywood and the music industry.

Religious imagery runs through many of the songs on the album, as on 'All I Believe'. The title track, especially, shows the struggle Brown had been having with religion and science and which would surface in his books. The lyrics reflect his difficulties reconciling these two disciplines, as well as good and evil, because in the song he is unable to tell the difference between angels and demons.

The liner notes also again credited his wife for her involvement. But perhaps more of note is the album's artwork, an ambigram by artist John Langdon, which he later used for the novel *Angels & Demons*. Ambigrams are words that, written in a certain graphic way, can be read upside down or right way up. Langdon's gothic style had caught Brown's attention so he decided to use it for the cover.

The new CD was released in 1995. It was to be his last. Its sales were not as high as Brown had hoped, but Lisa Rogak states in her book that Brown maintains one of the tracks from this was performed at the 1996 Olympics. Although the track, called 'Peace in Our Time', doesn't appear anywhere on the official Olympic collection of songs, there were many that were performed at Olympics events and ceremonies that were never officially recorded, so there is no reason to assume that Brown was not telling the truth. It may well be that his track was performed at a smaller event or two away from the cameras and crowds.

But whichever way it was considered, Dan Brown's music career was over. As he continued teaching, he turned his efforts now solely to writing.

CHAPTER FIVE

THE BIG IDEA

*I was taught early on at Phillips Exeter that one must write
what one knows. Like many aspects of my life, scenes from my
childhood, my relationship with my parents and family, my
student years, and my time in Spain all later emerged in my books.*

DAN BROWN

The novels of Dan Brown are thrillers that skilfully blend
fact and fiction and support this with technical and
historical information. They are books that send the reader
on a quest, but they are written to a formula.

On 20 April 2009 an article appeared in *The Guardian*
newspaper in which British writers Matt Lynn (the author
of *Death Force*, a military thriller), Alan Clements (a TV
producer who penned *Rogue Nation*, a political thriller)
and Martin Baker (the author of *Meltdown*, a financial
thriller) railed against what they called 'American
production-line' writing. The trio called themselves the
Curzon Group and the authors they singled out for criticism
were John Grisham, James Patterson and Dan Brown,
with Lynn stating that 'authors such as James Patterson
– who writes, with the aid of a team of co-authors, up to

eight books a year – have drained a lot of the life out of the market.'

'There haven't been any new writers coming through. It might be because there aren't any very good writers, or maybe it's because publishers and booksellers have been neglecting it – they've become obsessed with the big names, and because they've got a new James Patterson or John Grisham four to five times a year to put at the front of the bookshop, it crowds out all the new British authors who are coming through.' [18]

Authors such as Grisham, the Curzon Group claimed, produced excellent thrillers in their first few novels but as their popularity grew, Grisham's output had become 'very, very formulaic'. Tom Clancy and James Patterson were included in this criticism. 'Good writing should be done well, with passion and originality, but [the thriller genre is] becoming very cynical, which is what we're protesting about,' said Lynn.

What makes the Curzon Group particularly interesting is that they came up with five principles of good thriller writing. These are that the book must first entertain the reader; it should also reflect the world around it; that for popular fiction to be thrilling it doesn't need to follow formulas; that at the heart of every thriller should be an adventure both for the writer and the reader, and finally an edge-of-your-seat thriller can be written in an insightful, witty and stylish way.

At the heart of every Dan Brown novel is what he calls 'a big idea'. The inspiration for his first novel came from an unexpected source: while teaching at Phillips Exeter he heard of a student who'd been in trouble for writing an email jokingly threatening the President. 'The US Secret

Service came to the campus and detained one of the students claiming he was a threat to national security,' Brown said. 'As it turned out, the student had sent a private email to a friend saying how much he hated President Clinton and how he thought the President should be shot. The Secret Service came to campus to make sure the boy wasn't serious. After some interrogation the agents decided the student was harmless and not much came of it.'[19]

The incident stuck with Brown. How could the Secret Service have known what the student had written in his email? How would they have known where that person was, where he lived, and that he was a student if they hadn't been monitoring all traffic on the web? 'Email was brand new on the scene, and like most people, I assumed email was private,' he said. 'I couldn't figure out how the secret service knew what these students were saying in their email.'

Intrigued by the story, Brown began digging and discovered that the National Security Agency (NSA) was able to read people's email. The more research he did on the NSA and the moral issues surrounding civilian privacy and national security, the more Brown realised he had the basis of a brilliant thriller. 'I remember Blythe commenting that life seemed to be trying to tell me something,' Brown said. 'The music industry was clearly rejecting me, and the publishing industry seemed to be beckoning. The thrill of being a published author (*187 Men To Avoid*), combined with George Wieser's words of encouragement, my newfound fascination with NSA, and the vacation reading of Sidney Sheldon's *The Doomsday Conspiracy*, all had begun to give me confidence that I could indeed write a novel.' [20]

And so he began writing his first novel *Digital Fortress*

even though he had no firm commitment from any publisher. 'I literally woke up one day, sat up on the end of the bed, and said, "It's time to write a novel." My wife sort of just patted me on the head and said, "You go ahead. That's nice, dear. Have fun." I was working two jobs at the time. I would get up at four o'clock, write until eight, bike 12 miles to a junior high school, teach Spanish, bike 12 miles home, shower, race over and teach two afternoon classes at Phillips Exeter and then get up and do it all over again.'[21]

However, writing a book on spec is extremely difficult. Not knowing if anyone will ever be interested in it or if it will ever get sold can sap an author's spirit and many would-be writers have lost their way because they didn't have the motivation to keep going. Brown did and he had Blythe's support and encouragement. After more than a year of researching and writing the manuscript was as ready as it would ever be, but he had also decided that this was the last time he would write anything without having a publisher.

The manuscript now needed to be sold but the publishing industry had changed and companies now only wanted submissions from unknown authors through literary agents. The Browns turned again to George Wieser, who had secured an offer for *187 Men to Avoid*. He been running a small literary agency (Wieser and Wieser) with his wife Olga since 1975 and their claim to fame was that George had bought the film rights to Mario Puzo's *The Godfather*. They offered to send the *Digital Fortress* manuscript around to the publishers and three weeks later it was sold to St Martin's Press for one of their imprints, Thomas Dunne Books. At Dunne, editor Melissa Jacobs took the manuscript and worked with Brown to get it into shape for publishing.

Sadly, George Wieser died of cancer in 1998, but *Digital Fortress* was published that same year. It sold only a few thousand copies but it was a step forward for Brown. He was sure his next would be better: now that his first novel had been picked up by publishers, he could leave teaching and concentrate on writing full time and so he dived into the research for the second thriller that would become *Angels & Demons*.

It was in *Digital Fortress* that Brown began blending fact with fiction, stretching the facts to suit the story and the situation. In each novel he has honed this ability and perhaps that's the secret of his success: that he can tell a story in such a way that the reader is lost in a world that is, completely fictional on one hand but on the other still based in reality. 'I write in a very specific intentional way to blend fact and fiction and that's part of the fun,' he explained.

Bond author Ian Fleming suggested that for writing good thrillers, some part of the story should be based on fact so that there is an authenticity to the work that rings true and carries the reader along. In his first book, *Casino Royale*, he said, 'there are strong incidents in the book which are all based on fact. I extracted them from my wartime memories of the Naval Intelligence Division of the Admiralty, dolled them up, attached a hero, a villain and a heroine, and there was the book.'[22]

For Fleming the line between fact and fiction is a narrow one. 'I think I could trace most of the central incidents in my books to some real happenings,' he said. He also suggested that the author should know 'thrilling things'. 'Imagination alone isn't enough, but stories you hear from friends or read in the papers can be built up by a fertile imagination and a certain amount of research and documentation into incidents that will also ring true in fiction.'

Almost all Fleming's books were written when he went to Jamaica every year, and he pointed out, 'Your lack of friends and distractions will create a vacuum which should force you into a writing mood and, if your pocket is shallow, into a mood which will also make you write fast and with application.' Having a hideaway, as Fleming called it, is essential for creating this vacuum. While some may not be able to go to Jamaica every year to write, there are other alternatives: 'I can recommend hotel bedrooms as far removed from your usual life as possible.'

Fleming also said that a routine of writing is essential. He wrote for three hours in the morning and then another hour in the evening. 'The whole of this four hours of daily work is devoted to writing narrative. At the end of this I reward myself by numbering the pages and putting them away in a spring-back folder.' [23]

Fleming wrote his novels in a very short space of time without correction or looking back or checking anything. That came later, as he explained: 'If you interrupt the writing of fast narrative with too much introspection and self-criticism, you will be lucky if you write 500 words a day and you will be disgusted with them into the bargain. By following my formula, you write 2,000 words a day and you aren't disgusted with them until the book is finished, which will be in about six weeks.'

However, Brown takes a very long time to work on his novels, which is why he's turned out only five in 12 years. Because the research is so intensive, the subject matter has to hold his attention. Usually, there is a moral argument to each of his stories that he presents in such a way that the reader has to decide what is right and what is wrong, and Brown hopes they will go on a quest to discover the truths for themselves. Indeed, many books have been written since the success of *The Da Vinci Code*, trying to debunk the claims he makes in his books, or trying to explain and expand on some of the ancient myths, legends and mysteries that permeate each Dan Brown novel. The internet is full of people either searching for the facts that Brown includes in his novel or debunking them.

But back when he had just started writing *Digital Fortress*, Brown was juggling his writing time with teaching at Phillips Exeter. He had no choice but to set up a writing routine and it's interesting that that he still sticks to it today. That routine means he gets up at 4am every day and walks to his writing cottage which, he says, 'is not in the house – I have to walk to it. But there are times when I'm so excited I'll get up and go out in my pyjama bottoms and sweatshirt, because it is pitch black outside and no one is around.' [24]

According to some sources Brown keeps an antique hourglass on his desk so each time the sands run out, he stops to briefly do some exercises, such as sit-ups, push-ups and stretching to keep the circulation flowing.[25]

Another Brown legend says that he practises inversion therapy and hangs upside down in anti-gravity boots when he runs into difficulty with writing and can't find a solution to a problem. 'Not only does it increase the circulation to the head but you think differently upside down,' he said. 'I have this habit of painting Robert Langdon into a corner and saying, "You know what? I know I'll find a way out of this" and if you don't, you hang upside down and think about it from a different perspective and sometimes it works.' [26]

This practice is not for the faint of heart, or those people who have high blood pressure or heart disease. The idea is that hanging by the feet not only sends blood rushing to the head but each joint in the body is loaded in an opposite way to standing in the identical position. Proponents of inversion therapy say hanging upside down is good for the spine because it relieves pressure on the discs and the nerves, enabling the spine to return to its original shape.

There is no indication that Brown has back problems, so his use of anti-gravity boots is to see things from a different point of view. His writing cottage has no phone, email or internet but it does have his anti-gravity boots. 'It's a different perspective. You're hanging upside down you're seeing the world from a different point of view and you think differently,' he said.

Now we know how Brown writes, let's take a closer look at his literary formula. We have seen that the Sidney Sheldon book was Brown's eureka moment and inspired him to write thrillers, but he has also been influenced by Robert Ludlum's Jason Bourne series. 'Ludlum's early books are complex, smart, and yet still move at a lightning pace,' he pointed out. 'This series got me interested in the genre of big-concept, international thrillers.'[27] He has recurring themes that he brings into each of his novels – the hero pulled out of his or her familiar environment and plunged into a dangerous, unforgiving new setting where a life-and-death struggle needs to be resolved within a very short space of time.

Brown writes stories where good and evil battle it out. 'In all the ancient myths there are monsters that haunt your hero,' he said. 'I am always fascinated by the mythological resonance of these villains and they are by far the most interesting and pathetic. They are almost monsters but they are almost superhuman too and they are going up against somebody and your hero on some level is a little bit more than ordinary.'[28]

In three of his books the protagonist is symbologist Dr Robert Langdon, an academic and the kind of man the Brown would like to be. Largely because Langdon is prepared to take risks in order to solve his puzzle, Brown puts his character into danger so he can find the solution. 'He's very curious,' Brown said. 'Intellectually curious and that's what I hope these books will do for readers is make them intellectually curious. He's not an action hero and yet he finds himself in these situations where he finds himself uncovering ancient historical truths and having to decipher codes and puzzles to solve mysteries.'[29]

He has also said that he loves building tension in his novels. Having a female lead in his novels, either as a companion to Langdon or as the heroine of the story, gives the novel romantic and sexual tension, which in most cases is implied. This adds an extra dimension while also building the tension. Brown finds smart women very attractive so he has given Langdon that same trait.[30]

Brown also says his character must have some form of Achilles heel, some weakness otherwise he is simply a cardboard cutout. 'The classic weakness is hubris and Langdon doesn't have that. I would say that his fault is that he is curious to a fault. He puts himself in dangerous situations to find things out and that is something I would not do.'

Brown is fascinated by veiled or hidden power – those organisations that operate in the shadows. 'The idea that everything happens for reasons we're not quite seeing. It reminds me of religion a little. The power that religion has is that you think nothing is random. If there's a tragedy in my life, that's God testing me or sending me a message. That's what conspiracy theorists do. They say, "The economy's terrible? Oh, that's not random. That's a bunch of rich guys in Prague who sat down and…"'

Yet Brown still remains a sceptic. He is not a conspiracy theorist and doesn't believe in UFOs. 'I think one reason my books have found mainstream success is that they're written from a sceptical point of view,' Brown said. Langdon is a sceptic as well, which connects the reader with someone who will not take anything at face value but whose first reaction is disbelief. 'If I'm doing my job,' says Brown, 'then what happens is that you, the sceptical reader, move through my stories and start to say, "Oh my God. Maybe. Maybe."'[31]

The astonishing success of *The Da Vinci Code* not only propelled him into the spotlight but also brought detractors out of the woodwork. 'I am aware there are those out there who disagree with me,' Brown has said, 'who say awful things about me, who make little pictures and I know that a lot of them have published long lists of my shortcomings, my errors and my mistakes.'[32]

Because of that success people came out of the shadows to hang on Brown's coat-tails in any way they could. 'There is something that comes along with success that you have people who are gunning for you, who want to say, "That's not worthy. Why is everybody enjoying that?" and it comes with the territory.'[33]

Critics claim that his writing is awkward and that he is no literary genius. Brown's response is that he never set out to be a great literary author. The point is for the reader to have fun. 'There are some people who understand what I do and get on the train and go for a ride and have a great time, and there are other people who should read something else.'[34]

How Brown measures his success is how well he connects with his readers. His official website regularly gets hundreds of emails and most of those are complimentary. 'The nicest thing I ever hear and I often hear it and it makes me happy is that somebody will say, "After I got out of high school I really didn't read much but somebody made me read *The Da Vinci Code* – they hit me over the head with it and finally I read it and now I can't stop reading. You reintroduced me to the love of books" and for me that's the most gratifying and rewarding thing about it.'[35]

CHAPTER SIX

MRS BROWN, YOU'VE GOT A LOVELY HUSBAND

Both Angels & Demons and The Da Vinci Code are dedicated to Blythe, whom Brown has given a great deal of credit, stressing her invaluable help as a co-researcher.

DAVID A. SHUGARTS

The old saying that 'behind every successful man is a successful woman' is certainly true of Dan Brown. When Brown gave his evidence in the High Court at the Old Bailey in a detailed witness statement responding to two historians claiming that he plagiarised their ideas in *The Da Vinci Code* (which we will look at in detail later), he gave his fans a unique insight into the story behind the most successful thriller ever written.

Blythe has been the driving force in Brown's life ever since they met in Los Angeles, and together they make an impressive team. It was her networking that got him into the studio with top musicians and a top producer for his first CD. She sent out the press releases proclaiming Brown as the next big singer-songwriter. It was her contacting agents and publishing companies that got Brown the publishing deal for *187 Men to Avoid*.

He cites her as his inspiration but there is more to her than that. As an art history enthusiast and Leonardo da Vinci fan, she contributed some of the more interesting art ideas to the novel. As Joanna Walters and Alice O'Keeffe noted in *The Observer* in March 2006, 'The older, more glamorous half of the Browns is emerging as, if not the "real brains" behind *The Da Vinci Code*, then certainly a creative energy as indispensable to her husband as the Mona Lisa herself.'[36]

Blythe has had an influence on every Dan Brown novel with the exception of *Deception Point. Angels & Demons* is dedicated to Blythe, and Brown writes in his dedication for *The Da Vinci Code* 'For Blythe... again. More than ever.' Indeed, Brown says she is more than an inspiration, she is 'the intellectual catalyst, sounding board and initial judge.'[37]

Little is known about Blythe. He has described her in various interviews as an art historian, or as a history buff and a Da Vinci fanatic. Painting is her hobby, yet there is no indication that she ever graduated in art history.[38]

Blythe hails from Palmdale in California. As we have seen, she and Brown met in 1991 when she was Director of Artistic Development at the National Academy for Songwriters in L.A. By the time she headed east with Brown on the promise of a publishing deal for *187 Men To Avoid* they were lovers, and she must have been very committed to the relationship to leave her home and her job to pull up sticks and move to the other side of the country with him.

But without a doubt she is crucial to Brown's success. On the second CD, *Angels & Demons*, Brown thanked her for 'being my tireless co-writer, co-producer, second engineer, significant other and therapist'. Once in quiet

Exeter, Blythe provided essential research material while Brown concentrated on his writing. In 1997 the couple tied the knot and for several years lived in an old mill, until they hit the big time with *The Da Vinci Code* and moved to a discreet house tucked up a private drive near Rye on the New Hampshire coast.

According to Rogak, Blythe's input into Brown's first novel *Digital Fortress* was largely in an editing capacity. 'With the help of Blythe's keen editing eye, the material that made it to the final draft was only the tip of the iceberg. But what went unsaid made the characters deeper and the story line richer in the end.'[39]

While Blythe didn't get involved in the research on *Digital Fortress,* she did on the subsequent novels apart from *Deception Point,* when she swapped her research role for her editor's hat. 'Unfortunately for Blythe, the technological subject matter of *Deception Point* did not interest her much,' Brown said. 'She helped research some of the geology and glaciology, the architecture of the White House, Air Force One, etc., but she served more as a first class editor and sounding board.'[40]

With Brown's fascination for symbols, codes, Renaissance art and Blythe's love of all things Da Vinci, Brown had a winning combination. In Rogak's opinion: 'With her vibrant imagination and burgeoning knowledge in that direction, he hit the literary jackpot.'[41]

While Brown was researching *Angels & Demons*, Blythe became the author of another humour publication called *The Bald Book* which, Lisa Rogak said, 'could rightfully be considered to be a love letter to bald men everywhere.' Blythe approached Wieser and Wieser again and the agency sold it to Pinnacle Books. The book came out on 1 June

1998, four months after *Digital Fortress*. The author biography said, 'Artist Blythe Brown lives in New England and spends her days painting while her husband happily goes bald.' But although the book is attributed to Blythe, the copyright is held by Dan Brown.

In February 1998 when *Digital Fortress* was released, Blythe took on publicising the novel in addition to the work the publishers did, which wasn't much. She sent out press releases she'd written, she got on the phone to talk-show producers to book Brown and she contacted newspapers to set up interviews with her husband.

According to Rogak it is much harder to promote a book of fiction than it is a book of non-fiction where 'a publicist can market the title as a solution to a problem.' So, as an angle, Blythe set up a website that featured Brown as a source 'to advise readers and viewers on how to protect themselves online'. The material she developed to promote the book focused on the more paranoid aspects of who was reading people's email and who was watching people online. These two aspects made Brown a popular interview subject. Sometimes she had him doing up to four radio interviews a day. She also arranged for him to sign copies of his book in as many bookstores in New Hampshire as she could. Blythe also contacted the *Union Leader*, New Hampshire's largest daily newspaper, and got a reporter to attend a talk Brown was giving to the New Hampshire chapter of the American Society for Industrial Security. Despite all their efforts, the sales for *Digital Fortress* were poor, yet 'he basked in the attention the media had been giving him for *Digital Fortress*.'[42]

Later in 1998 Brown began work on his second novel, *Angels & Demons*. 'Of course, at this point I was an unknown, unpublished author,' he said. 'Money was tight, but we had enough to travel, something Blythe and I both love, and we decided to visit Rome.'

Unlike the first novel, Blythe would play a major part in this new project. 'Although I had researched *Digital Fortress* entirely on my own, for this new book Blythe became my research assistant,' said Brown. 'This was wonderful. We were able to work together as husband and wife; I now had a sounding board and a travel partner on research trips. Although Blythe's main interest and expertise was art, I did ask her for help researching specifics on scientific topics like Galileo, the Big Bang, particle accelerators, etc. She also served as a first-class set of eyes for new sections I was writing.'[43]

The couple walked for miles around Rome, taking hundreds of photographs 'exploring the city using all kinds of guidebooks, maps and tours.'

Angels & Demons came out under Simon & Schuster's Pocket Books imprint in April 2000. As with St Martin's Press the publicity for this book was poor and Blythe found herself winding up the publicity machine again. 'Unfortunately, when the book came out, my print run was slashed down to 12,000 copies with virtually no publicity at all,' said Brown. He was on his own. 'Blythe and I were heartbroken as we had put so much work into this book. The few readers who read *Angels & Demons* had gone wild for it, and Blythe and I really believed we had something – if we could only get it to a critical mass of readers.' [44]

In August 2001 *Deception Point* was published, the second half of the two-book deal he had with Simon & Schuster. But as with the two that went before it, the publicity for it was less than adequate and again Blythe began greasing the wheels of publicity. With *Angels & Demons* people had been emailing Brown; readers had bought the novel and gone over to Europe using it as a guidebook. All the places and names Brown had put into the book were real and people were saying how much they were enjoying the fact that he had described them as they were. For Blythe that was the angle to hang the promotion on, but with *Deception Point* there was nothing.

Blythe's involvement with *The Da Vinci Code* was far greater than anything previously. In her biography on Brown, Lisa Rogak states that for this fourth novel Brown and Blythe 'began to work more closely together' because Blythe's expertise lay 'in the primary subject of the book – the art of Leonardo da Vinci.' The subject matter of this book was much more complex than anything Brown had tackled before and more often than not he got bogged down in the intricate story line. Blythe's influence and passion for Da Vinci meant she could help Brown unblock his imagination. 'There are days when it helps to have somebody around who understands art and Da Vinci and is passionate about it,' he said.[45]

The day after submitting *Deception Point* to the publisher, Brown and Blythe had decided to head for Mexico on vacation. There they explored the Yucatan peninsula, and the ancient Mayan pyramids and archaeological ruins of Chichen-Itza and Tulum that got Brown's creative juices flowing again and he began to think about another book. 'In the case of *The Da Vinci Code*, Blythe and I spent a year or so travelling and conducting research,' Brown said. 'We met with historians and other academics and extended our travels from the Vatican and France to England and Scotland in order to investigate the historical underpinnings of the novel.'

The Da Vinci Code was Brown's most heavily researched work yet, and Blythe played a major part in this. Indeed, he tells us that a lot of his research books for the novel are marked 'with margin notes, sticky notes, underlining, highlighting, inserted pieces of paper, etc. A good portion of these notes (as with *Angels & Demons*) are in my wife's handwriting.'

While researching for *The Da Vinci Code* Blythe was passionate about learning as much as she could. 'In *Angels & Demons*, she may have found me the exact specifications of Bernini's *Fountain of the Four Rivers*,' said Brown. 'With *The Da Vinci Code*, however, she was reading entire books, highlighting exciting ideas, and urging me to read the material myself and find ways to work the ideas in to the plot.' Particularly inspiring for Blythe was the suppression of women by the Catholic Church. Brown tells us that 'she lobbied hard for me to make it a primary theme of the novel. Blythe also tends to save far more memorabilia than I do; many of the research notes were now hers, and more of them found their way into safe-keeping.'[46]

Blythe and Dan bought several books from which they would take the facts that Brown needed to tell his story. One of these books, *The Hiram Key*, Blythe marked quite heavily. 'In my childhood, I was taught never to write in books,' Brown said. 'To this day, I still have a strong aversion to it. For this reason, my margin notes often are very light or taken down on a separate piece of paper. Blythe does not share my idiosyncrasy, and she often marks books very heavily. She also often produced research documents for me as a result of her studies of the books. An example from *The Hiram Key* is "Hiram's Key Notes". It can be seen from that document that she included a number of page references which she thought I should consult.'

Not all the documents that Blythe prepared for her husband were what he wanted, however. He read everything she gave him with care but sometimes 'she prepared notes that were either too lengthy which I skimmed, ignored or seemed off-topic,' or the notes were more interesting to her than they were to Brown.

The couple worked very well together as a team, with Blythe providing research that Brown could not possibly have had the time to do if he had been working on his own. *The Da Vinci Code* is a highly complex novel and without Blythe it would have been much harder for him to write. 'She was becoming more and more intrigued by the information we were learning, and she wanted me to incorporate all of it which I could not possibly do,' Brown explained in his witness statement for the High Court. 'She often playfully chided me about my resolve to keep the novel fast-paced, always at the expense of her research. In return, I jokingly reminded her that I was trying to write a thriller, not a history book. In the end, we found a comfortable balance of pace and history, and we had a wonderful time throwing ideas back and forth. Blythe's female perspective was particularly helpful with this book, which deals so heavily with concepts like the Sacred Feminine, goddess worship and the feminine aspect of spirituality.'

Blythe played a hugely important role in researching the Sacred Feminine, which was one of the central themes of the book. Margaret Starbird had written about Mary Magdalene and this captured Blythe's imagination. 'Blythe reacted to Starbird's books with enormous passion and enthusiasm,' Brown said. 'In fact, I'm not sure I had ever seen Blythe as passionate about anything as she became for the historical figure of Mary Magdalene (particularly the idea that the church had unfairly maligned her).'[47] So enthralled was Blythe by Starbird's portrayal that she purchased a painting of Magdalene which she hung on the wall over her desk.

Starbird's books opened Blythe's and Brown's eyes to the way the Church had subjugated the Sacred Feminine. 'My wife ordered a series of three historical films by the film maker Donna Rea,' Brown explained. 'I found the films absolutely fascinating. I was amazed to learn of the existence of a church publication called *The Malleus Maleficarum.*' This book told its readers how to identify and then murder women who fitted the very broad definition of what the Church called a witch. 'I began to realise that history barely mentioned the Church's systemic subjugation of the Sacred Feminine,' Brown continued. 'The films also mentioned the Gnostic Gospels, prehistoric art honouring the female as life giver, the symbol of the inverted triangle – the womb, Catholicism, symbols, the serpent being linked to religion, the obliteration of 25,000 years of goddess worship by the ancient Greeks.'[48]

But Brown had still not decided what the 'big idea' of the book was going to be. He toyed with writing a few sections just to get a feel for the setting and especially for the characters, but the basis of the book was not yet fully formed in his mind. Enter Blythe with the solution. 'Blythe encouraged me to incorporate the theme of the Sacred Feminine and the goddess,' said Brown. On a note inserted into the inside cover of the *Woman's Dictionary of Symbols and Sacred Objects* 'Blythe has written a note "goddess section" and on page 202, she has written "read all" by the Goddess entry.'

So with encouragement from Blythe, the three films of

Donna Rea and Starbird's books, Brown was swayed to making the Sacred Feminine the central theme of his book. 'Margaret Starbird's books were a big inspiration – the image she created of Mary Magdalene being the bride, the lost sacred feminine, was very elegant – it seemed like the "big idea" – like the core of a classic fairy tale or enduring legend.'[49]

In his acknowledgements Brown thanked the two women closest to him, his wife Blythe and his mother, and noted that the novel 'draws heavily on the Sacred Feminine.' In his witness statement he added, 'If we spent half the intellect and money we spend on killing each other on solving problems, wouldn't that be great? I kind of equate that with testosterone.'[50]

It is highly likely that Blythe came up with most of the art references for *The Da Vinci Code*. One published account, according to David Shugarts, author of *The Dan Brown Revelations*, suggests that it was Blythe who came up with the reference to Rosslyn Chapel in Scotland.[51] In the book, this is one of the last settings and it is where Sophie finds her brother and grandmother. It is also where she discovers her background. 'The predominant source for my Rosslyn information was *The Hiram Key*, a lot of which is devoted to Rosslyn,' Brown said, adding that Blythe made notes throughout the book on Rosslyn. 'She also compiled two research documents called Rosslyn Castle Info and Rosslyn Highlights, much of which appears to come from *The Hiram Key*.'

A commonly held belief about writers is that they toil away in loneliness and isolation. Indeed, this is an image that we have seen Brown himself use in writing at 4am in his cottage. But clearly throughout the research phase of his writing Blythe was there with him – to the degree that they started sharing information via email. 'The reason for this,' Brown explained in his witness statement, 'is that more of our research was taking place on the internet, and email became the most efficient way of sharing information. For Blythe, sending me cut-and-paste text or a clickable link to a large website was easier than printing out dozens of pages in hard copy.'

Using email was especially useful for Blythe to send her husband images from particular websites. He claims that photos helped him to write out his descriptive passages but 'they printed poorly and ate up expensive printer toner; I preferred to see them online.'

Blythe would bring information and research together from a wide variety of sources and then type it up into a document for Brown to use. 'This new tool of email now meant that those research notes appeared in all kinds of different forms – her own extracts, clips from the internet, scans from source books, and website resource files. Sometimes I got a paper copy of those notes, usually an emailed copy, and sometimes both.'[52]

While Brown does his own research, Blythe's work in this field is key to providing the big picture, enabling him to produce what he regards as the most interesting parts for the reader. Most of the research is discarded for the final product. 'My tendency toward heavy editing ("trimming the fat" as I called it) fuelled the ongoing push-and-pull between Blythe and me. Blythe constantly urged me to add more facts and more history. I was always slashing out long descriptive passages in an effort to keep the pace moving,' Brown said. 'I remember Blythe once gave me an enormous set of architectural/historical notes for a short flashback

I was writing about Notre Dame Cathedral. When I had finished the section, she was frustrated by how little of work actually made the final cut. In these situations, I always remind Blythe I was trying to write a fast-moving page-turner.'[53]

One particular document that Blythe produced for Brown for *The Da Vinci Code* was titled *Constantine*. Much of it was taken directly from the source and wasn't in her own words. 'It is not unusual for her to do this when we are working together,' Brown said in his witness statement. 'I will tell her the outline of a section of a book I have written and then ask her to go away and make a note of more specific information about the topic which I can use to elaborate my text.

'She is better than me at producing a good summary of the material which we have looked at,' he added. 'If she finds a particular source which has many of the relevant facts collected together, she will make her note from that source. Sometimes she combines a number of sources in her notes to me. Sometimes she adds notes to me to look at other sources as well. There is no fixed pattern.'

One thing that makes this document on Constantine interesting is that a lot of it came from the book *Holy Blood and the Holy Grail,* whose authors launched a court case against Brown claiming he had plagiarised their work. (We will look at that in greater detail later.) A second thing is that Blythe often transcribed paragraphs directly from the work she was looking at, to ensure that her husband had the exact data he'd asked for.

Blythe doesn't just email a document over to her husband – she often peppers it with notes to draw her husband's attention to a particular point while he's writing. She explains: 'The document says, "Keep in mind these important references" and then there is a list of several points or themes and a corresponding source and page number.' She would pass notes to Dan pointing out something she felt was important, as she did with the Constantine document where she noted, 'Throughout my readings of all my books, this smell or perfume for some reason keeps coming up in relation to Mary Magdalene. I have seen this many times.' Brown said that she was referring to many references she'd discovered regarding a perfume that was connected to Mary Magdalene.

'Our studies into the origins of the Christian movement and the ancient mysteries continue to this day. Our research and Blythe's note taking is a continual process,' Brown said in his 2005 witness statement. Both he and Blythe knew that they had something with *The Da Vinci Code*, but before they began that project they went through the three preceding novels that were poorly promoted to see what could have been done better.

Even with Blythe's encouragement, support and collaboration on his first three novels, Brown had felt like giving up, so it's fair to say that without Blythe, Dan Brown would probably be nowhere.

CHAPTER SEVEN

DIGITAL FORTRESS

Initially I had been indignant that the NSA was reading emails. But subsequently I realised their work constituted a fascinating moral grey area.

Dan Brown

Digital Fortress was the first of Dan Brown's novels and was the only one he wrote on spec. 'The thrill of being a published author (*187 Men To Avoid*), combined with George Wieser's words of encouragement, my newfound fascination with NSA, and the vacation reading of Sidney Sheldon's *The Doomsday Conspiracy*, all had begun to give me confidence that I could indeed write a novel,' he said. 'I quite literally woke up one morning and decided to write a thriller that delved into NSA. That's when I started writing *Digital Fortress*.' [54]

Like all of Brown's books, the core of the story is built around a puzzle that the protagonist must solve in a short space of time. Brown builds the pace of the book deftly, taking the reader from Spain to Washington and back again many times. He uses flashbacks to build background information then brings the reader back into the present to push the story forward. So how does *Digital Fortress* stack up against the Curzon Group's five principles of thriller writing?

For its entertainment value, we can go to Brown for the answer: feedback from the *Digital Fortress* website was very positive. 'I get a lot of email from excited readers,' Brown said. 'It seems people have really connected with the timely "moral issues" in the novel.' Readers have also enjoyed the inside look at the National Security Agency (NSA) that Brown exposed in the book. 'Every now and then I get an irate letter from some technician telling me that the gadgets in *Digital Fortress* could never exist in real life (they all do), and I have to forward some article or photograph confirming my research.'[55]

But as we have seen, Brown is an author who is able to stretch or embellish the truth when it suits him. There is, however, no shortage of independent reviews of *Digital Fortress*. 'I found the book fast-paced and engaging,' said one. 'I almost literally didn't put it down until I was done. I don't take many forays into the world of fiction, but if you like cyber-thrillers I highly recommend you pick this book up and read it.'[56]

Another reviewer said it was an exciting read, that the subject matter was thought-provoking and that the plot was fascinating. '*Digital Fortress* is an example of the techno-thriller at its very best. But what makes *Digital Fortress* stand out from the crowd are its other elements: a real love story and an examination of the struggles between right and wrong and protection of the public versus the preservation of that same public's privacy.'[57]

John Barnes of the *Washington Pi Journal* reviewed *Digital Fortress* in 2004 and he too was complimentary. He said Brown had succeeded in taking him from one end of the story to the other in a single sitting. 'Twists and turns are Brown's stock in trade and he paces their unveiling in a manner that is properly sinister,' he wrote. 'I won't claim this is Pulitzer Prize literature but it is a jolly good read.'

The website *Curled Up With A Good Book*, concluded that Brown had written a 'cutting edge techno-thriller'. The reviewer also said that the book had pace like that of a speeding plane with copious amounts of suspense and with 'interesting characterisations and a romantic entanglement thrown in for good measure, *Digital Fortress* compels the reader to wonder whether big brother is really watching everything everywhere.'[58]

In his interview with Claire White, of the *Internet Writing Journal* web pages, Brown said that many people had emailed the website saying how much they enjoyed the book because it had other elements than computers. 'I worry sometimes that, because we talk about cryptography and the NSA that people think, "Oh, it's a computer book," but it's so much more than that.' [59]

The book was also reviewed on Amazon's website, where the general public get their chance to say what they think about a book. These are not professional reviews but the opinions of the readers must be taken into account in assessing how entertaining *Digital Fortress* is. 'There are enough twists and turns to keep you guessing and a lot of high, gee-whiz-level information about encryption, code breaking, and the role they play in international politics,' says one contributor. This reviewer also tells readers to take an entire afternoon and do nothing but read the book ensuring that you have enough 'finger food on hand for supper, because you'll probably want to read it from cover to cover.'

However, the reviews were not all roses. Brown has his detractors and once *The Da Vinci Code* had broken, sales of *Digital Fortress* rocketed, bringing the negative comments. Yet it may be that some of the bad reviews of *Digital Fortress* are by people who have an axe to grind with Brown because they disliked *The Da Vinci Code*.

For example, one reviewer said the romance in the book was cheesy and that it made a book 'about national-level cryptography seem oversimplified into a romance novel that was set against a life-or-death backdrop.' The reviewer went on to say that if the reader wanted to learn about the goings on at the NSA or about computer programming or codes then *Digital Fortress* was a good book to read but 'for plot and style, it's just the usual Dan Brown.'[60]

Another reviewer said, 'I was most disappointed to discover that the betraying character – which appears in all of his books and is, I think, supposed to shock readers – becomes ridiculously easy to identify.'[61]

Finally, a review by Magda Healey published on the *Bookbag* website in July 2004 condemned *Digital Fortress* as a book to read if the reader has nothing else to do. She said that the writing was worse 'than *The Da Vinci Code*,' and that his characters were unrealistic and the dialogue was wooden. She did not recommend the book at all, giving it just two stars.

So there are good reviews and bad – most are good – but is *Digital Fortress* an entertaining read? There is one easy way to tell: sales figures. In 2005 the *Times Online* published the figures for Brown's books and even then they were astounding. '*The Da Vinci Code* is estimated to have sold, 2,225,118 copies in Britain, and his two backlist titles *Digital Fortress* and *Deception Point*, previously unpublished here – have shifted over 600,000 copies each.'[62]

Based on the reviews, the comments emailed to Brown and the sales figures, we can say that *Digital Fortress* meets the Curzon Group's first principle of entertainment value and does so in spades. From the first page to the last it is filled with tension, pace and suspense. Whether it is good writing or not is another matter.

Digital Fortress is an interesting story. It's set inside the US National Security Agency (NSA), which monitors communications from around the world, via the internet and email, for anything that would be a threat to US security. The core of the NSA is a multi-billion dollar computer called TRANSLTR that has three million processors enabling it to decode any encrypted messages almost instantly and the NSA to pick up potential terrorist threats.

TRANSLTR is merrily decoding thousands of messages from around the world until suddenly it comes across a code that it can't break. The agency calls in its top cryptographer, beautiful mathematical genius Susan Fletcher, to help break the deadlock. Without her knowledge, the agency has also brought her fiancé, David Becker, into the equation. An expert in foreign languages and a professor who has assisted the NSA before, Becker is sent to Spain to retrieve the 'kill code' or pass key that will enable TRANSLTR to break the code.

As the story unravels, we discover that a former employee of NSA's Crypto division, the brilliant Ensei Tankado, has written this unbreakable code called Digital Fortress because he believes that TRANSLTR is immoral and that the world should be aware that the US is listening in to everything. However, Tankado is murdered in Spain before

Becker can get to him. Becker believes the code is written on a ring that Tankado gave to a tourist just before he died and Becker needs to find that ring. From this moment on Becker is in a race against the clock to get the ring back while being hunted by an assassin bent on killing him.

Meanwhile, Susan Fletcher is working hard to break the code and as she does, she uncovers layers of lies and deception. The plot twists and turns as people she thinks she can trust are the ones who can't be trusted and her world is turned on its head. She soon discovers that Digital Fortress is more than just an unbreakable code: it has the power to bring down the US government's entire security systems, which, once breached, will open up all of the US government secrets – including the launch codes for nuclear missiles – to hackers, terrorists and any other malignant attack!

As we have seen Brown got his 'big idea' for the book while he was teaching English at Phillips Exeter. 'In the spring of '95, two US Secret Service agents showed up on the campus of Phillips Exeter and detained one of our students claiming he was a threat to national security. ... He wasn't, of course, and not much came of it. The incident however really stuck with me.'[63]

Brown couldn't understand how the Secret Service had known what the student had written in his email. It bothered him, so he began to do research to find the answer. The more he looked, the more shocked he was. 'What I found out absolutely floored me. I found out there is an intelligence agency as large as the CIA... that only about two per cent of Americans knows exists.' That agency was the NSA. 'The agency functions like an enormous vacuum cleaner sucking in intelligence data from around the globe and processing it for subversive material. The NSA's supercomputers scan email and other communiqués, looking for dangerous word combinations like "kill" and "Clinton" in the same sentence. The more I learned about this ultra-secret agency and the fascinating moral issues surrounding national security and civilian privacy, the more I realised it was a great backdrop for a novel. That's when I started writing *Digital Fortress*.'

The second of the five principles of the Curzon Group is insight, so does the book reflect the world around it and provide insight on the subject matter? Brown researches all his novels meticulously. Most of this investigative work has been done with Blythe but the fact-finding for *Digital Fortress* he did himself and the research is evident throughout the novel. For example, in the opening chapters of *Digital Fortress*, Brown tells us about how NSA's technical people were easily able to intercept email. This, he states, was in the early days of the internet in the 1980s: 'The internet was not the new home computer revelation that most believed. It had been created by the Department of Defence three decades earlier – an enormous network of computers designed to provide secure government communication in the event of nuclear war.'

In the same section Brown goes on to write about how email became more difficult for the NSA to crack. He claims it was made more secure by the use of public-key encryption: 'It consisted of easy-to-use, home-computer software that scrambled personal email messages in such a way that they were totally unreadable.' At the other end of the email process, messages would come out looking like random letters and numbers. According to Brown, the only way to unscramble the email message 'was to enter the sender's "pass-key" – a secret series of characters that functioned much like a PIN number at an automatic teller.'

This idea of a pass-key is crucial to the story, because this is what is supposed to unlock Tankado's code and stop the meltdown of all the secrets in the NSA's databanks. 'The pass-keys were generally quite long and complex; they carried all the information necessary to instruct the encryption algorithm, exactly what mathematical operations to follow to recreate the original message.'[64]

In the book Brown states that the new pass-keys used chaos theory and multiple symbolic alphabets to scramble the messages into complete nonsense. The NSA's computers were able to handle the first pass-keys because they were short and relatively easy to break using trial and error. 'If a desired pass-key had ten digits, a computer was programmed to try every possibility between 0000000000 and 9999999999. Sooner or later the computer hit the correct sequence.'

Brown goes on tell us that this method was known as 'brute force attack', which, while time-consuming, was guaranteed to work. However, the pass-keys got longer because the 'world got wise to the power of brute-force code-breaking.' The time to break the codes increased from days to weeks, then to months and to years. By the mid-1990s the pass-keys used the full 256-character ASCII alphabet of letters, numbers and symbols, and 'the number of different possibilities was in the neighbourhood of 10120th with 120 zeros behind it.'

Brown then states that at the time the NSA's fastest computer, the Cray/Josephson II, took more than 19 years to break a 64-bit code in a brute force attack. To break this deadlock and speed up the code-breaking, the NSA set out to build a computer that was lightning fast. 'The last of the three million stamp-sized processors was hand-soldered in place, the final internal programme was finished, the ceramic shell was welded shut. TRANSLTR had been born.'

This new supercomputer had three million processors working in parallel to break any code that it intercepted. It would use 'the power of parallel processing as well as some highly classified advances in cleartext assessment to guess pass-keys and break codes,' Brown writes in *Digital Fortress*. 'It would derive its power not only from its staggering number of processors but also from new advances in quantum computing – an emerging technology that allowed information to be stored as quantum-mechanical states rather than solely as binary data.'

Research is the key to Brown's craft. 'I did read a lot of books about cryptography and the NSA's advanced technology. The hardest part was sifting through the techno babble and simmering it down to something fairly non-technical that anyone could understand and that would not bog down the plot.'[65]

But he had to be sure that his research was as accurate as it could be, so he read as much as he could about cryptography. 'I posted some questions to a cryptographic newsgroup,' he said in an interview with Claire White on the *Internet Writing Journal*. 'I ended up talking to some people whom I later found out were former NSA people. I was also fortunate to meet face to face with a Trusted Agent with the US Commission on Secrecy. Although these people never shared anything classified they helped me sort through a lot of recently declassified data through the Freedom of Information Act.'

Brown also turned to a wide variety of sources and spent a lot of time on Usenet groups on the internet. These are forums where like-minded people can discuss or post questions to people interested in specific topics. 'Brown has said that he relied on Usenet groups to ask questions pertinent to his research, and in some cases these initial queries developed into close friendships later on,' says Lisa Rogak in her biography of Brown.[66]

Brown's research revealed some startling information. 'There are a number of intelligence sources who have written extensive white papers on the NSA,' he said. The writer discovered that the US government's eavesdropping on their citizens and on countries around the world was far more insidious that he'd thought. 'They certainly buried the hooks they need to monitor traffic. They also have satellites that can listen to cellular phone calls and all sorts of other electronic eavesdropping devices.'

'A particularly influential book, at the time, was James Bamford's *The Puzzle Palace*,' Brown said. 'Although dated, it is still one of the seminal books on the covert world of America's premier intelligence agency, describing how the NSA pulls in intelligence data from around the globe, processing it for subversive material.'[67]

Brown was indignant at this massive invasion of privacy. However, he believes that even with this technology listening to everyone, the NSA isn't really interested in the ordinary person. 'Agencies like the NSA are far more interested in terrorists than in the average citizen and most of us have nothing to worry about. Of course, the pros and cons of living in an Orwellian "Big Brother is watching" kind of society can be debated forever.'

One of the former NSA cryptographers also faxed him a transcript of a Senate Judiciary Hearing, 'where the then director of the FBI, Louis Freech, testified that in one year alone – I believe the year was 1994 – the NSA's ability to infiltrate civilian communication had thwarted the downing of two US commercial airliners and a chemical weapons attack on US soil.'[68]

In the review posted on *Curled up With a Good Book*, Brown's research was singled out for praise. 'Dan Brown's laudable detailed research makes this book so realistic it's scary. Moreover, it will provoke readers to think and wonder if this loss of privacy and violation of human rights is justified by the number of horrific terrorist plots foiled and lives spared daily. It's an interesting dilemma.'[69]

It is this research that gives *Digital Fortress* its authority and certainly provides the reader with insight into cryptography and the NSA. Brown tells us that President Truman founded the NSA on the morning of 4 November 1952 but the Congressional Record did not record this event in any way. The role of this new super secret agency was to wage information war by stealing the secrets of people and governments hostile to the US. 'Today the agency has a $12 billion annual budget, about 25,000 employees, and an 86-acre heavily armed compound in Fort Meade, Maryland. It is home to the world's most potent computers as well as some of the most brilliant cryptographers, mathematicians, technicians, and analysts,' says Brown in *Digital Fortress*.

Even though Brown spent considerable time researching the book there are many who believe that some of the information is inaccurate. 'As a computer programmer myself, I found some of the research a bit weak,' said one critic. 'For example in this book, a computer program could have bugs in it if the programmer typed in a comma instead of a full stop. In the real world this program wouldn't compile, let alone run!'[70]

So what about the characters, the people who populate *Digital Fortress*?

Some reviewers have labelled his characters unbelievable and unreal. Some – such as Healey – have been unable to suspend disbelief at the improbability of finding anyone who speaks the way the characters do in *Digital Fortress*. 'The dialogue is in a class of its own: people simply don't speak like that,' was Healey's opinion.

She is referring to a section in the book where Brown describes David Becker, Susan Fletcher's fiancé, who happens to be one of the youngest professors ever at an American university and is paid such a pittance that he resorts to freelance translation work to 're-string his old Dunlop with gut'. She tells us the biggest problem 'with writing about characters with an IQ of 170 employed in highly responsible, management positions is that all credibility is lost if the writer makes them behave and speak like temp office juniors.'[71]

Brown tells us that they are composites of people he knows. 'They are also a bit larger than life (something for which a few people have criticised me), but this is an escapist, fun novel, and I personally enjoy reading about characters that have exceptional talents like code-breaking or multiple language skills,' he said. 'We run into boring people all day long, so why not read about some interesting ones?'[72]

This makes sense. If a writer wrote about tedious people no one would read the book. *Digital Fortress* is anything but boring. The characters are sometimes a little wooden, and the ending, where it takes some of the greatest minds to figure out a very simple clue does take some believing. But that's not the point: we have to remember that this was his first attempt at writing a thriller. Many, many writers never get their work published but he did, before the world went mad for *The Da Vinci Code.*

While the characterisation in some cases might not be as up to the mark as Le Carré, there is still a lot of warmth and depth to them that Healey must have skimmed over. For example, Brown gives Susan a moment of reflection before he introduces another character. She is worried about her fiancé in Spain. 'Despite her efforts to forget her morning conversation with David, the words played over and over in her head. She knew she'd been hard on him. She prayed he was okay in Spain.' These moments of reflection advance the plot and provide greater anxiety later in the novel, increasing the tension for the reader when she learns that someone has been sent to kill David.

Brown puts his heroes into a situation where they are on the run, or on an adventure in completely unfamiliar settings. 'The hero of *Digital Fortress*, David Becker, finds himself on the run through a landscape of ancient Moorish towers, Sevillian barrios, and the Cathedral of Seville,' Brown said. 'Much of the early work is to place these locations in a workable sequence such that the characters can move from one to the next in a logical manner.'[73]

'In trying to craft a suspenseful framework, I decided to throw Becker into a world he did not understand,' Brown explained in his witness statement. 'I also took him away from the heroine, his fiancée, Susan Fletcher. A lot of the suspense of this novel derives from wondering if these two will be reunited. In general, my plots drive my need for specifics (such as the precise vehicle a character will use to move from point A to B) rather than vice versa.'

In Spain, David Becker speaks some simple Spanish, but Brown takes his characterisation that one step further:

'Becker affected his Spanish with a thick German accent. "Hola, hablas aleman?"'

One of the crucial points about *Digital Fortress* is that it relies on Susan Fletcher's feelings to push the story forward. When Susan discovers her fellow cryptographer Greg Hale – a man with a dodgy past, bad cologne and a penchant for snooping through other people's computers – is Tankado's partner, she is stunned. The book continues: 'Susan could not accept what she was seeing. True, Greg Hale was obnoxious and arrogant – but he wasn't a traitor. He knew what *Digital Fortress* would do to the NSA; there was no way he was involved in a plot to release it!'

In the book there are several sublevels beneath the main floor of the building that houses the supercomputer. These levels are for the generators needed to keep TRANSLTR cool and, given its size, the generators that cool it with Freon gas would also have to be pretty big, as the novel states: 'The heat generated by three million processors would rise to treacherous levels – perhaps even igniting the silicone chips and resulting in a fiery meltdown.' This information is Brown giving us a taste of what's to come and what the characters face.

The book is littered with red herrings and turning points. It's the characters who push the story forward, such as when Susan is in the bathroom and overhears a muffled conversation through the air vents from two people standing on the catwalks below. She recognises one of the voices, commenting that: 'One voice was shrill and angry. It sounded like Phil Chartrukian.'

This particular character is a systems security officer. After Susan overhears this conversation, the power goes out and moments later the sirens begin to blare, announcing that TRANSLTR is overheating. Here Brown borrows a little from the movie *Alien,* when Ripley is moving through the atmosphere processor searching for the little girl Newt when the entire installation is about to blow a whole in the ground the size of Nebraska. Sirens blare incessantly and compressed superheated steam shoots out of red-hot pipes.

In *Digital Fortress* Brown raises the tension and suspense by several notches. We find out that Chartrukian has been thrown over the catwalk onto the generators below, causing enough damage for the generators to stop working: 'Phil Chartrukian was sprawled across the sharp iron fins of the main generator. His body was darkened and burned. His fall had shorted out Cyrpto's main power supply.'

Then all hell breaks loose when the warning horns start blaring. This is a crucial turning point because now the reader is faced with characters who are trapped inside with a giant computer that not only has a virus that threatens all the NSA data banks but that same computer is about to blow. To make matters worse, she discovers her fiancé is in grave danger when she reads the suicide note left by Greg Hale, who supposedly shot himself: 'And above all, I am truly sorry about David Becker. Forgive me, I was blinded by ambition.'

But it isn't only Susan Fletcher whose world is turned upside down. Brown uses his supporting characters to push the plot forward as well. In Spain, David runs across several smaller characters, from a fat German tourist with a prostitute to the assassin Hulaholt, who is trying to kill him. In between, he runs into punks, an old French Canadian and a girl with spiked punk hair who has Tankado's ring.

Brown believes the setting is critical to the story. A parking lot, he tells us, is probably not the best place to set a love story. 'Set the scene in a location that has an interest factor so that the setting itself is interesting,' he says. In his case, Brown has set his first thriller inside a super-secret American agency with a giant supercomputer where everything goes badly wrong. 'Reveal your setting in such a way that the setting is interesting,' Brown said. 'If you wrote a story in a private school and didn't reveal any inside information about what life's like to work or study at a private school, then you've got a boring setting.'[74]

The other thing to remember is that *Digital Fortress* was not turned out in a fortnight. It was a labour of love and sometimes of hate, as Brown tells us. 'The toughest part was believing in the story even when things were going badly.' Indeed, he had to force himself to spend five to eight hours each day writing, even when he felt he had lost direction and that the book wouldn't work.

To write *Digital Fortress*, Brown followed a simple approach. The first, as we have seen, is to get the 'big idea', which has to be something that will hold his interest for a long time because his novels are so research-intensive. 'Therefore, I choose a subject which is not black and white, but rather contains a grey area,' Brown said in his witness statement. 'The ideal topic has no clear right and wrong, no definite good and evil, and makes for great debate. I have some favourite subjects, which I wove into the *Digital Fortress* story once I had my "big idea" in place.'

Those favourite subjects include secret organisations, puzzles, codes and treasure hunts. 'My books are all "treasure hunts" of sorts. In each of my books, the treasure is an object,' Brown explained. 'I think people enjoy this sort of quest, especially trying to stay a step ahead of the hero by deciphering the clues along the way.'[75]

All of his books deal with secrecy – covert agencies, conspiracies, 'classified technologies, and secret history'. David Becker signs his messages to Susan 'without wax' – a code that Susan has real problems breaking, much to the delight of David. Brown reveals this code at the end of the book when he includes a little bit of history:

During the Renaissance, Spanish sculptors who made mistakes while carving expensive marble often patched their flaws with *cera* – "wax". A statue that has no flaws and required no patching was hailed as a "sculpture sin cera" or a "sculpture without wax". The phrase eventually came to mean anything honest or true. The English word "sincere" evolved from the Spanish *sin cera* – "without wax". David's secret code was no great mystery – he was simply signing his letters "Sincerely". Somehow he suspected Susan would not be amused.

After writing the novel Brown wanted to share some of the research he'd discovered, so he posted it on the *Digital Fortress* website. 'While I was researching the book there was so much information about the National Security Agency, about global terrorism, about intelligence gathering that couldn't be worked into the novel,' he said. He wanted people to see that what he was writing about was, in fact, true, saying, 'People would email me to say that there was no way that there's an agency that can do this. I would simply respond, "Go to the website and have a look – it's real."' (At the time of writing, however, the website didn't contain anything to do with the NSA and was an advertisement site for everything from digital voice recorders to night-vision goggles. The only mention of Dan Brown was where the reader could pick up a copy of the book – cheap.)

If we apply the five principles for thriller-writing to *Digital Fortress*, then by and large the book meets four of the five principles. First it is entertaining, as we've seen from the reviews. It provides an insight to the NSA and reflects the world around it through the settings in Spain, Washington, the use of email, gadgets and so on. At its heart it is an adventure. Brown cuts back and forth between the NSA where everything is going wrong, and with Spain where Becker is racing against time to find the ring. It is a stylish, edge-of-your-seat thriller. The one thing it doesn't have is humour but this is made up for by lashings of suspense, pace and tension.

Is it formula writing? Is it possible to have a formula when writing a first novel? The best way to answer that is to look at Brown's work in total. His next novel would be a departure from *Digital Fortress*.

CHAPTER EIGHT

ANGELS AND DEMONS

Science and religion was a very large part of my life from grade school all the way through college and I wanted to make them harmonious on a personal level.

DAN BROWN

Once *Digital Fortress* had been sold to Pocket Books in 1996, Brown went full tilt into researching his next novel, *Angels & Demons*. It would be a full 18 months before his first novel hit the shelves and all that time he was working on the new one, even though he didn't yet have his main theme.

'Sometime after completing *Digital Fortress,* I had several other ideas in development but hadn't yet decided on a direction,' Brown explained. 'I had enjoyed writing about the NSA, computers, technology and, of course, "secrets". I had read about CERN – Conseil European pour la Recherche Nucleaire – which is the world's largest scientific research facility.'

The idea of Europe was certainly an interesting one to Brown. As he had one character saying in the finished version: 'Most Americans do not see Europe as the world leader in scientific research. They see us as nothing but a quaint shopping district – an odd perception if you consider the nationalities of men like Einstein, Galileo and Newton.'

Brown and Blythe travelled to Rome and it was on this trip that he got his big idea for novel number two. It was an off-the-cuff remark by a tour guide that switched the light bulb on. 'We were beneath Vatican City touring a tunnel called *Il Passetto* – a concealed passageway used by the early Popes to escape in event of enemy attack,' said Brown. 'It runs from the Vatican to Castle Saint Angelo. According to the tour guide, one of the Vatican's most feared ancient enemies was a group of early scientists who had vowed revenge against the Vatican for crimes against scientists like Galileo and Copernicus. History had called them many things – the enlightened ones, the Illuminati, the Cult of Galileo.'

Brown was fascinated by the idea of the Illuminati and when the guide said that some people believed the Illuminati were still active and had strong political influence around the world today, despite the fact that most scholars believed they were long gone, the big idea for the new novel suddenly became clear. Brown decided there and then to base the book on the fact that the Illuminati were still very much alive in the shadows and had a sinister plan to bring down the Catholic Church.

Brown and Blythe took two trips to Rome for Brown to get what he needed for the novel. On the first one they walked for miles and took hundreds of photos, 'and explored the city using all kinds of guidebooks, maps and tours.'

Researching religion, architecture and art were the stuff of dreams to Brown and very exciting. He was lucky that Blythe also found the subjects enthralling. 'Once I started to look at artwork for inclusion in the story, I began to focus on particular artists,' Brown recalled. 'I knew Gianlorenzo Bernini had had problems with the Church. For example, his sculpture *The Ecstasy of St Teresa*, which I mention in the book, had been controversial.'

This controversy was the trigger for Brown to use Bernini in the book. He'd studied the artist in Spain and gained a lot of knowledge about the man's work. 'I was intrigued by the concept that Bernini's artwork might contain hidden messages; I learnt in art history classes that artists like Bernini, when commissioned to create religious art that may have been contrary to their own beliefs, often placed second levels of meaning in their art.'

'Langdon looked up at the towering monuments and felt totally disorientated. Two pyramids, each with a shining elliptical medallion. They were about as un-Christian as sculpture could get. The pyramids, the stars above, the signs of the Zodiac. All interior adornments are those of Gianlorenzo Bernini.' (*Angels & Demons*)

On their second trip, Brown and Blythe were accompanied by an art expert friend who had ties to the Vatican, and who helped them gain access to places that most people wouldn't see. 'The Vatican has a staggering collection of Renaissance masters such as Michelangelo, Raphael and Bernini,' Brown said. 'We spent a week in Rome, and our contact facilitated our gaining special access to the unclassified sections of the Vatican archives, as well as our seeing the Pope, both at a mass and in his audience hall.'[76]

In the book Brown goes into detail about the secret Vatican archives but he never actually saw them himself. According to Brown, only three Americans have managed to gain access to these secure and priceless collections of antiquities and documents, and he was not one of them. 'I was allowed inside the Vatican library and the Vatican archives, but not the Vatican secret archives.'[77] As Brown told the same interviewer, 'Secrets, I think, interest everybody and the concept of secret societies – especially after I visited the Vatican – just really captured my imagination.' [78]

Brown has said that he'd read that there are four miles of shelves in the Vatican secret archives, and that he 'became captivated by the prospect of what might be kept down there.' He tried many times to petition the Vatican to gain access but was always refused. Still, there were other unusual areas he could visit. 'Our contact there generously arranged for us to see several restricted areas of the Vatican, including the Necropolis (the city of the dead buried beneath the Vatican), St Peter's actual crypt (which we learned is not where most people think it is), and some perilous sections of the roof high above the Basilica; all of which featured in *Angels & Demons*.'[79]

After the European trips Brown had two main ideas, the Illuminati and the research he'd already started gathering on CERN. Located in Switzerland, CERN employs more than 3,000 scientists from around the world. When Brown began researching it, he discovered that they were working on antimatter, which has potential as a renewable energy source. But antimatter has its darker side. Its volatility and massive energy release mean it could also be used as a weapon of mass destruction. This dichotomy fascinated Brown. 'This science could be used for good or evil; to power the world or create a deadly weapon. I thought this would make a good plot element for a novel.'[80]

As Brown looked into the Illuminati, he was stunned by some of the things he discovered. 'I read conspiracy theories

... that included infiltration of the British Parliament and US Treasury, secret involvement with the Masons, affiliation with covert satanic cults, a plan for a New World Order, and even the resurgence of their ancient pact to destroy Vatican City.' He also found there was a huge amount of what he calls 'misinformation': 'Some theorists claim the plethora of information is actually generated by the Illuminati themselves in an effort to discredit any factual information that may have surfaced. This concealment tactic – known as "data-sowing" – is often employed by US intelligence agencies.'[81]

But who were the original Illuminati? Brown describes them as enlightened early men of science, such as Galileo, who were expelled from Rome by the Vatican because they adhered to science rather than the accepted beliefs of religion. 'The Illuminati fled and went into hiding in Bavaria where they began mixing with other refugee groups fleeing the Catholic purges – mystics, alchemists, scientists, occultists, Muslims, Jews. From this mixing pot, new Illuminati emerged. A darker Illuminati. A deeply anti-Christian Illuminati.'

According to Brown, the Illuminati became very powerful by infiltrating powerful organisations across the world, 'employing mysterious rites, retaining deadly secrecy, and vowing someday to rise again and take revenge on the Catholic Church. *Angels & Demons* is a thriller about the Illuminati's long-awaited resurgence and vengeance against their oppressors.' And in the middle of this is Robert Langdon who has to figure everything out.[82]

So Brown realised that he had the makings of a thriller, not only with antimatter and its possibility for good or evil but also with science versus religion. His challenge was how to combine the two. He had grown up in an atmosphere where both lived in harmony. His father was a mathematician and his mother was a church organist. He had studied science in school but also gone to church camp. At college, he had completed a cosmology course that included a section on Copernicus, Bruno, Galileo, and the Vatican Inquisition against science.

'Science and religion seem to be two different languages attempting to tell the same story, yet the battle between them has been raging for centuries and continues today,' said Brown, referring to the debate over whether to teach Creationism or Darwinism in schools. 'We live in an exciting era, though, because for the first time in human history, the line between science and religion is starting to blur. Particle physicists exploring the subatomic level are suddenly witnessing an interconnectivity of all things and having religious experiences... Buddhist monks are reading physics books and learning about experiments that confirm what they have believed in their hearts for centuries and have been unable to quantify.'[83]

Sensing he'd stumbled across something big, Brown began to dig deeper. At first he turned to the internet for his research, posting questions and comments to Usenet groups. 'The Freedom of Information Act, of course, is a great resource, primarily because it can lead to specific individuals who are knowledgeable in a given field and sometimes are willing to talk about it,' Brown said of his research. 'In many cases, understandably, these contacts prefer to remain nameless, but sometimes depending on what they've told you, they like being acknowledged in the book.

'Occasionally, research is simply a matter of finding the proper printed resource. For example, the detailed description in *Angels & Demons* depicting the intimate ritual of Vatican conclave – the threaded necklace of ballots... the mixing of chemicals... the burning of the ballots – much of that was from a book published on Harvard University Press by a Jesuit scholar who had interviewed more than a hundred cardinals, which is obviously something I never would have had the time or connections to do.'[84]

The books Brown read included *The Quark and the Jaguar*, *The Tao of Physics*, *The God Particle* and *The Physics of Immortality*, among many others. To his surprise he discovered that science and religion were working in common areas. 'The grey area that interested me was the ongoing battle between science and religion, and the faint hope of reconciliation between the two,' he said. 'This was my "big idea" and my "grey area". I thought I had hit on something that really would keep my attention for the next two years.'[85]

Around this time, the editor at Pocket Books who had brought Brown to the publisher and backed him left the company, leaving Brown in a state of flux. He had become a writer without an editor championing his book inside a big company. However, Brown simply cracked on with what he was doing, relying on Blythe to be his sounding board as well as his research partner.

A new editor, Jason Kaufman, came on board with the publisher shortly after the old one left. 'A month after he had started working at the Simon & Schuster imprint, a higher-up made him responsible for overseeing the two books Brown was contractually obligated to write for the publisher.'[86]

The book has several ambigrams within its pages and the premise of the book is built around an ambigram of the word Illuminati. Brown finds them fascinating. 'Ambigrams can be very unnerving when you first see them, and almost everyone who sees the ambigram on the novel's cover invariably stands there for several minutes rotating the book over and over, perplexed.'[87] Eventually he would get his new editor to include an ambigram on the cover of the book, although only first editions had it.

With *Angels & Demons* Brown made a few key departures – he called them 'advances' – from *Digital Fortress*. The first of these was the idea of writing a thriller that was also an academic lecture. He wanted to write a book that he would love to read himself. 'The kind of books I enjoy are those in which you learn,' he said. 'My hope was that readers would be entertained and also learn enough to want to use the book as a point of departure for more reading.' As he explored his main subjects further, he found items that he thought readers would love to know about. 'Rome was a location that allowed me to immerse myself in the history of religion, art, and architecture.'

When Brown visited the Pantheon in Rome, the docent told him about the building's history. This is reflected in the humorous scene in the book where Robert Langdon is desperately searching for the killer while a zealous cardinal reels off facts and figures about the building: 'Langdon's progress around his side of the Pantheon was being hampered somewhat by the guide on his heels, now continuing his tireless narration as Langdon prepared to check the final alcove.'

Hidden information and secret societies feature prominently in all of Brown's work. In *Angels & Demons* he was honing his ability to put them at the very heart of his narrative. 'For example, the design of the Great Seal on the

US dollar bill includes an illustration of a pyramid – an object which arguably has nothing to do with American history,' Brown explained. In the *Angels & Demons* section of his witness statement Brown said the pyramid was, 'actually an Egyptian occult symbol representing a convergence upward toward the ultimate source of illumination: in this case, an all-seeing eye. The eye inside the triangle is a pagan symbol adopted by the Illuminati to signify the brotherhood's ability to infiltrate and watch all things. In addition, the triangle (Greek Delta) is the scientific symbol for change.'

Brown's fascination with secret societies comes from growing up in New England, where he was influenced by the clandestine clubs of Ivy League universities, Masonic lodges and so on. He recalled that he saw 'New England as having a long tradition of elite private clubs, fraternities, and secrecy.' He had friends at Harvard who were members of a secret finals club and he also knew about the Skull & Bones club at Yale. 'In the town where I grew up, there was a Masonic lodge, and nobody could (or would) tell me what happened behind those closed doors. All of this secrecy captivated me as a young man.'[88]

Writing about secret societies and material keeps Brown interested in the project. 'Because a novel can take upwards of a year to write, I need to be constantly learning as I write, or I lose interest,' he said. 'Researching and writing about secretive topics helps remind me how much fun it is to "spy" into unseen worlds and it motivates me to try to give the reader that same experience. My goal is always to make the characters and plot so engaging that readers don't realise how much they are learning along the way.'[89]

But the novel is not a religious book. It is quite simply 'a chase and a love story'. The action takes place inside the

Vatican and Brown believes that 'most people understand that an organisation as old and powerful as the Vatican could not possibly have risen to power without acquiring a few skeletons in their closets.' But perhaps the reason why the novel raised eyebrows in certain circles is because it 'opens some Vatican closets most people don't even know exist.'[90]

As with *Digital Fortress*, codes and treasure hunts feature prominently. In the first novel it was a straight binary code that had to be cracked but in the second Brown put the clues in a series of poems or riddles, which he saw as 'useful tools for releasing information and moving the plot to the next stage.'

'I accomplished this by delivering the code in short snippets of verse, which enables the reader a chance to stay one step ahead of Langdon,' explained Brown. 'Langdon, as a teacher, symbologist and art historian, satisfies dual prerequisites for my hero – that of being a credible teacher and also of being knowledgeable enough to decipher the clues in the artistic treasure hunts I create.'

Brown has said that he feels that *Angels & Demons* has a superior plot and is better written than *Digital Fortress*. 'I wanted every single chapter to compel the reader to turn to the next page. I was taught that efficiency of words is the way an author respects his readers' time, and so I trimmed the novel heavily while I was writing.'[91]

To build pace and tension he compressed the plot into a 24-hour time span. 'I tried to keep the reader abreast of where the characters were physically, at all times. That seems to help the reader's feeling that he is right there the entire time. In addition, I tried to end every chapter with a cliffhanger.'

All five of Brown's novels are written to a similar style or structure. He believes it is this formula that makes his books so compelling for his readers. Essentially, his books have a hero who is pulled out of their routine and put into unfamiliar and dangerous situations that they don't understand. Each of his books have very strong female characters who interact with the male character to create romance and implied sexuality. Travel, interesting locations and the countdown all add to the story. 'I think that it is not so much what I write which is compelling but how I say it,' Brown said. 'I must admit, however, that I did not realise this until my first three novels became huge bestsellers after *The Da Vinci Code*.'

The story of *Angels & Demons* revolves around the main character of Harvard symbologist Robert Langdon as he tries to stop the Illuminati from destroying Vatican City with antimatter. The book begins with Robert Langdon getting a fax from CERN director Maximilian Kohler that shows the ambigram of the Illuminati branded into a dead man's chest. This man is, or was, Leonardo Vetra, one of the top and most respected physicists at CERN. In addition, one of Vetra's eyes is missing.

Kohler has discovered the body but not called the police. Instead he contacts Langdon and has him flown over to authenticate the symbol, which he does. The meaning of this is that the Illuminati, a long extinct secret society, is operating again. But things are more serious than that. Kohler has called in Vetra's daughter, the beautiful Vittoria, who takes them down to the lab where she and her father were working. They discover that a canister of antimatter has been stolen. Because of its volatile nature the antimatter is suspended inside the canister in a high vacuum by a magnetic field, which ensures it cannot come in contact with matter and unleash its tremendous destructive power. The canister is maintained by electricity at CERN but if it is taken away its backup battery lasts only 24 hours. When the battery fails, the antimatter will fall, touch the base of the canister and explode.

The canister, its digital clock ticking down, is hidden somewhere inside the Vatican City with a stolen security camera focused on the readout. The camera is wireless and feeds back to the security monitors in Vatican City but the Swiss Guard, the Vatican's elite security force, have no idea where the canister is.

To make matters worse, as a result of the recent death of the most recent Pope, a papal enclave to elect a new one is under way at the Vatican. The most likely candidates for the post are four cardinals known as the Preferiti, and they are missing. Langdon and Vittoria arrive at Vatican City and begin searching for them, hoping they will also find the canister and the people responsible for Vetra's murder. Tradition says that all the cardinals in Vatican City have to be sealed in the enclave until a new Pope is elected. With all the cardinals isolated, the man left in charge is the late Pope's closest aide, Camerlengo Carlo Ventresca. Along with Commander Olivetti, Captain Rocher and Lieutenant Chartrand, the Camerlengo helps the two heroes in the search.

Langdon is convinced the only way to find the Preferiti is to retrace the Path of Illumination, an ancient and complex process the Illuminati used to induct new recruits into the fold. Prospective inductees had to follow a series of clues in and around Rome. If done correctly, the candidate would discover the secret meeting place of the Illuminati and be granted membership. Langdon and Vittoria set off on the path to uncover the clues that will lead them to the Preferiti and ultimately the canister.

An unknown assassin, working for a shadowy Illuminati master known only as Janus, has said he will kill the four cardinals in four different places, one each hour starting at 8pm. Using ancient texts written by Galileo and through his extensive knowledge of religious symbology and history, Langdon believes that there are four locations in Rome that the Illuminati believed represented Earth, Air, Fire, and Water. Each time Langdon and Vittoria arrive at a location, they find one of the cardinals murdered in a way appropriate to the element. The first cardinal is found with soil down his throat and branded with an Earth ambigram, while the second has had his lungs punctured and been branded with an ambigram of Air.

After finding the first two bodies, Langdon heads for the third location at Santa Maria della Vittoria Basilica, where he discovers the assassin has set the third cardinal on fire. But the assassin hasn't left: he kills Olivetti, tries to kill Langdon and kidnaps Vittoria. Langdon meets the assassin again at a fountain, the landmark for the final element of Water, where the fourth cardinal is drowned.

But Langdon is determined to finish the Path of Illumination, which leads him to the Castel Sant' Angelo and a secret underground tunnel leading directly to the Pope's chambers in the Vatican. Langdon finds Vittoria and frees her. They face the assassin together and manage to kill him by pushing him several hundred feet to his grisly death. The two heroes race back to St Peter's Basilica, only to find that Kohler has arrived to confront the Camerlengo, who points the finger at Kohler, saying that he is Janus. The Camerlengo is branded with the Illuminati Diamond and screams in agony. Hearing his screams, the Swiss Guard break into the Pope's chambers and shoot Kohler.

The Camerlengo then accuses Captain Rocher of being one of the Illuminati and orders Lieutenant Chartrand to shoot him, which he does. Kohler, however, has managed to hang on long enough to give Langdon a video tape that he says will explain everything.

Time is running out. They decide to evacuate the Basilica but the Camerlengo suddenly goes into a trance and refuses to go. He says he's had a vision from God and now knows where the canister is. He tears into the catacombs under the Basilica with Langdon, Vittoria and others in hot pursuit. They arrive at St Peter's Tomb to find the canister sitting there, the clock dangerously close to the end.

With only five minutes left, Langdon and the Camerlengo grab the canister and head for a helicopter. They manage to get into the air well above the city when the thing explodes, causing no damage to the city below. The Camerlengo parachutes safely down onto the roof of St Peter's Basilica and stands triumphantly before the crowds in the Square. But what has happened to Langdon? There was only one parachute in the helicopter.

Everyone sees the survival of the Camerlengo as a miracle, so the cardinals in the conclave say that Catholic law should be made to elect the Camerlengo as the new Pope. But Langdon has survived by managing to use a window cover from the chopper as a parachute and landing heavily in the Tiber River. He is hurt, but the injuries aren't serious and he manages to get back to the Basilica and views Kohler's tape with the College of Cardinals. Kohler was right: it does tell the truth and Langdon, Vittoria and the cardinals confront the Camerlengo in the Sistine Chapel.

At this point we find that the Pope had been due to meet Vetra to discuss his work on antimatter at CERN. Vetra, a devout Catholic, believed he'd found a way through his research to bring science and religion together, linking Man and God. This was an anathema to the Camerlengo, who strongly felt that only the Church should have domain over God. The Pope had revealed to the Camerlengo when discussing Vetra that science had given him a son. This had been done through artificial insemination.

The Camerlengo had looked up to the Pope, seeing him as a holy man who was completely against science. Enraged and feeling betrayed the Camerlengo plotted to stop the Pope and Vetra. His first step was to poison the Pope. He then took the guise of the Illuminati master Janus and recruited the assassin, setting the wheels in motion for the murder of Vetra, stealing the canister and murdering the four cardinals.

As Langdon has suspected from the beginning, the real Illuminati had nothing to do with the plot. The secret order has long since gone and the whole thing was a plot by the Camerlengo to carry out his evil plans. But there is a sting in the tail for the Camerlengo when he discovers that he was the Pope's son through artificial insemination. Overcome with grief, the Camerlengo sets fire to himself in St Peter's Square for all to see. In the conclave a new Pope is elected.

Langdon and Vittoria end up in bed together in the Hotel Bernini, where Lieutenant Chartrand delivers the Illuminati Diamond from the new Pope for Langdon to keep on loan indefinitely.[92]

While the plot may sound far-fetched, the true test is what people think of it and what the reviews say about it. On Amazon, one reviewer (Kelly Flynn) called *Angels*

& Demons 'a no-holds-barred, pull-out-all-the-stops, breathless tangle of a thriller – think Katherine Neville's *The Eight* (but cleverer) or Umberto Eco's *Foucault's Pendulum* (but more accessible).'[93] This review also says the book is 'a heck of a good read' and 'tasty brain candy'.

Another reviewer said that *Angels & Demons* was better than *The Da Vinci Code*. 'A fast-paced, exciting read. For my money, I think this is a more interesting and surprising book than *The Da Vinci Code* and I recommend it to any fan of *The Da Vinci Code*.'[94]

And again. . .

'Even for me with the attention span of a fly I could not put this book down! Full of twists and turns it leaves you guessing till the end. Beautifully written, great plot, every chapter leaves you fully engaged and excited to read more!!'[95]

Not all the reviews are so positive. One reader gave the book a single star saying, 'My wife asked me to read this book before we went to Rome so that I would know some of the places we would visit... this is the only use for this book. Now, before I start, can I just say that I know this is a work of fiction, BUT when the author begins by making claims of fact and clearly trying to make out that the story is true, then it deserves to be judged on how realistic it is. The story is undoubtedly exciting, but the ending is so preposterous that it completely blows away any lingering sense of realism. Also the death of one of the characters is a total anticlimax, and is at odds with the level of suspense that had been built up to that point. I certainly won't be rushing back to read more Dan Brown on the basis of this book.'[96]

Another Amazon reviewer called it a book 'stuffed

with hackneyed clichés, it's worse than Mills & Boon or a 16-year-old on a creative writing course. Obviously for the less discerning reader yet it has sold millions. A literary snob? Damn right I am. There's enough junk in life these days as it is.'[97]

The reactions to *Angels & Demons* covers both ends of the spectrum and everything in between. As one reviewer put it, 'you either hate it or you love it.' Many reviewers give the book five stars while others give it one star, but the majority of reader reactions are positive, such as: 'The book starts slowly but as you begin to get into the thick of it, the book picks up pace and takes you on an astounding journey, fast-paced, intriguing and all in all a fantastic read.'[98]

One of the themes running through many reviews, good and bad, is that there are many inaccuracies in the book. Indeed, the Wikipedia entry on *Angels & Demons* states that in the first edition some of the locations in Rome were wrong as was the use of Italian, which was corrected in subsequent editions.

Where the real problems lie is in the areas of science, technology and history. For example, the antimatter discussions that take place in the book claim that the substance can be produced in practical quantities that could lead to a limitless source of energy. But CERN has published a paper on the facts – which Brown placed in the book – stating that it takes more energy to create antimatter than the substance actually produces.

Here's what Brown said about antimatter in the *Angels & Demons* section of his witness statement: 'Antimatter is the ultimate energy source. It releases energy with 100% efficiency (nuclear fission is 1.5% efficient). Antimatter is 100,000 times more powerful than rocket fuel. A single gram contains the energy of a 20 kiloton atomic bomb – the size of the bomb dropped on Hiroshima. In addition to being highly explosive, antimatter is extremely unstable and ignites when it comes in contact with anything... even air.'

Brown also claimed that antimatter can only be stored by suspending it inside a vacuum in an electromagnetic field. Once that field fails, the antimatter collides with its container, resulting in a matter/antimatter conversion known by physicists as annihilation. 'CERN is now regularly producing small quantities of antimatter in their research for future energy sources. Antimatter holds tremendous promise; it creates no pollution or radiation, and a single droplet could power New York City for a full day.'

However, on 10 May 2009 an American cable television network aired a documentary called *Angels & Demons Decoded*. In it an official from CERN suggested that the organisation had only been able to produce approximately 10 billionths of a gram of antimatter over the previous 20 years and that the explosive potential of that amount was not much more than a firecracker – certainly not as powerful as Brown had claimed.[99]

Still, this book stacks up well against the five principles of thriller writing. People consider it to be an entertaining, fast-paced read. Brown's research into the Vatican, the art in Vatican City, the architecture of Rome and its churches, and the secret society of the Illuminati provides the reader with insight into the inner workings of the Vatican, reflecting the world around the characters. Like Brown's other books, this one is written to a formula that Brown himself has described – essentially blending fact with fiction and taking a character out of his comfort zone and pitting them against a ticking clock and some ruthless villains. At its heart is the adventure – in this case a treasure hunt to find the codes that lead to the discovery of the canister. And finally, it is written in a stylish way that Brown has developed since *Digital Fortress.*

Although the book has sold well since *The Da Vinci Code,* initial sales were very poor. Though Brown's publisher had changed from St Martin's Press to Simon & Schuster, the promised publicity campaigns never happened. 'They promised to give the book considerably more publicity and support than my previous publishers,' Brown explained. 'Their proposed publicity included a much larger print run (60,000), advertising in major newspapers, web advertising, a 12-city tour, an e-book release, and other exciting prospects.'[100]

Despite good reviews, the poor sales of both his novels left Brown struggling with the desire to write a third one. But he had to do it. He was contracted to the publisher for a third novel. The only thing that kept him going was the possibility that one of the novels might be optioned for a feature film. 'At the time, that was a big financial incentive,' Brown said. 'I did receive numerous offers for the film rights to *Angels & Demons,* but I turned them down as they were not enough money and not with major studios.' [101]

Strapped for cash, Brown and Blythe found themselves visiting low-profile publishing events where they sold copies of *Angels & Demons* out of the boot of their car. Brown was seriously considering giving up writing and returning to teaching but he and Blythe knew that they had something special from the feedback they were getting. 'The few readers who read *Angels & Demons* had gone wild for it,' Brown said in his witness statement. 'The store where we buy most of our books, The Water Street Bookstore in

Exeter, New Hampshire, was hand-selling my books, but the superstores still did not even know my name.'

Brown kept on trying to get the book known but failed. 'I was told that the window of opportunity in book publishing was only a few weeks and that an author needed to reach a critical mass of readers very quickly after release or the bookstores would return his books to the publisher to make room for the next round of new books. This is why large scale, coordinated launches are needed to make a success of most books. I realised I could not do it alone, no matter how hard I tried.'

CHAPTER NINE

DECEPTION POINT

Commander James D Swanson of the United States Navy was short, plump and crowding forty. He had jet black hair topping a pink cherubic face, and with the deep permanent creases of laughter lines radiating from his eyes and curving round his mouth he was a dead ringer for the cheerful, happy-go-lucky extrovert who is the life and soul of the party where the guests park their brains along with their hats and coats. That, anyway, was how he struck me at first glance but on the reasonable assumption that I might very likely find some other qualities in the man picked to command the latest and most powerful nuclear submarine afloat I took a second and closer look at him and this time I saw what I should have seen the first time if the dank grey fog and winter dusk settling down over the Firth of Clyde hadn't made seeing so difficult. His eyes. Whatever his eyes were they weren't those of the gladhanding wisecracking bon vivant. They were the coolest, clearest grey eyes I'd ever seen.[102]

The above quote is the opening to Alistair MacLean's *Ice Station Zebra*. It sets the stage for a fast-paced, tension-filled, edge-of-your-seat thriller. There are similarities to Brown's *Deception Point*: MacLean's story takes the reader straight into the action as does the prologue to *Deception Point*. But from the Prologue onwards *Deception Point* takes more than a hundred pages for the story to really begin. From that point on, Brown builds the tension to the final nail-biting climax. But *Deception Point* is essentially an American novel set against the backdrop of a presidential election. If the reader has no interest in American politics then those first hundred pages will be tedious indeed.

Brown's 'big idea' for this book was based on the press stories about the string of failures that the National Aeronautics and Space Administration (NASA) had suffered and the calls to hand the agency over to the private sector. 'I became very interested in the question of whether it made sense for my tax dollars to fund trips to Mars while the very school in which I was teaching could barely afford an art teacher.'[103]

Brown built his story around this premise, weaving in characters and locations, again blending fact with fiction. But while MacLean tells his story in the narrow, confined location of a submarine and an ice station on a glacier in the Arctic Circle, Brown uses a much broader canvas to tell his story: from a glacier off Canada's Ellesmere Island to Washington DC to a research vessel off the coast of New Jersey. And while MacLean tells his story simply and with minimal fuss, Brown peppers his novel with a wide variety of information covering technical equipment, geological data, physics and much more.

Why compare Brown with MacLean, *Deception Point* with *Ice Station Zebra*? Both books have similar plots and similar locations. In *Deception Point* a meteorite has been found buried in the ice of a glacier and a team of experts has been sent up there to authenticate NASA's claims of extraterrestrial life found as fossils in the meteorite. But all isn't what it appears to be and soon it all unravels as the protagonist finds someone is trying to kill her to stop her from telling the world about what is really going on.

In *Ice Station Zebra* a US nuclear submarine is sent up to the Arctic Circle in response to a distress call from a British ice station that has suffered a catastrophic fire. The boat goes there to pick up survivors and find out what happened. However, it is soon apparent that the fire was deliberate and that the expedition is far more than a rescue. It is to retrieve a capsule of microfilm that has been ejected from a Russian spy satellite and landed near Zebra. The film contains images of all the nuclear missile installations around the world and the Russians want it back.

While *Ice Station Zebra* is a much older novel than *Deception Point*, it is an excellent example of the formula thriller writing that made MacLean's early work so good. The question is, does *Deception Point* stack up against it?

Ice Station Zebra feels real. The reader goes right into the story along with the narrator. The description of the cold and the lonely icecap comes from MacLean's own experiences as an able seaman aboard *HMS Royalist* during the Second World War. MacLean did two tours aboard this cruiser on the Arctic Convoys and learned about numbing cold first-hand. The same ship later took him to the Pacific theatre where he saw action escorting carrier groups against Japanese targets in Sumatra, Burma and Malaysia. This wartime experience can be seen in his early works, including *Ice Station Zebra*.

Having been at sea for most of the war MacLean knew the sea and what life was like aboard ship. He understood the mind-numbing cold and the bleakness of the Arctic

Circle from his days in the Arctic Convoys. For example: 'We flitted through the howling darkness of that nightmare lunar landscape. We were no longer bowed under the weight of heavy packs. Our backs were to that gale-force wind so that for every laborious plodding step we had made on our way to Zebra, we now covered five.' Or: 'After perhaps four hundred yards the ice wall ended so abruptly, leading to so sudden and unexpected an exposure to the whistling fury of the ice-storm that I was bowled completely off my feet.'

Ian Fleming said the key to writing a good thriller is to write about what you know, to base the book on something that happened and build it from there. MacLean used his personal experiences in his books, but what about Brown? There is no record that Brown ever served aboard a ship or that he spent any length of time in the Arctic Circle, so for him to write about being stuck out in the open on a glacier and make it sound real, must be from a combination of painstaking research and a vivid imagination.

'Outside the habisphere, the katabatic wind roaring down the glacier was nothing like the ocean winds Tolland was accustomed to. On the ocean, wind was a function of tides and pressure fronts and came in gusting ebbs and flows. The katabatic, however, was a slave to simple physics – heavy cold air rushing down a glacial incline like a tidal wave. It was the most resolute gale force Tolland had ever experienced.'

So how does *Deception Point* stack up against the Curzon Group's five elements of a good thriller ?

The 'big idea' for *Deception Point* came from the research

Brown had done on *Digital Fortress*. He'd finished writing *Angels & Demons* and needed a break, as he explained in his witness statement. 'I was exhausted from the research and writing of such a complicated religious thriller,' he said. 'Even though I had lots of viable material left over from all of my research on religion/art/Rome and the Templars etc., I felt like I needed a change of pace. I decided to write what I later termed a "palate cleanser".'

Having researched and written about the covert and secretive organisations (the National Security Agency in *Digital Fortress* and the clandestine brotherhood of the Illuminati in *Angels & Demons*), Brown needed something different to write about. 'I found myself hard pressed to come up with a more secretive topic,' he said. 'Fortunately, I had recently learned of another US intelligence agency, more covert even than the National Security Agency. This new agency, the National Reconnaissance Office (NRO), figured prominently in my third novel, *Deception Point*.'[104]

At the same time, the press had also been commenting on NASA's string of failures, saying that the agency was becoming a bottomless pit for taxpayer's money without much coming back in return. Weren't there more important things closer to home for taxpayers' money to be spent on? 'Then again,' Brown said, 'could we as human beings really give up our quest for discovery in space? *Deception Point* centred on issues of morality in politics, human progress, national security, and classified technology. The crux of the novel was the link between NASA, the military, and the political pressures of big budget technology.'

Up until the point in the book when the meteorite is discovered with fossils embedded into it, the anti-NASA feeling espoused by the President's opponent has been growing but then this amazing discovery puts NASA back on the map. Or does it?

The protagonist in *Deception Point* is the top intelligence analyst to the White House, Rachel Sexton. She is the daughter of Senator Sedgewick Sexton, a presidential candidate with his eyes fixed firmly on the White House. It is he who is running the anti-NASA campaign with great success. Rachel – who is in her mid-thirties, single and described as attractive – works for the National Reconnaissance Office (NRO) as a 'gister'. As the book explains, gisting (or data reduction) requires analysing complex reports and distilling their essence (or gist) into concise, single-page briefs. Rachel holds the NRO's premier gisting post – intelligence liaison to the White House.

At the opening of the book Senator Sexton's presidential campaign is rolling forward. The polls show he is more popular than the besieged President Zachary Herney. The President knows of Rachel because of the daily intelligence briefs she sends to his National Security Advisor.

Unknown to Senator Sexton, to Rachel or anyone else outside of NASA, the President has sent a team of scientific experts to authenticate NASA's findings in the meteorite buried deep within the Milne Ice Shelf off Ellesmere Island in the Arctic. The meteorite was found by NASA's new Polar Orbiting Density Scanner (PODS), one of a collection of satellites orbiting earth and monitoring the planet for any signs of large-scale change. Embedded in the meteorite are insect fossils that are similar to – but not the same as –those found on earth, so NASA claims these fossils are evidence of extraterrestrial life. Rachel is sent up to join this team of experts and act as an independent authenticator.

Senator Sexton is using the NASA failures to fuel his campaign and the general public are buying into it. Why send missions to Mars when there are people in the US without education, clothing, housing etc.? Sexton wants to abolish NASA and use its funding for schools across the country. NASA is desperate for good news. Because of its poor standing, the President has sent four scientists – TV personality and oceanographer Michael Tolland (who also owns the boat involved, the *Goya*), an eccentric but brilliant astrophysicist Corky Marlinson, glaciologist Norah Mangor, and palaeontologist Wailee Ming – to authenticate and verify the findings.

But while the scientists and NASA employees are embedded in relative warmth and comfort in a giant habisphere on the ice shelf, outside a Delta Force team is monitoring the discovery for a mysterious boss known only as The Controller. In the pit from which the meteorite has been extracted, Ming spots an irregularity that shouldn't be there if NASA's data is correct. Leaning into the pit to get a sample of the water, he is attacked by a microbot operated by the Delta Force team, falls into the water and drowns.

Tolland also spots the irregularity in the water and quickly tells Marlinson and Rachel, who report their concerns to Mangor. She realises there is seawater in the closed area of the pit where there should only be freshwater – melted ice from extracting the meteorite. To make sure they are right, the four scientists go outside onto the ice shelf to scan the ice from a distance. On the scan they discover Ming's body in the water pit and a column of frozen sea beneath the opening from which the meteorite was extracted. This leads to the conclusion that the meteorite was drilled up from the bottom of the ice.

While they are considering the implications of this, they are attacked by the Delta Force team and Mangor is left dead. The other three manage to get away in a nail-biting chase across the ice that sees them plunge over a cliff and end up on a piece of ice that has broken away from the main glacier. Sure they are going to die, Rachel remembers that the US has hydroplanes mounted on sea floors around the world. She begins banging on the ice, and this is picked up by a submarine. The three survivors are rescued, while the Delta Force team believe they have perished in the freezing ocean.

From the submarine Rachel contacts the President's security advisor, telling her about their discovery, as well as contacting her boss at the NRO, William Pickering. He has them airlifted from the submarine by helicopter away from the danger zone to an airfield in Greenland, from where they are flown to Washington.

The real motive for Senator Sexton wanting to get rid of NASA eventually comes out. Private companies want to see space exploration privatised and Sexton has been receiving large amounts from these people for his campaign. Rachel's relationship with him is strained as she blames him for her mother's untimely death and she is unaware of her father's true motivation. She believes the President and NASA are part of a conspiracy to kill them to cover up the fact that the meteorite is a fake. It is a massive PR exercise designed to bolster the incumbent President in the upcoming election.

Rachel, Tolland and Marlinson need one last bit of evidence to prove the whole thing is a sham and that can be found aboard Tolland's ship anchored off the coast of New Jersey. The Delta Force team learn that the three survivors are now aboard this ship and arrive via helicopter gunship to kill them. Rachel manages to send a fax to her father asking for help just before the team arrive.

Aboard the *Goya*, Rachel, Tolland and Marlinson manage to stop the Delta Force team, but they are still at the mercy of The Controller in the helicopter gunship. When it touches down on the heaving vessel, Rachel is stunned to see her boss William Pickering emerge – he is The Controller, the one who has really been trying to kill her and her friends. He tells her about her father's true motives and how he (Pickering) masterminded the fake meteorite to attack Sexton's campaign and, in his eyes, protect the American people. However, it all went wrong when the President sent the scientists to the Arctic to authenticate the findings. At that point Pickering realised they would discover his plot, so anyone who knew about it had to be eliminated. Violence erupts as the three scientists try to get away. The Delta Force team have been immobilised in the claws of a submersible on the ship's deck but Pickering grabs a machine gun and fires several bursts at them.

The ship is anchored on a magma plume that sends hot water racing to the surface from the bottom of the sea, causing an inverted tornado in the sea. The vessel is crippled in the fight and starts heeling over. The helicopter gunship slides off the deck into the sea with Delta One still in it. The hot magna ignites its Hellfire missiles, creating a water vortex and the gunship is sucked down to the bottom with William Pickering still aboard.

Sexton reads the fax that Rachel sent him and realises with this news, nothing can stop him on the way to the Oval Office. He decides to go public but instead of sending copies of the fax to the press, incriminating evidence comes to light and he is publicly humiliated – his campaign is in ruins. President Herney tells the American people the truth and presumably gets his second term. At the novel's end, Rachel and Tolland are romantically involved.

That's the story of *Deception Point*. Brown does take considerable time building up the discovery itself before he reveals it's a fraud and getting the protagonist into a situation where her life is in danger. Indeed, it's not until she arrives at the glacier that the pace really starts to take off. But there are plenty of hints that something isn't quite right. While NASA is working to extract the meteorite from the ice and believing they've found evidence of life outside the planet, a Delta Force team is using sophisticated technology to monitor the activity. So the reader knows something's wrong. Why would a Delta Force team be on the ice shelf if everything was okay? It is Ming's discovery that is the turning point. Our heroes then realise their lives are in mortal danger and from that point on Brown takes us on a roller-coaster chase.

But is it any good? Again, the reviews are similar to those of the first two books, largely positive but some negative. *Bookreporter* said that Brown was 'quite the craftsman, displaying a knack for character sleight-of-hand while always playing fair with his audience.' No one in the book is what they appear to be, except perhaps the three heroes, Rachel Sexton, Michael Tolland and the hugely annoying Corky Marlinson. 'The only certainty is that Brown, within the space of a few novels, has developed into one of the best of the authors labouring in the suspense field.'[105]

A reviewer on *Bookbrowser* said that Brown had masterfully blended 'science, history and politics in his critically acclaimed thriller *Angels & Demons*' and with *Deception Point* he 'has crafted another novel in which nothing is as it seems – and behind every corner is a stunning surprise. *Deception Point* is pulse-pounding fiction at its best.'[106]

Publisher's Weekly said that *Deception Point* was 'an excellent thriller, a big yet believable story unfolding at breakneck pace, with convincing settings and just the right blend of likable and hateful characters.'[107] *The Library Journal* added to the accolades by saying that it had 'intrigue aplenty, both in the Arctic and in Washington, and Brown does not disappoint with this genuine page-turner.'[108]

Not everyone was so enthusiastic. One reviewer on *Kirkus Review* called the book a 'tedious techno-thriller', saying that the characters were wooden and that the gadgets were more believable than the people. 'Brown's scientific knowledge isn't what ultimately dooms the book. The story, which has an initial rush to it, bogs down once it starts plodding through all the government shenanigans and secret plots. Although Brown is a more astute storyteller than most of his brethren in the techno-thriller vein, and won't lose any fans this time out, he's never able to convincingly marry the technical and the human sides of *Deception Point*.'

Other reviews called the book predictable. 'You can turn your nose up at the pointless love interest,' sniped one on Amazon. However the criticism of predictability is tempered by the reviewer's description of the book's climax: 'The final action scene was brilliantly choreographed, a masterpiece of cause and effect. Initially a "samey" feel, yet after a quarter of the book you'll be hooked and won't put it down until it's all over.'[109]

While the positive reviews number in the hundreds, there is a theme that runs through many of the negative ones, criticising Brown for just scratching the surface of his characters. 'You never feel as if you really get to know them properly,' said one such reviewer, 'which makes it difficult to know just how you feel towards them. In the end I settled for ambivalence. I'd have liked to have known more about Rachel and her relationship with her father, what makes Michael Tolland tick, and with several other characters we only had an outline sketch, with no colour added. On the basis of a school report I'd say, "Dan must try harder with his characterisations."'[110]

In addition, some reviewers complained that Brown writes his books on a formula, one saying: '*Deception Point* follows the same path as his other works, with only the basic premise of the story and the characters' names and professions changing. For *Deception Point* (the one about the thing NASA found), substitute *The Da Vinci Code* (the one about the Holy Grail), or try *Digital Fortress* (the one about the unbreakable code). In *Deception Point*, Brown gets away with this formula, but I'm not sure how much longer he'll manage this.'

Like his first two novels, *Deception Point* is indeed formula writing, which Brown has admitted. 'Of course, there is a twist in the tail, as there is in all my books. Like its predecessors, *Deception Point* incorporates my usual elements – a secretive organisation, a love story, a chase, and plenty of academic lecture. At the heart, however, my books are all essentially treasure hunts set within a 24-hour period.' [111]

In truth, the formula aspect is difficult to escape. The interchangeable plot is essentially highly intelligent people caught up in a situation that puts their lives in danger as they try to work out the clues, and along the way two of them fall in love. The details change with each novel but the characters remain essentially the same. Rachel Sexton is interchangeable with Susan Fletcher in *Digital Fortress*. The Commander in *Digital Fortress* is William Pickering in *Deception Point*. Michael Tolland in *Deception Point* is David in *Digital Fortress* with a key difference being that Rachel and Michael's relationship is just beginning while David and Susan's is already well established in *Digital Fortress*. The object of the treasure hunt in *Deception Point* is the meteorite while in *Digital Fortress* it was the ring.

Stacked up against the five principles of good thriller writing, the book has to entertain the reader and *Deception Point* does that, as we can see from the largely positive reviews and comments. (*Deception Point* gets a 3.5 star customer rating.)

It should also reflect the world around it, which Brown has done through his extensive research into a wide variety of topics, mostly technical, to give the story authenticity. For example, 'Presidential Decision Directive 25(PDD 25) grants Delta Force soldiers "freedom from all legal accountability" including exception from the 1876 Posse Comitatus Act, a statute imposing criminal penalties for anyone using the military for personal gain, domestic law enforcement, or unsanctioned covert operations.'

The third principle is that a good thriller doesn't need to follow formulas. This is where Brown falls down. He uses an interchangeable plot with interchangeable characters based in different settings on a different treasure hunt for different reasons.

A good thriller also needs to take the writer and the reader on an adventure. We know that Brown has done this in *Deception Point* because of the reviews, many of which have said that all his books are 'packed full of suspense'.

Deception Point is filled with twists and turns to keep the reader guessing. The plots cuts back and forth between locations and Brown uses his short chapters with cliffhanger endings to keep the pace moving. Once the action kicks in he moves it with lightning speed and the climax at the end is a finely crafted and skilled piece of writing equal to that of MacLean's work.

But there is one element that MacLean peppers his works with and is difficult to find in *Deception Point* – humour. For Brown his third novel was meant to be fun and easier than the first two, but halfway through he began to think that he might have made a mistake because he was bored by politics and he felt uncomfortable using a female lead. 'I had been far more interested in the Vatican, Langdon, codes, symbology, and art,' he said. 'I had no money, and I found myself wondering once again if I should give up. Fortunately, my wife has always been a tremendous support system and she encouraged me to keep at it.'[112]

Brown's first two books had been commercial duds. The sales of *Deception Point* would prove to be no better. The next one had to be good if he was to survive as a novelist. It was his last hope.

PART TWO

THE BIG TIME

The hard part of writing a novel is not the ideas but rather the nuts and bolts of the plot and language and making it all work.

CHAPTER TEN

THE LAST HOPE

Rumours of this conspiracy have been whispered for centuries in countless languages, including the languages of art, music, and literature [113]

Brown had fulfilled his two-book deal with Simon & Schuster and to say he was disappointed with the publisher is an understatement. 'My lone advocate at Simon & Schuster seemed to be my editor, Jason Kaufman, with whom I had developed a friendship and level of trust,' Brown said. 'He too had become deeply frustrated with the lack of publisher support I was receiving at Simon & Schuster.'

As with *Angels & Demons* the promise for *Deception Point* was high but never materialised. The book was published in August 2001 fifteen months after *Angels & Demons* and a month later the unthinkable happened. The terrorist attacks of 11 September scuppered the sales of his third novel. No books of fiction or non-fiction did well that autumn – people's minds were elsewhere. As Lisa Rogak noted in her book on Brown, 'Many details of the typical thriller novel suddenly seemed too frivolous.' [114]

Broke and disheartened in the months after sending

Deception Point to the publishers, Brown realised that something needed to be done if he was to remain a full-time author. He had to have success.

The pressure was intense. The first thing he did was to change his agent. He left Jake Ellwell at Wieser and Wieser and found a friendly face at Sanford J. Greenburger Associates. Based in New York, the agency represented authors of commercial and literary fiction as well as non-fiction, and the friendly face was Heidi Lange.

Dan and Blythe Brown met with Heidi to look at the first two novels (*Deception Point* hadn't been published yet) with a critical eye. *Digital Fortress* had received a lot of attention from the press because it was a topic that was prominent in the news in those days. Email was relatively new at the time but most people used it at some point in their day and the revelation that the government read everyone's email was a shocking one.

Brown needed locations he could travel to fairly easily, so the day after he submitted the manuscript for *Deception Point*, he and Blythe went on holiday to Mexico. 'It was there on the Yucatan Peninsula, exploring the ancient Mayan pyramids and archaeological ruins of Chichen-Itza and Tulum, that I was (at last) able to leave behind the high tech world of *Deception Point*,' he recalled. In Mexico Brown was immersed in ancient ruins, myths and legends, 'and this intriguing history was tickling my imagination again. I began to muster the sense that I might be able to write another novel. At that point, I had no doubt who my hero would be – I would return to the world of Robert Langdon.'[115]

According to Rogak, Dan, Blythe and Heidi continued their analysis, and Brown went back to the research for

Angels & Demons that he hadn't been able to use. Was there anything he could use that would shock people or even offend them? 'He remembered that, after *Angels & Demons* had been published, he'd got a lot of grief for describing the face on Bernini's statue of St Teresa as looking like she was in the midst of a 'toe-curling orgasm.'[116]

What he was looking for was something controversial. 'This particular story kept knocking on my door until I answered,' he said.

In his witness statement Brown says he had first learned of the mysteries hidden in Da Vinci's paintings while studying art history at the university in Seville. He came across Da Vinci again while researching *Angels & Demons*. 'I arranged a trip to the Louvre Museum where I was fortunate enough to view the originals of some of Da Vinci's most famous works as well as discuss them with an art historian who helped me better understand the mystery behind their surprising anomalies. From then on, I was captivated.'

The trio's analysis had shown three things: that he needed a topic people knew and used in their daily lives, that he needed to present it in a way that would knock people's understanding of that topic on its head, and that he had to reveal something that was shocking, even upsetting. By combining sex with religion he was almost guaranteed a certain level of push back and when he remembered his art class in Seville where the professor had pointed out the secrets in Da Vinci's painting of the Last Supper, he realised he had the foundation upon which he could build the book.[117] With his wife Blythe being a Da Vinci fan as well, it made sense to bring Da Vinci into the story.

Bringing Langdon back was also perfect for the plot because Langdon is a professor of religious history and symbolism. He is also an art historian. 'In choosing what characters to include in a novel, I select characters who have sets of skills that help move the plot along and also permit me to introduce information,' Brown said in his witness statement. 'His expertise in symbology and iconography affords him the luxury of potentially limitless adventures in exotic locales.'

Langdon is also close to Brown in personality. Indeed, Brown has said that he wishes he was Langdon, largely because his character takes chances that he (Brown) wouldn't to uncover the truth about some ancient mystery. He has the same interests as Brown does, which makes sense because Brown takes so long to research and write his books that the subject matter has to keep his attention. He also feels more comfortable writing about Langdon.

With all of these ingredients in place, Brown got to work researching and writing *The Da Vinci Code*. 'His fourth novel would be a culmination of every interest and influence he'd ever had in his life: religion, codes, art and secret societies.'[118]

Sifting through the research left over from *Angels & Demons*, he made notes on areas where he still required more research and got busy. What happened if this book didn't work? It just didn't bear thinking about. He would have to change again, perhaps return to teaching full time.

At the heart of the book is a battle between two secret societies, the Priory of Sion and Opus Dei over the possibility that Jesus Christ of Nazareth had been married to Mary Magdalene and that the bloodline from their union is the Holy Grail. 'It's been chronicled for centuries,' Brown explained, 'so there are thousands of sources to draw from. In addition, I was surprised how eager historians were to share their expertise with me. One academic told me her enthusiasm for *The Da Vinci Code* was based in part on her hope that this ancient mystery would be unveiled to a wider audience.'[119]

'The secret I reveal is one that has been whispered for centuries,' Brown told one interviewer. 'It is not my own. Admittedly, this may be the first time the secret has been unveiled within the format of a popular thriller, but the information is anything but new.'

Recalling his art history classes 15 years earlier in Seville, Brown said, 'One morning our professor began a lecture in a very strange way. He showed us a slide of Da Vinci's famous painting *The Last Supper*, which depicts Jesus and his disciples sharing a glass of wine on their last night together. I'd seen this painting many times but somehow I'd never seen the anomalies that the professor began pointing out – a hand clutching a dagger, a disciple making a threatening gesture across the neck of another, the strange arrangement and architecture of individuals at the table and much to my surprise a rather obvious omission – the apparent absence on the table of the holy cup of Christ.'

Brown is referring to the cup that Christ used to share the wine with the disciples. For some reason Da Vinci chose not to put this into the painting and Brown was intrigued. 'So all of us in class are scratching our heads as if we are seeing the painting for the first time and the professor said to us that these oddities that he'd just revealed to us were really the tip of the iceberg.

'I was instantly fascinated. The further I progressed in my research the more troublesome it became to me,' Brown added. 'I don't see much truth in the stories of UFOs, crop circles or the Bermuda triangle or any other conspiracy theories you might have in pop culture.'[120]

However, a strange thing happened as Brown immersed himself in the research. His ideas on religion and spirituality began to change. 'I began writing this book as a sceptic and I expected as I was researching it to dispute it.' Instead, after two years of research and numerous trips to Europe, Brown became a believer. 'It's important to remember that this is a novel about a theory that has been out there for a long time and this theory makes more sense to me than what I was taught as a child.'[121]

Much of the information he was researching Brown found hard to accept. The theories he was looking at didn't match the dogma he'd been taught at school and in the church. 'Troubled by these findings I asked a historian friend of mine, "How do historians balance contrary accounts of the same event?" This man responded in what I thought was a brilliant way.' His friend made two big points, which most people don't take into account. 'When we read and interpret history we are not interpreting the events themselves but written accounts of the events. In essence we are interpreting people's interpretations. Second, since the beginning of recorded time history has always been written by the winners.'[122]

The mountain of research was daunting. Brown wanted to cram as much of it into the book as he could because there was so much to say. From the art history and the religious theories to the locations in Paris and London to the description of the Louvre and Da Vinci's paintings, the amount of information was staggering. 'Writing an informative yet compact thriller is a lot like making maple sugar candy. You have to tap hundreds of trees... boil vats and vats of raw sap... evaporate the water... and keep boiling until you've distilled a tiny nugget that encapsulates the essence,' he said.[123]

Brown found himself using the delete key a lot as he

pared down the text. 'In many ways, editing yourself is the most important part of being a novelist... carving away superfluous text until your story stands crystal clear before your reader. For every page in *The Da Vinci Code*, I wrote ten that ended up in the trash.'[124]

Having written three novels about secret societies, Brown had built up several contacts around the world in the circles he talks about in his books. Through them he was able to gain access to areas of the Louvre that the public doesn't see – including ones he didn't know existed, such as the restoration labs – which, Rogak tells us, Brown describes in the book. Despite the trips, according to Lisa Rogak, Brown spent most of his research reading books by noted and respected historians and academics.

The Sacred Feminine figures prominently in *The Da Vinci Code*, and this came as a result of his research. 'Two thousand years ago we lived in a world of gods and goddesses,' Brown said. 'Today we live in a world solely of gods. Women in most cultures have been stripped of their spiritual power. The novel touches on the question of how and why this shift occurred.'

It wasn't just the research that inspired him to write about the Sacred Feminine. Brown says it was also partly because of his mother, who has a strong spiritual and religious conviction but is also open to change. It was also partly due to falling in love with Blythe as well as studying religions that were not Christianity, such as paganism and the concept of Mother Earth. 'And some of it came from looking at the destructive force of man and saying, "What if we embraced our feminine side – the more creative, passive, loving side?" It's a gross generalisation, but all those things added up to my celebrating the Sacred Feminine.'[125]

For the more obscure facts Brown turned to the Ohio University research librarian Stan Planton, who had helped him on *Angels & Demons* and *Deception Point*. While Brown used his own extensive research on religion, spiritualism, art history and symbology, he used Planton and other researchers to help him with the more obscure facts on Da Vinci's paintings and the hidden codes within them, and on the secret sects of the Priory of Sion and Opus Dei.[126]

Brown claims that in *The Da Vinci Code* he worked very hard to ensure there was a balanced and fair view of Opus Dei. 'While [it] is a very positive force in the lives of many people, for others affiliation with Opus Dei has been a profoundly negative experience.' Brown states his view of the organisation comes from reading more than a dozen books on it and through his own interviews with former and current members of this secretive society.[127]

But while Brown was beavering away every day, there was no guarantee that any resulting book would ever be published. In the 1990s large conglomerates had started to buy up as many independent publishers as they could because they saw there was money to be made, especially when a book could be tied into a film or other media channels that the corporation might happen to own. The days of nurturing talent quickly disappeared and that meant if an author's first couple of books didn't have a readership that was rising all the time then no further contract would be issued. This was all about money and Brown's record so far was poor. Despite any critical acclaim, sales had been low on all three novels. *Deception Point* had had the poorest figures of the lot, so Brown's prospects weren't good.

In addition, Jason Kaufman, Brown's editor at Simon &

Schuster, had jumped ship in search of another publisher but he and Brown had developed a friendship and Kaufman wasn't about to abandon Brown. Kaufman stipulated that the next position he took would be on the condition that Dan Brown came on board as well.

The publisher that Kaufman signed on with was Doubleday. Initially they said no to Kaufman's condition but when Doubleday president Stephen Rubin read Brown's outline for *The Da Vinci Code* it made him read *Angels & Demons*. From that point Kaufman came on board and Brown came with him. Brown's new agent Heidi Lange negotiated an advance that for Brown must have been startling: $400,000 for a two-book contract.[128]

Had Simon & Schuster offered Brown a new contract for *The Da Vinci Code* one has to wonder if they would have publicised it the way they did his second and third novels: a few review copies distributed to the press and a small print run of a few thousand. With hindsight they must have been kicking themselves as they had lost the chance to have the biggest-selling novel of all time. It sounds similar to the time when the Decca record company turned down The Beatles only to find that the band became the most popular group on the planet.

Finally Brown had some backing and this time it was big money, but that also meant the book had to be good, so he and Blythe continued working hard on it.

There are many strands running through *The Da Vinci Code* and Brown spent many days researching them. 'The novel's themes include: the Sacred Feminine; goddess worship; the Holy Grail; symbology; paganism; the history of the Bible and its accuracy, including the lost Gnostic Gospels; Templar history; the suppression of information by the church; the genealogy of Jesus; religious zealotry; and nature's grand design as evidence for the existence of God,' Brown wrote in his witness statement.

According to the author, these themes have been explored for centuries in literature, art and music. They are the themes of man's past that seem to have been lost, become legend, muddied in the waters of time. 'Of course, it is impossible when looking at secret history to know how much is truth, and how much is myth or fanciful invention,' Brown said. 'By attempting to rigidly classify ethereal concepts like faith, we end up debating semantics to the point where we entirely miss the obvious – that is, that we are all trying to decipher life's big mysteries, and we're each following our own paths of enlightenment.'[129]

He was also intrigued by the way Da Vinci blended fact and myth. 'It's one of the reasons why I love Leonardo da Vinci. Some of the most dramatic hints to possible lost "secret history" can be found in the paintings of Leonardo da Vinci, which seem to overflow with mystifying symbolism, anomalies, and codes.'[130]

But beyond all the codes and secret societies Brown is quick to point out that *The Da Vinci Code* is 'at its core, a treasure hunt through Paris, London, and Edinburgh. The story is a blend of historical fact, legend, myth, and fiction.' He also says 'the paintings, locations, historical documents, and organisations described in the novel all exist.'[131]

After he'd sent the manuscript in to Doubleday, Brown waited. The pressure was still there. He'd had an amazing advance but if the book suffered the fate of the first three, he would have to think of something else to do.

However, Doubleday did not treat the book the way Simon & Schuster had handled his second and third novels.

The publicity department sent out 10,000 advance copies months before the book was due to be published. They also did something his other publishers hadn't done, which was to listen to his ideas about the book's front and back covers.

Brown suggested that both have codes about the story for readers to spot and to work out, giving them an all-round experience of the book. Brown also had a say in designing the inside cover. 'In my previous novels I hid codes in the text just for fun,' he said. 'I discovered that Leonardo da Vinci hid codes in his artwork and decided wouldn't it be fun to hide codes right on the jacket of this book in plain view? Shortly after this book was published there were just a few readers who stepped forward and said, "Am I seeing this correctly? Have I found a code?" Of course they had.' [132]

Brown has said there are at least four codes visible to the naked eye on the cover of his book, explaining: 'What Doubleday has done is rather than blurting out where the code is, they've said, "Let's make it fun."' Doubleday set up a website, *thedavincicode.com*, where readers of the book could go to look at clues or work out riddles that would give them the location of the codes.

The launch of the novel is still considered to be one of the best in publishing history. 'Articles have been written specifically on *The Da Vinci Code* launch,' Brown said in his witness statement. 'Steve Rubin and his team should get the credit for the success.' Months before the book came out, Rubin sent Brown on the road to meet the booksellers. 'Many booksellers were in love with the book when they read the advance reader copies.' What made it more amazing was that these copies were based on the first draft of the novel and not the final one.

'I must admit, somewhat embarrassingly,' Brown said, 'that until *The Da Vinci Code* launch, with the tremendous support booksellers have showed my book, I did not fully understand the role of word of mouth in the process and its power to generate buzz and excitement.'

The 10,000 advance copies were more than the first printings of his three other novels put together. Realising the book had mass appeal, the publisher initiated an unusual grassroots marketing campaign to try and frontload some name recognition for Brown. The idea was to generate interest among the booksellers before the book was released, rather than buy massive advertising campaigns afterwards. The plan worked and bookstores started doubling and tripling their orders before the book came out.[133]

This time it was the publisher that was scheduling the interviews, creating publicity material and sending out press releases – Blythe no longer needed to be her husband's press agent. 'I've had the experience of writing a book and not having many people care, and this has been the exact opposite,' Brown said. 'It poses many challenges as far as my time, privacy and level of visibility – all of which I'm very hesitant to complain about, because they're all problems that most writers in the world wish they had.'[134]

Early indications from the advance copies were extremely positive, so based on the orders that were flooding in, Doubleday took a gamble and ordered a print run of 230,000 copies, setting the publication date for 18 March 2003. Of course it could have all backfired and sales could have been nowhere near expectations, but one other thing happened that helped to push the novel skyward.

The day before *The Da Vinci Code* was due to be published, the *New York Times* ran a hugely positive review by the paper's book critic, Janet Maslin. It was filled with accolades such as 'an erudite suspense thriller' and 'the book moves at breakneck pace'. Maslin's review set the wheels in motion when she compared the book to J.K. Rowling's Harry Potter novels. Brown believes this was largely because of the secret rituals, codes and other mystery elements in Harry Potter that people found in his work. According to Lisa Rogak, he likened it to a more mature version of Harry Potter. [135]

Momentum was building. The booksellers could see the book had tremendous potential and so could the publisher. Everyone worked together to help the book succeed. By the end of the first week it had sold more than 24,000 copies. Brown was in Seattle on a book tour when he heard the news that *The Da Vinci Code* had hit the bestseller lists. It must been a sweet moment, because Brown has stated that had he stayed with Pocket Books, he feels *The Da Vinci Code* would have failed as his second and third books did. 'Equally, I think *Angels & Demons* would have been a big success if published by Random House with as much fanfare as they brought to *The Da Vinci Code*.'[136]

The first print run of 230,000 copies sold out very quickly and Brown became one of the publisher's top authors in terms of money generated. He'd gone from a nobody to a very big somebody almost overnight.

In her book, *The Man Behind the Da Vinci Code: An Unauthorised Biography*, Lisa Rogak states that Brown's agent Heidi Lange renegotiated his contract, landing him a four-book deal with Robert Langdon being the main character in each one. Not wanting to take the chance that Brown might go elsewhere after providing them with the second book to fulfill the original contract by, Doubleday agreed to the new contract. They wanted their new cash cow to stay put. Brown had become an industry in his own right.

In Britain, the *New Statesman* suggested that Dan Brown should be the *New Statesman Man of the Year*. This tongue-in-cheek claim was the title of an article in the magazine on 13 December 2004 but the facts in the story by Jason Cowley speak for themselves. At the time of writing his piece, *The Da Vinci Code* was the bestselling novel in Britain and in the US. More than eight million copies had been sold worldwide and Sony Pictures had bought the film rights in a multi-million dollar deal which would eventually become a Hollywood blockbuster starring Tom Hanks as Robert Langdon.

'Books are being written and scholarly articles published to refute its more outlandish claims and theological speculations,' wrote Cowley. 'The author's previous three novels – *Deception Point*, *Angels and Demons*, *Digital Fortress* – are, as I write, second, third and fourth on the UK paperback fiction bestseller lists as well as being in the Top 10 in the US.'

But Cowley also suggested that something significant was taking place that the cultural elite seemed to be ignoring. 'Like the *Harry Potter* books that are so popular with adults, it is a hugely accomplished escapist narrative,' he wrote. 'Brown knows exactly what he is doing, what he wants to say and how to say it. Beyond its huge generic accomplishment and obvious readability, *The Da Vinci Code* has something else to offer: it is a fascinating political text, underscored by an intense eschatological anxiety. In the aftermath of the events of 11 September 2001 and the invasion of Iraq, in a world where a mysterious and opaque global network of religious terrorists called al-Qaeda threatens the West as well as, it is believed, communicating via encoded messages, a novel such as *The Da Vinci Code* carries a powerful political charge.'[137]

As part of the publicity campaign for the book, Brown had appeared on ABC's *Good Morning America* peak-time TV show to talk about the issues in *The Da Vinci Code* and Cowley claimed the sales of the book hadn't stopped climbing since.

In his article, Cowley wondered how seriously we should take Dan Brown. Very seriously indeed was the answer, 'not least because eight million people have bought *The Da Vinci Code* in less than 18 months and many millions more will do so in the months ahead. Many of these readers will enjoy the book and think no more of it; some will throw it across the room in derision. But others, judging by the number of dedicated websites it has spawned, will believe it just as some believe the astrological guides that are published each morning in the newspaper. They will believe that it is *historically* true.'

And yet Cowley himself, in considering Brown and his fourth novel, had only done what many others have done: jump on the Dan Brown bandwagon, caught up in the hype and momentum that is the Dan Brown industry. 'With its pseudo-scholarship, religious zeal and conspiracy theories,' he wrote, '*The Da Vinci Code* occupies the ambiguous space of all our "if onlys" while offering us its own stairway to heaven. Not a bad combination, then; in fact, a sure-fire winner.' [138]

And it was a winner more than anyone could ever have anticipated. A million copies were sold in the US alone in its first ten weeks. A full year after it was published *The Da*

Vinci Code had sold more than 6.5 million copies in the US and after two years that figure jumped to 10 million copies.

After the long, lean, hard years Brown had hit the big time with a novel that had captured the imagination of millions of people. The sales were climbing and he was smiling but what happened next was something that no one in the publishing world had seen before and Brown would discover there was a price to pay for the success he had finally found.

CHAPTER ELEVEN

STRIKING IT RICH

I'm not really a pretender. I like complicated ideas presented in a fun way. My best teachers were the teachers that made learning fun. There are hundreds of books that deal with the topic of The Da Vinci Code that are pretty hard to read. And here's one that isn't [139].

After *The Da Vinci Code* was published, the millions of readers who'd devoured *The Da Vinci Code* decided they wanted more Dan Brown, so they began to buy his first three novels. Both publishers of his earlier books were taken completely by surprise by the demand and at first had difficulty handling the volume of orders. As the two publishers finally managed to get their houses in order to handle the volume, the phenomenon happened. All four books appeared on the bestsellers' lists in the same week, which was completely unheard of. *Digital Fortress* made the list five years after it had been published.[140] 'I really got the sense that people were ready for this story,' Brown said. 'It was the type of thing people were just ready to hear.'

In addition, the controversy in *The Da Vinci Code* – the claim that Jesus had married Mary Magdalene and that they'd had a child – heightened the sales still further, whether out of curiosity or anger.

During the last interview he did before he began promoting *The Lost Symbol* in 2009, Brown said that the controversy was welcomed. 'Whether someone agrees or disagrees with these ideas, at least we're talking about them, and that can only be good,' he said on *Entertainment Weekly*, going on to caution that everyone should remember that *The Da Vinci Code* is a work of fiction and not an academic tome or historical document. 'All of the references in the book – whether it's the documents or secret societies – all of that information is drawn from fact. But anyone who turns to popular fiction as some sort of historical textbook – I don't think anybody is doing that.'

Brown believes he is presenting ideas that are controversial and people are looking for ways to either embrace or dispute them. 'Everyone is entitled to their opinion. I think it's great that people are talking about it. To my critics, I usually say, "Thank you, thank you for being passionate about a topic for which most people feel only apathy."'[141]

One interesting fact that Lisa Rogak tells us about in her book is that Brown changed the acknowledgements page of subsequent editions of *Angels & Demons*. Originally, he had thanked his first agent Jake Ellwell and the agency Wieser and Wieser. He even went so far as to refer to Ellwell as his friend. However, once the sales for his fourth novel went through the roof, Brown went back to *Angels & Demons* and thanked his new agent Heidi Lange for giving new life to the book. Ellwell is pushed down several paragraphs and is no longer referred to as Brown's friend.[142]

We can only speculate as to why he did this. Nitpicking? Possibly, but he remains an enigma as he has also built a shrine in his house to all the publishers who have supported him. This he calls the Fortress of Gratitude and it contains more than 500 volumes – 'one copy of every edition of my books that have been published all around the world,' he told Matt Lauer of *The Today Show*. 'I have five books but they have come out in hardcover, paperback, movie tie-in editions, and it is a reminder of the good fortune I've had and all the great relationships I've made with foreign publishers around the world. It's a good reminder of all the great stuff that has happened.'[143]

The more the fourth novel sold, the more Brown was compared with other bestselling thriller writers like Grisham or Clancy. This success took a long time to register with Brown, who was still used to lean times. 'I'm overwhelmed by the success of *The Da Vinci Code*, and I don't tend to read my reviews, good or bad,' he said. 'I live a fairly isolated existence as far as the press goes. I've been on talk shows and things, but as far as buying in to what the media is saying – the next Grisham, the next Clancy, whatever – that doesn't really change my situation. Every morning I look at a blank piece of paper, and no matter what name people want to give me, I still have to create an engaging, intellectually challenging plot.'[144]

As the book continued to grow, Brown went on *Good Morning America* in November 2003. Doubleday had set up an online site for people to take part in a treasure hunt where they could decipher clues to crack four codes – the ones on the cover of the book. More than 40,000 people managed to decipher all four of these and hundreds of thousands more tried but failed. Essentially, once a person had cracked all four codes they could then add their name on the site. 'When I heard that 40k had finished and that hundreds of thousands had played, I didn't know what to think,' admitted Brown.

In the studio there was a giant blow-up of the cover of *The Da Vinci Code* on which Brown and the show's host Charles Gibson could point out the clues to the audience and the viewers. 'There are four codes visible to the naked eye on this jacket,' Brown said. But he also admitted that there might be more. 'Perhaps you need to turn the jacket a bit, use some good light,' he said. 'Perhaps even a magnifying glass might help.'

Pointing to the massively enlarged cover, Brown provided Gibson with some hints on where the codes were. On the flap where it said 'while in Paris on business' Brown said, 'There is something different about the word business. It is a very simple code to see.' For viewers at home he continued, 'If readers go to thedavincicode.com they will find a simple riddle that will see the very first location of the first code.'

Brown then showed Gibson more clues. 'This here is a darkened letter and if you follow the word symbologist you'll find the letter s and you'll get a phrase that is a distress call for a secret society,' he said. 'Technically this isn't a code – it's just a hidden language,' he said referring to the darkened letters.

Elsewhere, Brown pointed out a very faint latitude and longitude, which he said was for 'an American sculptor of Kryptos at the CIA headquarters,' he said. 'It has a very strange message.' This strange message from Kryptos is 'Only WW Knows', which Brown claims refers to William Webster. 'He was head of CIA. I've had some people tongue in cheek refer to it as an ambigram of the initials for Mary Magdalene.'

From the forty thousand successful participants, one name was chosen. Mr Brian Shay won the contest and promptly asked his girlfriend to marry him on the show. It had taken him around 40 minutes to work out all the clues, which Brown said was a record. What he won was a trip for two to Paris, where the book is set. 'They'll be sent for a number of days, and I will send with them a list of a number of secret locations in Paris for their own explorations.'[145]

By the time of the contest, Christmas 2003, Brown's fourth novel had sold more than five-and-a-half million copies. For Brown it was 'entirely shocking'. It was also a complete life-changer. 'I am fairly private person,' he said to Matt Lauer. 'I sacrificed a fair amount of privacy when *The Da Vinci Code* came out.' But he was happy to give that up in exchange for what he terms the wonderful things that have happened. 'It makes research a little bit tricky because you can't just walk in and say hey I'm writing a book, what can you tell me?' [146]

The success of *The Da Vinci Code* gave Brown opportunities he would never have had before. Of course there is the financial gain but also Brown found himself having access to 'an enormous number of fascinating people with fascinating ideas,' he told Lauer. 'At the same time, I have much less privacy. I'm recognised often, and there are intrusions to privacy that are a challenge. But nothing good comes without challenges.'

Brown travels extensively while researching his books and has sometimes sat beside someone on a plane who was reading his book. 'I often like to say, "Is that thing any good?" Just see what they think, maybe engage them in a conversation a little bit about the book without giving them any idea who I am. That's always fun.'

On one occasion he and Blythe were walking along a beach on a remote island and they found someone reading

The Da Vinci Code. 'And I'll just walk up and say, "How is that?" And they'll look up just sort of stunned. So it's always a strange sort of experience for people,' he told Lauer.

Even though he's now worth millions, Brown maintains a simple life. 'We really feel our life needs to stay as normal as possible. We travel a lot, but we always have. We enjoy antiques but we always have.' Brown has put a lot of his newfound wealth into charities, as he explained. 'My father's an educator. I grew up a teacher, certainly education is important. I'm a member of Big Brothers/Big Sisters of America and I have a little brother that I see all the time, and I'm sure we'll want to help them out.'

The fame also brought with it added pressure for him to produce another blockbuster. 'The reality is that putting pressure on yourself, whether you are a creative person or not, it really interferes with your performance,' he said. 'You have to breathe in, exhale and give it to them when it's done.'[147]

When *The Da Vinci Code* hit the big time, Brown's editor, Jason Kaufman, also found the limelight in the publishing world was suddenly squarely upon him. Before *The Da Vinci Code* broke, Kaufman's projects had covered everything from fiction to non-fiction topics, but he'd had no massive break-out book. With Brown's blockbuster success, Kaufman suddenly found himself inundated by agents trying to sell him pale imitations of *The Da Vinci Code* or of Brown's other books. Lisa Rogak tells us that in the year after *The Da Vinci Code* was published, Kaufman bought only one fiction book.[148]

Brown had a difficult time buying into his new celebrity status, as he told Matt Lauer. 'It changes your life dramatically. I'm sitting on the *Today Show*, talking to

Matt Lauer. That's a new experience. The same time, I'm a writer. I spend my life essentially alone at a computer. That doesn't change. I have the same challenges every day.'

As the momentum of the novel's success grew and his celebrity status along with it, Brown became much more reclusive, going into what he termed retirement to write his next book. 'There's enormous change,' he said. 'There are changes to your amount of privacy. Your amount of visibility. Your workload.'[149]

Unfortunately, that book soon became delayed as Brown's exhaustive schedule of media interviews grew to keep pace with the runaway success of *The Da Vinci Code*. While the publishers wanted the follow-up book as soon as they could get it, they also wanted Brown to stay on the media trail to promote his bestseller, so his writing schedule began to suffer. 'I have personal deadlines,' he said. 'I would like to spend no more than a year-and-a-half writing this book. Hopefully, it's closer to a year.'[150]

Brown denied that Doubleday were putting the pressure on him to provide a new Robert Langdon book: that pressure was coming mostly from himself. 'They say, "Take the time that you need to write a terrific sequel to *The Da Vinci Code*... We'd rather wait for a great book than pressure you to write something that's mediocre."'

Brown is a dedicated author and says that the process of writing can't be pushed. 'I work every single morning; I'm up at 4am every day, seven days a week, at my desk. I will work five, six hours sometimes straight.'[151]

Inevitably interviewers asked Brown about his next novel and Doubleday advised him to drop a few little crumbs to keep people's interest but not to say more. The best he could say was that the next book would be set in Washington and that it was another Robert Langdon book with a plot that revolved around Freemasons, but that was as far as he was able to go.

At the same time other authors began asking him to pen a blurb or a foreword for their work, or to read their manuscripts or provide a positive recommendation so they could ride on the coat-tails of his success. He said that if he'd read every one of the manuscripts that were sent to him he wouldn't have the time to write.[152]

By mid 2005 the book had been published in 44 different languages as publishers all over the world clamoured to buy the rights for their countries. Had Brown ever thought that *The Da Vinci Code* would be such a massive hit? He admitted that he'd had his suspicions it could prove popular. 'There were definitely moments in writing *The Da Vinci Code* that I got shivers and thought, "Wow, if this material is exciting *me* this much, and I've just spent a year-and-a-half with it, imagine how a fresh reader would react to this,"' he said. 'I never imagined in my wildest dreams that it would be this big a hit.'

With such a massive success, Hollywood also took an interest and came knocking on Brown's door. At first he was reluctant to sell the rights to the movie capital for a variety of reasons. 'One of the beauties of the reading experience is that everybody pictures Langdon in his or her perfect way,' Brown said. 'The second you slap a character [in a script] – no matter how you describe Langdon or any other character – they picture Ben Affleck or Hugh Jackman or whoever it happens to be.'[153]

Brown's reluctance also stemmed from his experiences in Hollywood when he'd been trying to make it with his music. He'd learned the ins and outs of how the place worked so he understood the thought processes. 'Hollywood has a way of taking a story like this and turning it into a car chase through Paris with machine guns and karate chops,' was how he described it.

Another difficulty was that in optioning the book for a film, Brown was essentially optioning the Langdon franchise, which was why he wouldn't do it unless he had 'exceptional amounts of control'.

'The publishing industry, contrary to popular belief, is more lucrative than film, so you need to really protect yourself. Authors who have *New York Times* bestselling books make so much more in royalties than they do from optioning or selling screen rights, that, when they have series characters, they definitely need to be careful.'[154]

Eventually Brown sold the rights to Ron Howard, with Tom Hanks playing the character of Robert Langdon.

Along with the positive response, the phenomenal book sales, something else happened: the level of criticism and controversy began to grow. 'When you are on top of the world, everybody is out to get you,' Brown said. 'People come after you and make all sorts of crazy claims or threats or whatever. But 99 per cent of the contact you have with people is adulation and it's praise and it's wonderful.'[155]

He had certainly been nervous about the response he would get – especially from the Catholic Church. 'The response from priests, nuns – all sorts of people in the church – for the most part, has been overwhelmingly positive,' Brown said.

But there were other people who took a different view and who would prove to be thorns in his side. Brown found himself embroiled in a court case after author Lewis Perdue wrote a letter to Doubleday claiming that Brown had plagiarised two of his novels, *The Da Vinci Legacy* and *Daughter of God,* published in 1983 and 2000 respectively. A writer of several novels and non-fiction books, Perdue alleged that Brown had liberally borrowed his themes and plots for the foundation of *The Da Vinci Code.*

Originally, Perdue had no intention of suing. He wanted clarification and recognition. 'In one novel the heroine is named Sophie, in the other a pivotal character is named Sophia. In both, a major figure in the art world is killed, leaving a mysterious last clue, and there ensues a headlong search for the dark secrets from the past that have been covered up by the Catholic Church – secrets so explosive they could destroy Christianity. And both claim to be based on fact.'[156]

Indeed, Dan Burstein, in the *Secrets of the Code*, says that the head of the UK Forensic Linguistics Institute, John Olsson, claimed it was one of the most blatant examples of plagiarism he'd run across. Perdue claimed he was only convinced after he'd seen Olsson's analysis of the three books. 'He did this out of the goodness of his heart,' Perdue said. 'People can make their own judgement about this professional analysis. I still believe my characters and his were essentially the same people doing the same things with the same motivations.'[157]

Doubleday's reaction to the letter was that the claims were unfounded and that Perdue would find himself facing legal costs if he chose to pursue the issue. In fact they went even further and filed a lawsuit against him, asking the court to find that Perdue's claims had no foundation at all and that there were no substantial similarities, nor could Perdue show any similarities between his books and Brown's. They claimed that any similarities that did exist were 'nothing more than abstract ideas, stock elements common to mysteries and thrillers, or the use of similar factual theories'.

Perdue insisted all along that he wasn't interested in money. What he wanted was recognition in *The Da Vinci Code* that Brown had used his work, and he maintained that the lawsuit could have been prevented if everyone had sat down and talked civilly with one another. 'I maintain that *The Da Vinci Code* duplicates my specific expression in most of *Daughter of God*'s and *The Da Vinci Legacy*'s key elements – even the mistakes,' Perdue said. 'I said Leonardo wrote on parchment but the great artist never did. He wrote on linen. *The Da Vinci Code* repeats that mistake.'

However, after the Doubleday lawsuit, Perdue countersued, claiming that there were enough similarities that Brown's expression of the Divine Feminine and its suppression by the Catholic Church was the same as his. He also claimed there were many details common to both stories – 'the physical evidence of the divine feminine ... similarities between Opus Dei and my Congregation for the Doctrine of Faith ... the fact that both novels incorporate the use of a gold key.'[158]

Perdue lost the case. Judge George B. Daniels handed down a decision in favour of Random House, stating that the 'feel, theme, characters, plot, sequence, pace and setting are not substantially similar.' Judge Daniels said that Brown's book was a hunt for treasure that focused on codes, clues and hidden messages and that it was an intellectual story, while Perdue's was more violent and packed with action – 'several gunfights and violent deaths and sex scenes'.[159]

Perdue's lawyers launched an appeal and Perdue vowed to take it to the Supreme Court if necessary. He pointed out that in *The Da Vinci Legacy* there is a secret sect calling themselves the Elect Brothers of St Peter, who are sworn to protect a secret that would destroy the Catholic Church. That secret is that the Brotherhood are the bloodline of St Peter and even hold his bones. Their sole purpose is to protect the secret and ensure the bloodline continues. 'The only difference here, as far as I am concerned, is that in *The Da Vinci Code*, the Elect Brothers of St Peter have been replaced by the Priory of Sion.'[160]

Does the premise sound similar? Perhaps. But Brown wasn't amused by Perdue's claims. 'Apparently, this happens all the time to bestselling authors,' Brown sighed. 'I actually got a lot of calls from bestselling authors, calls with congratulations, and also of warnings saying, "Well, get ready, because there are going to be people that you've never heard of coming out of the woodwork sort of wanting to ride on the coat-tails." And all I can really tell you about Mr Perdue is I've never heard of him, I've never heard of his work.'[161]

Brown calls this a dubious badge of honour for authors who hit the bestsellers list. But for him, this controversy was just the tip of the iceberg. Little did he know he would soon find himself embroiled in another court case, this time at the Old Bailey in London.

CHAPTER TWELVE

THE CHURCH ATTACKS

But why all this pretence of fact and research without the more common authorial note – that fact, fiction, and speculation have been uniquely combined in the imagination of the novelist?[162]

Even before the Perdue affair, Brown had found himself running the gauntlet of criticism from the Catholic Church and other religious and Christian organisations. The intensity of this criticism of *The Da Vinci Code* had grown until finally the Catholic Church, through the archbishop of Genoa, Cardinal Tarcisio Bertone, officially attacked it when he called the book a 'sack full of lies' two years after its publication. But why had it taken so long?

Looking at the Vatican history, two years isn't so long. 'It took the Church more than 350 years to reverse its condemnation of Galileo.'[163] It wasn't until Pope John Paul II's time in office that the Vatican finally apologised for the crimes of the Crusaders. But the Vatican itself had remained silent for almost two years after the release of the book. These were senior people within the Church in predominantly Catholic countries who were not speaking out against the book.

On the other hand, religious groups, local priests, theologians and religious leaders at grass roots level couldn't stop talking about *The Da Vinci Code*. In the US, for example, 'from California to Connecticut, some priests urged their parishioners to read the book, join church-sponsored book discussion groups, and even go to the weekend retreats devoted to the issues raised by it.'[164]

At the time, most Catholic leaders were critical of the novel because of its treatment of Christian history and theological issues. But some were more interested in the debate around the book humanising Jesus and elevating Mary Magdalene as one of Christ's more prominent followers.

There was widespread condemnation of the book in Catholic magazines and articles but the central theme was engaging in debate and open discussion. The idea of banning the book came from Cardinal Bertone. The 70-year-old archbishop called for banning the novel on the Italian radio show *Il Giornale* and his comments made global headlines. He said that the Church couldn't and shouldn't keep quiet about the truth when 'faced with all the lies and all the inventions in this book.' Bertone went on to say that he was shocked that such a book full of so many errors and lies 'could have such success.'[165]

What was he talking about? Brown asserts that almost everything in the book is factual and true. David A. Shugarts, author of *The Dan Brown Revelations*, suggests that Brown mixes fact and fiction very well. 'Did he not know when he was writing *Angels & Demons* and later *The Da Vinci Code* what kind of fishbowl he would be in, and therefore thought there would be no problem mixing established fact with speculation and imagination?'[166]

Indeed, Shugarts suggests that Brown creates his own

'home-cooked stew of fact and fiction'. He also states that the biggest sources of annoyance and anxiety about *The Da Vinci Code* are not just the technical errors but the versions of religious history and theology he provides in the novel. 'There is no obvious winner in the question of who is more factual in their rendering of the life of Jesus,' Shugarts writes. 'Those who believe the Bible is entirely factual, or Dan Brown who says he believes his rendering is entirely factual.'

The irate cardinal was afraid that people who read Brown's novel would believe the theories he was espousing in the book were the truth rather than what the Church had to say about Jesus and what the Scriptures say about Christ. He went on to say that Brown had perverted the Holy Grail story, saying that it did not in any way refer to the bloodline of the union between Mary and Jesus, adding: 'It astounds and worries me that so many people believe these lies.' Maureen Dowd's chapter in *Secrets of the Code, The Vatican Code* suggests Cardinal Bertone urged people not to buy the book and not to read it because it was 'rotten food'.

Banning books is certainly nothing new to the Church: it has been banning books it deemed heretical for more than five centuries. Dowd tells us that they would use just about any means necessary to rid themselves of works that they felt were unacceptable for their followers to read, resulting in a dreadful bloody and painful history – 'from the Inquisition, to burning the philosopher-scientist Giordano Bruno at the stake, to the trial and house arrest of Galileo.'

In the 1960s the Church became a little more open and enlightened and the practice of banning books was stopped, which makes Bertone's comments strange. Was he suggesting, Dowd asks, that the Church should return to the days when they felt 'they could win intellectual and philosophical arguments by simply banning or suppressing certain ideas'?

According to Dowd few people actually took any notice of Bertone's call and some high-ranking officials within the Vatican distanced themselves from the outspoken archbishop. One such was Monsignor Jose Maria Pinheiro, Bishop of Sao Paulo, who urged people to try to separate the fact from the fiction in Brown's novel. He suggested that there was no reason at all for people not to buy or read the book. [167]

So what was Bertone up to? Scholars have pointed out that the Pope John Paul II had two years to come out against the novel. In the past he'd commented on popular culture and had, in his younger days, written some poetry and even a few plays. But he said nothing. At the time of Bertone's comments the Pope's health was poor and he was going rapidly downhill. Waiting in the wings was a conclave to elect the next Pope and Bertone was in the running. There are some who believe that his outburst was a thinly veiled attempt at electioneering. 'Cardinal Bertone was calling attention to the need to strengthen the purity of church doctrine by selecting the new pope from among those in his conservative faction.'[168]

For all of Bertone's vitriol, if he'd bothered to read the end of the book or if some Vatican lackey had briefed him on it, he would have found there was no need to call for a ban. Because even though the story is about the Sacred Feminine and the Holy Grail is the Jesus/Mary bloodline, at the end the main female character, Sophie, says that there is no need for the truth to come out, 'that women should stay silent and submissive, letting the men who run the church continue to run it with men.'[169]

an Brown poses for a publicity shot before a reading of *The Da Vinci Code* in Exeter,
ew Hampshire in 2003.

As well as selling in phenomenal numbers, *The Da Vinci Code* proved to be extremely controversial. In early 2006 Brown (*above right*) appeared at a High Court trial in London, after two of the authors of *The Holy Blood and the Holy Grail*, Richard Leigh and Michael Baigent (*below*), accused Brown of plagiarism and sued his publisher Random House for breach of copyright.

Above: Perhaps the most famous painting in the world: Leonardo Da Vinci's Mona Lisa, which hangs in the Louvre. Officials agreed to allow Ron Howard to shoot scenes from the film of *The Da Vinci Code* inside the museum itself.
©*Rex Features*

Below: A black cloth covers an enormous poster promoting the film in Rome, after leading figures in the Catholic Church complained, saying the poster was 'causing a problem'.
©*PA Photos*

Above: Filipino Catholics on their way to a book burning in Manila in May 2006.

Below: Despite the controversy surrounding it – and some poor reviews – the film of *The Da Vinci Code* went on to perform extremely well at the box office. Here, Japanese movie-goers queue for a ticket at a Tokyo cinema.

an Brown arrives at the opening event of the 59th Cannes Film Festival in France, 2006
companied by his wife, Blythe Newlon Brown.   ©PA Photos

Above: Brown pictured in Rome in 2009 with the key cast and the director of the follow up film, *Angels and Demons*: (*l to r*) Tom Hanks, Ayelet Zurer, Ewan McGregor, Pierfrancesco Favino, Dan Brown and Ron Howard.

Below: Brown arriving at the Rome premiere.

Dan Brown posing with director Ron Howard and Tom Hanks, who plays
protagonist Robert Langdon.

©*Rex Features*

Above: Staff at Waterstone's at Piccadilly in London prepare for the launch of Brown's most recent novel, *The Lost Symbol*, in 2009.

©PA Photo

Below: Dan Brown on NBC's *Today* show in December, 2010.

©PA Photo

Why does this character do this? According to the novel, the story is being told in a quiet way through music, art, and books, which is helping to bring about a change for women. So like the book itself, the motivations of people may not be what they seem. Shugarts said that Brown had created his own version of religious history and theology that was 'interesting, speculative, plausible, but not necessarily fact.'

Still, the controversy continued and someone must have heard Bertone, because the book was banned in Lebanon in 2004 and the government ordered that any books that were on the shelves were to be removed.

In the US the United States Conference of Catholic Bishops set up a website, *Jesus Decoded*, to debunk the claims Brown makes within the book. On 28 April 2006 the then secretary of the Congregation for the Doctrine of the Faith, Archbishop Angelo Amato, called for a boycott on the film of *The Da Vinci Code* which had recently been released. He said the film was full of mistakes and 'calumnies, offences and historical and theological errors.' [170]

'What this novel does to Leonardo's Last Supper, it does to Christianity as such,' said the Conference's website. 'It asks people to consider equivalent to the mainstream Christian tradition quite a few odd claims. Some are merely distortions of hypotheses advanced by serious scholars who do serious research. Others, however, are inaccurate or false.'[171]

The main criticism of the book stems from the accusations that the novel contains so many mistakes and inaccuracies that Brown says are true. Most of his critics felt that if he could not get the little things right, then it stands to reason that the big themes of the book – such as the fact Brown puts forward that Jesus and Mary were married and had a child – must also be wrong. 'In *The Da Vinci Code* he failed to depict simple elements like routes to the Louvre and the American Embassy correctly,' says Shugarts in *The Dan Brown Revelations*.

This could be because Brown doesn't know French particularly well and can't read a guidebook written in French. But he spends considerable time and energy researching his books so you would have thought that he would be very careful to get the route to the American Embassy correct. 'It seems as though the in-depth, meticulous research claimed by Brown and praised so highly by some of the initial rave reviewers of his books is rather deeply flawed,' Shugarts says. [172]

According to the website *Jesus Decoded*, 'One false claim in the book is that the Emperor Constantine, for political reasons of his own, decided to make a god out of Jesus Christ who was solely a Jewish rabbi for whom neither he nor his first followers ever asserted a divine origin. This claim cannot be sustained on the basis of the existing evidence, which demonstrates that Constantine did no such thing.'[173]

Shugarts says that one of the crucial plot elements of the novel is the scene with the tracking dot embedded in a bar of soap in the Louvre's bathroom. This segment with Robert and Sophie takes up several pages, but the bathroom doesn't have bars of soap, just liquid soap. Nor does it have a window, so that tracking dot 'could not have been embedded in a nonexistent bar of soap, nor could it have been hurled out the nonexistent window.'

This sounds like sour grapes but Shugarts' argument is that Brown should not have stated that almost everything was fact when clearly it isn't. The book has many technical mistakes, plot problems and a 'fast and loose approach to calling anything that comes out of research – even from dubious sources – a "fact".'

'Reporters have asked whether even a bestselling novel can seriously damage a Church of one billion believers,' says the *Jesus Decoded* website. 'No, in the long run, it cannot. But that is not the point. The pastoral concern of the Church is for each and every person. If only one person were to come away with a distorted impression of Jesus Christ or His Church, our concern is for that person as if he or she were the whole world.'[174]

Tim O'Neil, a religious historian from Sydney, Australia, set up a website to look at the claims in the book from a non-Christian historical objective perspective. He spent more than a year-and-a-half researching Brown's claims. In his summing up he wonders why Brown, who we know studied art history at Seville, and Blythe, who though not officially an art historian is a fanatic about Da Vinci, would need to 'use a paperback conspiracy theory by two amateurs with zero expertise in the field of Renaissance art as his main source of "information", while ignoring what actual experts have to say. Just as it is strange how he consistently refers to Leonardo as "Da Vinci" and incorrectly calls his mural a "fresco". One would almost assume that he had little knowledge of the subject at all.'[175] The two amateurs he refers to are the authors of *The Holy Blood and the Holy Grail* (published in the US as *Holy Blood, Holy Grail*) who would later become a pain in Brown's backside.

The internet is full of websites from religious organisations detailing the errors in *The Da Vinci Code* and urging their fellowships to disregard Brown's claims that almost everything in the book is fact. For example,

Catholic Answers published a detailed listing of the main points in Brown's novel that they claimed were incorrect. Their overriding concern was that Christians would take *The Da Vinci Code* seriously. The story, *Cracking The Da Vinci Code*, maintains that Brown implies that current Christian faith is false and that the version he puts forward is more accurate. But, they point out, *Catholic World News*, one of many entries on the Acknowledgements page of Brown's official website, had no knowledge of Brown ever contacting them for research. Since the stories they publish on the site are there for anyone to look at, Brown may simply have gone there and pulled off what he needed. 'The acknowledgements of museums, libraries, and similar institutions may mean no more than that he used their facilities and that they did nothing special to assist his research.'[176]

The same article goes to Brown's official web page and lists some of the titles he used to research his novel. They include three books by authors Michael Baigent, Richard Leigh and Henry Lincoln: *The Holy Blood and the Holy Grail*, *The Messianic Legacy* and *The Dead Sea Scrolls Deception*. Books by Margaret Starbird are also listed and the article calls these speculative works that focus on 'alleged secret societies and conspiracy theories, attempt to reinterpret the Christian faith, and are imbued with radical feminist agendas. Historians and religious scholars do not take these works seriously.' Could that be because most of these religious scholars are men?

Brown was heavily dependent on these books, especially those of Starbird, for the basis of his plot for *The Da Vinci Code*. 'Margaret Starbird's books were a big inspiration,' he said in his witness statement. 'This concept of the lost

Sacred Feminine became the backbone of *The Da Vinci Code* and would become the central theme of the novel.'

The fierce criticism of the book continued and some of it was aimed directly at Brown, questioning his Christianity and his faith. Many books have been written by various scholars analysing his novel or trying to explain some of the so-called facts in the text.

One error that his critics have lambasted him for is the Priory of Sion. In the book Brown portrays it as an ancient organisation involved in goddess worship, but the true story is that a con-man named Pierre Plantard, along with Andre Bonhomme and some of their friends, founded the organisation in 1956 for fun. They named the Priory after a nearby French mountain and not the ancient Mount Zion in the Bible. Establishing the authenticity of the Priory were a set of documents called *Les Dossiers Secrets* which were fakes created for Plantard by Philippe de Cherisey. These documents form the basis of some of the books Brown relied upon for his research, specifically *The Holy Blood and the Holy Grail* and *The Messianic Legacy*. But Plantard eventually confessed under oath that the whole thing had been fabricated, and Bonhomme went on record in 1996 saying 'the whole thing had been a hoax right from the start.'[177]

According to Simon Cox in *The Dan Brown Companion*, scholars believe that Plantard connived with De Cherisey to place the forged documents in the Bibliothèque nationale in Paris 'and in one fell swoop the Priory Documents were born. The idea was to create a false trail of evidence that would be stumbled upon by later researchers.'[178]

The documents detailed the Priory of Sion's pedigree as a secret society. The authors of *The Holy Blood and the*

Holy Grail picked up on these and used them as the basis of their book, as did Brown for *The Da Vinci Code*. Plantard actually met the authors of *The Holy Blood and the Holy Grail* and spun them the story, which they 'accepted in good faith'. The book became a bestseller and turned the Priory of Sion from a 'French phenomenon to a worldwide sensation and today it is a minor industry all of its own,' Simon Cox says.

Several books have been published criticising the story of the Priory of Sion as depicted in *The Holy Blood and the Holy Grail* book, but in Brown's novel these documents are purported to be real. Another of Brown's sources, the book *The Templar Revelations*, also considers the secret dossiers to be complete fabrications.

Yet *The Da Vinci Code* has art historians and academics agreeing that *Les Dossier Secrets* confirmed what 'historians had suspected for a long time.' Indeed, Brown has Langdon saying that the Priory of Sion was founded in AD 1099 is incontrovertible, 'that men like Newton and Leonardo da Vinci were members, and that the Priory protects a bloodline descended from Jesus and Mary Magdalene.'

According to the Wikipedia entry on the Priory of Sion, 'Langdon explains to a sceptic that it is only the influence of the Bible that keeps the public from realising these astounding historical facts. The Church is in denial, but academics and even "educated Christians" realise what the Priory has been guarding down the centuries.'[179]

In addition, Cox writes in *The Dan Brown Companion*, 'Certain elements of Dan Brown's version of the Priory appear to be pure invention by the novelist, quite unconnected to the pre-existing Priory lore he otherwise draws on (and presents as "fact" in his preface).'

One idea that *is* pure fiction is Brown's invention of the legend of a 'keystone', a kind of coded map that points the way to where the Holy Grail is hidden. This sort of thing goes down very well with Brown and shows us his love of puzzles, treasure hunts, ancient maps and legends. The keystone turns out to be a cryptex that is absolutely central to Brown's plot.

Further criticism of the novel came when a documentary, narrated by Tony Robinson of *Time Team* fame, was aired by Channel 4 in 2005. *The Real Da Vinci Code* featured interviews with people such as Arnaud de Sède, son of Gérard de Sède, one of the people who had perpetrated the hoax along with Plantard, who was adamant that his father and Plantard had created the hoax surrounding the Priory of Sion and that it was all 'piffle'. 'The programme also cast severe doubt on the alleged expatriation of Mary Magdalene to France and any connection between the Merovingians and Jesus.'[180]

More pain came for Brown when Baigent and Leigh, two of the authors of the *The Holy Blood and the Holy Grail*, filed a plagiarism lawsuit against Random House, Brown's publishing company, claiming he had plagiarised significant parts of their book and so violated their copyright.

Brown was completely taken aback by the lawsuit. 'Messrs Baigent and Leigh are only two of a number of authors who have written about the bloodline story, and yet I went out of my way to mention them for being the ones who brought the theory to mainstream attention. I have been shocked at their reaction: Furthermore I do not really understand it.'[181]

The case was heard in the Old Bailey and Baigent and Leigh lost. According to the judge, because they had presented their arguments as fact, historically accurate and not as fiction, then any novelist could use those facts in the context of a fictional story. If those facts were spurious to begin with, that made no difference.

Yet in 2007 Brown's web pages were still saying that Priory of Sion was an ancient order: the same things that the book had claimed on the Fact page of the novel. 'In 1975, Paris's Bibliothèque Nationale discovered parchments known as *Les Dossiers Secrets*, identifying numerous members of the Priory of Sion, including Sir Isaac Newton, Victor Hugo, Botticelli, and Leonardo da Vinci.'[182]

'This,' Wikipedia says, 'would indicate that Dan Brown still ignores the unanimous conclusion of scholars and serious investigators: that the Priory was a 20th-century hoax, and that the famous people listed never had anything to do with it.'

Brown says in his defence that he described the Priory as 'the pagan goddess worship cult and in order to further steer the emphasis of the novel towards Mary Magdalene and the lost feminine. This portrayal of the role and ideology of the Priory was my personal interpretation.'[183]

Then there is Brown's depiction of Opus Dei. He describes this real-life religious society as a personal prelature and says it has monks among its members, not least the murderous self-flagellating Silas, an assassin who creates havoc and mayhem while doing the Lord's work. The truth is that there are no real monks in Opus Dei and while some members have in the past practised self-flagellation or voluntary mortification of the flesh, the society encourages its members to avoid these practices because of the perception it would create to the outside world.

The criticism levelled at Brown over his interpretation of

the society accuses him of exaggerating the self-mortification within the membership as well as treating the society as 'misogynistic, a claim which the society's defenders say has no basis in reality, because half of the leadership positions in Opus Dei are held by women.'[184]

In November 2006 the US Prelature of Opus Dei sent a letter of protest to Random House complaining about some of the inaccuracies in the book. For example, the 'allegations of dealings between John Paul II and the society concerning the Vatican Bank also have no basis in reality.'

Brown also misrepresented the hierarchy within the society. His interpretation was that the head of Opus Dei travelled alone and made decisions affecting the society in the same way that a chief executive officer of a large organisation might make decisions – alone. But according to the Wikipedia entry on *The Da Vinci Code*, the reality is that the head of Opus Dei has one vote and rarely travels alone.

Of course, as a novelist Brown can easily stretch the truth or invent it as he needs to in order to advance the plot. We know that Brown is highly adept at blending fact with fiction so that the border between the two is virtually undetectable. Brown puts the following about Opus Dei in the fact page: 'The Vatican prelature known as Opus Dei is a deeply devout Catholic sect that has been the topic of recent controversy due to reports of brainwashing, coercion, and a dangerous practice known as "corporal mortification". Opus Dei has just completed construction of a $47 million National Headquarters at 243 Lexington Avenue in New York City.'

The response from the society itself was straightforward: '*The Da Vinci Code*'s depiction of Opus Dei is inaccurate, both in the overall impression and in many details, and it would be irresponsible to form any opinion of Opus Dei based on *The Da Vinci Code*.' And: 'We would like to remind them that *The Da Vinci Code* is a work of fiction, and it is not a reliable source of information on these matters.'[185]

In his defence of his depiction of Opus Dei, Brown said in his witness statement that he wanted to show that religion was not as cut and dried as it is made out to be. 'In *The Da Vinci Code* I also wanted to include the grey area in religion and did so by including Opus Dei,' Brown explained. 'Opus Dei is a very devout Catholic group, which like many fervent religious groups is met with suspicion and mistrust; only some of which is justified.' Brown went on to say that the society is 'a very positive force in the lives of many people.' However, based on interviews he conducted with members and former members of the society he found that some had had profoundly negative experiences while they were part of Opus Dei. 'Their portrayal in the novel is based on books written about Opus Dei as well as my own personal interviews,' he said. 'I wanted to demonstrate that very few things are black and white; all bad or all good.'

As for the practice of self-flagellation, Brown based his portrayal of it from his time in Spain, where he had seen the practice as part of modern Spanish Catholicism. 'Every year on Easter prominent bankers and lawyers put chains on their legs and march through the streets as their yearly penance. The practice itself is not uncommon.'[186]

Another area where Brown has been severely criticised is in his claim that the Roman Emperor Constantine commissioned a new Bible from which our modern Bibles are derived. In *The Da Vinci Code*, Leigh Teabing, a religious historian, tells

Sophie Neveu that Constantine changed Jesus' status from mortal man to Son of God four centuries after Christ had died. He explains to Sophie that 'thousands of documents already existed chronicling His life as a mortal man. To rewrite the history books, Constantine knew he would need a bold stroke. From this sprang the most profound moment in Christian history. ... Constantine commissioned and financed a new Bible, which omitted those gospels that spoke of Christ's human traits and embellished those gospels that made Him godlike. The earlier gospels were outlawed, gathered up, and burned.'[187]

It would appear that Brown got the idea that Constantine had commissioned a new Bible from the fact that he ordered 50 copies of the existing and accepted Christian texts to be created. The man Constantine ordered to produce these 50 copies was Eusebius. 'Brown totally misrepresents this enterprise as creating "a new Bible", whereas, in fact, the texts Eusebius oversaw had already been accepted for over 150 years,' says Tim O'Neill on his excellent website, *History vs The Da Vinci Code*. 'These texts included the gospels of Matthew, Mark, Luke and John, which had long been considered the oldest and most authentic accounts of Jesus' life. These gospels actually emphasised both Jesus' human aspects and his supposed supernatural nature and they did not, as Brown claims, emphasise the latter over the former. Many of the books the accepted canon rejected, on the other hand (such as the Gnostic works), portrayed Jesus as purely spiritual and not human at all; despite Brown's claim that they presented a "more human" Jesus. On the contrary, they were actually rejected largely because they portrayed a Jesus who was not human enough. Once again, Brown gets his history backwards.'[188]

Brown said he did not set out to write the book to 'stir up a hornet's nest. I am not the first person to tell this story of Mary Magdalene and the Holy Grail,' he explained in his High Court witness statement. 'This idea is centuries old and I am one in a long line of people who have offered up this alternative history. The book describes history as I have come to understand it through many years of research, reading, conducting interviews and exploration.'

Along with the criticism came other books attempting to unravel the secrets within *The Da Vinci Code*, such as Dan Burstein's *Secrets of the Code*, which is an attempt to study the mysteries behind the secrets of the novel. Burstein's book is a collection of articles, interviews and essays with scholars both for and against Brown's interpretation of religious history. Another book is *The Dan Brown Companion, the Truth Behind The Fiction*, by Simon Cox. These two are just the tip of the iceberg.

Back in 2004, Dan Brown had given a talk to the New Hampshire Writer's Project at the Capitol Centre for the Arts in Concord, New Hampshire. At the time, he felt the books being written about his novel were 'absolutely wonderful' and that the dialogue the book had created was very positive. 'The more we can debate these topics the better our understanding of our own history. Most theologians will agree that religion really only has one true enemy and it's not me, it's apathy,' he told the 800-strong audience. 'Apathy has a good antidote and that is passionate debate and I am thrilled to see so much of it. Debate makes us think about what we believe and why we believe it.'

Brown said he felt the debate around religion created by his novel was healthy and invigorating. He assumed his opponents had the best of intentions but cautioned his audience to remember that 'the same way I was out on the talk shows trying to sell my book, they are now out trying to sell their book and it is in their best interest to generate as much controversy as possible and make as much of my book as possible, oftentimes making inflammatory claims.'

Brown's response to people who called his own religious beliefs into question was to go into a little detail about his life in a religious family. 'I was raised Christian, I sang in the choir, I went to Sunday School and I spent summers at church camp. To this day I try to live my life following the basic tenets of the teachings of Christ.'

Being a Christian, Brown said, is different for each individual. 'If you ask three people what it means to be a Christian you will get three different answers. Some feel it means to be a Christian just to be baptised into a Christian church. Others feel that you must accept the Bible as immutable proof of historical fact, while others require a belief that all those that do not accept Christ as their personal saviour are doomed to Hell.'

From this we can see that Brown believes there is a vast grey area around what it means to be Christian and while millions of readers may fall into the first category, the really vitriolic criticisms of his books have largely come from those who fall into the other two camps.

But what of science and religion, another theme that Brown explores throughout his books? 'When science starts tackling the really tough questions, it starts using phrases like uncertainty principle, margin of error, theory of relativity,' he told his audience. 'Slowly physics turns into metaphysics and numbers become imaginary numbers and even matter itself comes into question. Particle physicists now believe that matter that is everything around us is really just trapped energy.'

He then went on to say that 'these same physicists are now quietly asking if it is merely coincidence if the vast majority of ancient religious texts, including the Bible, describe God as energy and God as all around us.'

This interplay of science and religion, he continued, was what fascinated him about Leonardo da Vinci. 'Right now for the first time in history the line between science and religion is starting to blur. Particle physicists exploring sub-atomic levels are witnessing an inter-connectivity of all things and they are having religious experiences. At the same time Buddhist monks are reading physics books and learning about things they have believed in their hearts forever and yet have been unable to quantify.'

Perhaps key to understanding the way in which Brown weaves science and religion together in his books is his understanding and acceptance of science and religion as partners. 'They are simply two different languages telling the same story and are both manifestations of man's quest to understand the divine. While science falls on the answers religion savours the questions.'

Brown also told the crowd that no one is born a Christian and there is nothing in the make up of our genes or DNA that determines what religion a newborn baby will be. 'We are born into a culture where we worship the God of our fathers,' he said. 'It is truly that simple. Now more than ever there is enormous danger in believing that our version of the truth is absolute, that everyone who doesn't think like we do is wrong and therefore an enemy.'

Brown claimed he wrote *The Da Vinci Code* to explore how the shift away from the world of gods and goddesses occurred and why it took place. He said he wrote it partly as a personal spiritual quest and not as something that would be as controversial as the book had become. 'I am aware there are those out there who disagree with me who say awful things about me who make little pictures and I know that a lot of them have published long lists of my shortcoming, my errors and my mistakes.' But he felt that a lot of the critics had completely missed his main point that 'prior to 2000 years ago we lived in a world of gods and goddesses. Today we live in a world solely of gods.'

He continued by saying that in most of the religions around the world women are, what he called, 'second class citizens' and there is no reason there shouldn't be women priests. 'Why is this even an issue?'

But Brown is also happy with multiple versions of where we came from. He told the crowd about one of his critics going on radio proclaiming he was on the air because he'd been called by God to fix the errors Brown had written in the novel. 'He told the interviewer that he was angry with me for teaching inaccurate history. The interviewer pointed out that some scientists might consider this scholar guilty of the same thing for having taught his own children that evolution never happened and that they had come from two people named Adam and Eve. Everyone is entitled to believe what they believe. If you find someone's ideas absurd or offensive just listen to somebody else.'

During this talk, it was clear that Brown was wearying of the criticism levelled at him saying that even the media were getting tired of the name-calling and the absurd debunking 'with several going so far as to quote Shakespeare's line from *Hamlet* about protesting too much.'

He told the audience that his critics had clearly read different books and been taught by different teachers in different schools than he had. 'Some of these people sound absolutely certain about their truths and of that I am envious,' he said, adding that he still had a lot of questions. 'But I have written a novel in which fictional characters explore some of these questions for possible answers. I think readers can decide for themselves how much of this novel they want to believe. As far as us all making a bit too much of this, a very wise British priest noted that Christian theology has survived the writings of Galileo and the writings of Darwin and will surely survive the writings of some novelist from New Hampshire.'[189]

But instead of waning as Brown had hoped, the tide of criticism and controversy was to get worse and two years later he found himself in the witness box at the Old Bailey.

CHAPTER THIRTEEN

MEDIA FRENZY AT THE OLD BAILEY

While Brown was facing an ever-increasing attack from the Church and religious groups in America and around the world, he again found himself entangled in a court case. It seemed to be never-ending.

In August 2005, Lewis Perdue brought a lawsuit against Brown, claiming he had plagiarised his two novels, *The Da Vinci Legacy* and *Daughter of God*. When Perdue lost his case, Brown breathed a sigh of relief. With that out of the way he'd hoped he could concentrate on his next book, but that hope proved to be short-lived. Nine months later he found himself embroiled in another court case and this one was at the Old Bailey.

The authors of one of the books Brown had used as his research – and had credited in his novel – decided Brown had infringed their copyright and mounted a lawsuit against his publisher, Random House, in the UK. These authors were Michael Baigent and Richard Leigh who, together with Henry Lincoln, had written *The Holy Blood and the Holy Grail*, published in 1982. The central idea to their book was that Mary Magdalene and Jesus had married and had a child, and the bloodline of that union continues today.

Brown was stunned by their action. 'I have been shocked at their reaction,' he said in his High Court witness statement, and why shouldn't he be? He'd given them an accolade in the novel itself when he created the character of Sir Leigh Teabing, an anagram of Baigent and Leigh.

Brown hadn't thought up Teabing until he was well into researching and writing the book. 'I initially conceived the character because Langdon and Sophie needed somewhere to rest and eat before moving on to London,' he explained. 'As well as providing a safe haven for Sophie and Langdon, I needed to create a character who could say some of the more far-fetched and controversial things that I initially had Langdon saying.' In his witness statement Brown said he wanted to ensure Langdon's integrity was preserved, enabling him to play devil's advocate, provide some historical detail and allow Langdon to stand back a little.

So Brown decided to use the character of Teabing as a nod to the two authors. He had several reasons for doing this. The first was because *The Holy Blood and the Holy Grail* was in his opinion a more traditional book than many of the other sources he was using. 'It seemed a more fitting match for my Teabing character, whom I had crafted as an old British knight.'[190]

One of Brown's traits as a writer is to use the names of people he knows and cares about or respects, which was another reason he included Baigent and Leigh. Though he didn't know them, he respected their book because it was the first to bring 'the idea of the bloodline into the mainstream,' Brown explained. 'I decided to use the name Leigh Teabing as a playful tribute to Mr Baigent and Mr Leigh. I have never once used a novel to denigrate anyone, and most certainly my use of the name Leigh Teabing was no exception.' Brown was hurt that the two authors would have brought a lawsuit against him when he had paid them a tribute in his novel. Perhaps he hadn't counted on *The Da Vinci Code* being so phenomenally successful or that Baigent and Leigh might want to ride on his coat-tails in the hope that their book sales would also skyrocket?

In his witness statement Brown said he saw a document, titled *General Statements*, during the lawsuit. This, he said, made 'a number of serious allegations against me. The document contains numerous sweeping statements which seem to me to be completely fanciful.' Indeed, it concluded that Brown had lifted the overall design of *The Holy Blood and the Holy Grail* – its governing themes, its logic, its arguments – for his own novel. 'This is simply not true,' he asserted.

Brown claimed that there were vast amounts of information in *The Holy Blood and the Holy Grail* that he never used for his novel. In his witness statement he said that comparing the first half of the two books would illustrate that there is enough of a gulf between them that no one could say the design, logic and arguments were the same. 'And where there is overlap of ideas,' Brown said, 'the fact remains that I used *The Holy Blood and the Holy Grail* merely as one of a number of reference sources for some of the information which *The Da Vinci Code* sets out.' One of the central questions in *The Holy Blood and the Holy Grail* is whether Christ really did die on the cross. 'This is not an idea that I would ever have found appealing.'[191]

Bringing the resurrection of Christ into question is something Brown would never go near. In his witness statement he made it plain that having been raised a Christian and gone to Bible camp he was fully aware that the crucifixion and the resurrection were absolutely central to Christian faith. 'The resurrection is perhaps the sole controversial Christian topic about which I would not dare write. Suggesting a married Jesus is one thing, but undermining the resurrection strikes at the very heart of Christian belief.'

As the lawsuit got under way Brown was still reeling from the accusations against him. 'I find it absurd to suggest that I have organised and presented my novel in accordance with the same general principles as those in *The Holy Blood and the Holy Grail*,' he said. The accusation that he had copied the facts as well as 'the relationship between the facts and the evidence to support the facts, is simply not true.' Brown also maintained that *The Holy Blood and the Holy Grail* was one of four books that he mentions by name in his novel. The other three were *The Templar Revelation* by Lynn Picknett and Clive Prince, *The Woman with the Alabaster Jar* by Margaret Starbird and *The Goddess in the Gospels*, also by Starbird.[192]

'I have received a letter of thanks from Margaret Starbird,' Brown said, 'and Blythe remains in friendly contact with her. Margaret's career has really taken off since publication of *The Da Vinci Code*. We see her on television specials all the time, and her books are now bestsellers. Lynn Picknett and Clive Prince also sent me a kind letter through their publisher, saying they were very happy with the newfound attention to their books, that they were fans of my work.'

Another accusation levelled at him was that he made Teabing a cripple to reflect the disability of Henry Lincoln, the third author of *The Holy Blood and the Holy Grail*. 'I have read an allegation that I made Leigh Teabing a polio victim and a cripple because it was my cruel way of including Mr Lincoln (who apparently walks with a severe limp) in my anagram. This is both untrue and unthinkable to me.'

Brown claimed he had never met Lincoln and so didn't know he had a disability. Nor did he know that Lincoln had worked for the BBC until he was advised of the fact by his British lawyers. What's the significance of this? Brown had used the BBC 'as a device to give Langdon and Teabing a history together,' he explained in the witness statement. The idea was that this would give Teabing status so that Langdon could easily turn to him for advice. 'I used the BBC in *Angels & Demons* as well; the BBC is the only British news agency with which American readers are familiar, and it adds credibility.'[193]

The media frenzy around the court case began in October 2005 when BBC News published a story on their website stating that the two authors had launched a lawsuit against the publishers of *The Da Vinci Code,* saying that Brown had 'infringed upon their ideas.'[194] Ironically, the publisher, Random House, was also the publisher of *The Holy Blood and the Holy Grail* and had recently reissued it under their Century imprint.

The article reported that a High Court hearing would take place the following week with the trial coming up the following year. Baigent and Leigh were claiming Brown had stolen the theme that Jesus and Mary Magdalene were married and had children. 'The authors had been struck by alleged similarities to their history book,' stated the spokeswoman for Baigent and Leigh. Brown, they also claimed, had lifted huge chunks from their book for *The Da Vinci Code*. Baigent and Leigh's book also featured 'cryptically coded parchments, secret societies, the Knights Templar' and links them to 'a dynasty of obscure French kings' and the Holy Grail. [195]

Six days later another article appeared on BBC News

announcing that a trial date had been set for 27 February 2006. This story also said Baigent and Leigh felt that Brown's book, 'which explores similar ideas, constitutes "theft of intellectual property".'[196]

The Daily Telegraph entered the fray with an article on 28 February 2006. According to the newspaper, Baigent and Leigh said that Brown had 'lifted the whole architecture and theme' from their book. Baigent, a 52-year-old New Zealander living in Britain and Leigh, a 62-year-old American living in London, said that a lot of people noticed the similarities between their book and *The Da Vinci Code*, which, the article said, was what had motivated the two men to bring the lawsuit. *The Daily Telegraph* stated that Leigh felt no animosity towards Brown as a person but thought Brown had written 'a pretty bad novel'.

The two authors were suing Random House, Brown's UK publisher, in the High Court for past royalties and future earnings, even though their book was a bestseller as well. *The Daily Telegraph* article also stated that Jonathan Rayner James QC, barrister for Baigent and Leigh, listed 15 incidents 'where the central theme of the earlier book is copied in Brown's novel.' Rayner James also stated that 'Brown worked from notes researched by his wife Blythe to give "plausibility" to his work.'[197]

Indeed, Rayner James said Brown had done more than just copy facts from Baigent and Leigh's book – he had copied the connections joining the facts. 'He and/or Blythe has intentionally used *The Holy Blood and the Holy Grail* in order to save time and effort that independent research would have required,' *The Daily Telegraph* reported.

Even though Brown denied these accusations, he could not deny that one of the characters in his book, Jacques

Saunière, has the same surname as Berenger Saunière, a real person who figures prominently in *The Holy Blood and the Holy Grail*. 'One of the characters, Sir Leigh Teabing, picks the book off a shelf and gives his opinion of it. "To my taste, the authors made some dubious leaps of faith in their analysis," he tells another character. But their fundamental premise is sound, and to their credit, they finally brought the idea of Christ's bloodline into the mainstream.'[198]

The Daily Mail joined the frenzy with an online article stating the lawsuit had done wonders for both books. 'Ever since the High Court case began over claims that the central theme of Dan Brown's blockbuster, *The Da Vinci Code*, was copied from *The Holy Blood and the Holy Grail*, both books have been flying off the shelves. And both are published by Random House.'

At that time, four million copies of *The Da Vinci Code* had been sold in the UK with 40 million sold worldwide. *The Mail Online* article stated that the trial had seen a phenomenal rise in sales of *The Holy Blood and the Holy Grail* from 350 a week, already a good run, to 3,000 a week as interest in the trial grew.[199]

With journalists from all over the world covering the story, sales for both books would have risen dramatically across the globe, the article continued, 'But whoever loses may be faced with the total legal costs which legal experts are estimating could greatly exceed £1 million.' Those same experts, the *Mail Online* claimed, were saying the legal fees could reach £2 million because of the massive amount of time taken in studying the books page by page to find the similarities.[200]

For Baigent, the week he spent in the witness box was one of the worst experiences of his life, according to a

Guardian article published in May 2006. 'I could hardly bear it,' he said. 'I was expecting it to be tough, but I was not prepared for the intensity, the ferocity and the personal quality of the attack. There were days when I had to fight the impulse to stand up and walk out of the court and just keep walking.'[201]

Cross-examined by Random House's QC, John Baldwin, Baigent seemed to get paler and thinner each day he was in the witness stand. As Baldwin presented page after page for him to point out the passages that Brown allegedly copied, there were long silences as Baigent tried to find the answers.

'On one occasion, when he was invited to examine a passage in *The Da Vinci Code* and point out exactly which words proved the plagiarism from his own book, the silence lasted for two minutes and 30 seconds, during which time you could hear a clock tick, pages rustle, pens squeak across paper,' *The Guardian* reported. For what seemed an eternity Baigent searched the page for the answer but in the end he turned to the judge, admitting that there was nothing on the page shown that proved it had been plagiarised from his book.[202]

Meanwhile, *The Guardian* continued, the case had became an international media circus thanks to the reclusive Dan Brown's daily appearance in court, 'as neat as if he had just been boil-washed and steam-ironed.'

Facing this kind of pressure one wonders why Baigent and Leigh brought the case in the first place. Maev Kennedy's article in *The Guardian* said the authors believed they had no choice but to bring the lawsuit against Random House. Their intention had never been for the case to go to court. All they wanted was 'proper acknowledgment of our work and that would be that.' But since they couldn't get the publishers to discuss the matter, they decided they had no other choice but to sue.

The BBC kept up regular coverage of the trial. On 10 March 2006 an article posted on the News web pages reported the latest developments. This time Richard Leigh was questioned by Mr Baldwin QC, who accused him of copying ideas from other books for *The Holy Blood and the Holy Grail*. Baldwin asked Leigh if he had copied the idea of Jesus not dying on the cross but marrying Mary Magdalene and having children with her from other sources. Leigh said he'd repeated the facts and not copied them.

Baldwin then attacked Leigh's assertion that the crucifixion was a fraud – the central theme of *The Holy Blood and the Holy Grail* – was also a central theme in *The Da Vinci Code*. As Baldwin pointed out, this idea didn't appear anywhere in Brown's novel.[203]

Baldwin then pointed out that the section in *The Holy Blood and the Holy Grail* on the Knights Templar being formed as an administrative arm of the Priory of Sion and their destruction in the Middle Ages, Leigh had used the same wording of the facts as in other texts. Leigh replied, 'The facts are common historical knowledge being expressed in straightforward language and could well look the same.' He continued by telling the court, 'Much of the wording is my own but there are certain turns of phrase that are in common use. If some phrases are not mine, it is something I liked sufficiently to hijack it.'

Across the pond in America, the National Public Radio network were reporting on the case during their *All Things Considered* programme. They interviewed Katherine Rushton, a reporter for *Bookseller* magazine, who was covering the trial in London.[204]

Rushton painted an interesting picture of the scene when Brown came to give his evidence. The courtroom was crammed, she told programme host Robert Siegel. Journalists from around the world were attending, along with conspiracy theorists and authors hoping to speak to the publishers, and with people fighting over the seats, the scene resembled a circus rather than a courtroom. Rushton said the conspiracy theorists would shake their heads whenever specific details from *The Holy Blood and the Holy Grail* were discussed by the judge as if they believed the truth was something different. 'The judge, a large guy with this sort of big black walrus moustache, speaks very gently and inserts his own jokes, and he knows the subject as well,' she said. 'He'll correct all the authors, on dates if he thinks they've got them wrong.'[205]

When Siegel asked Rushton about the publicity aspects for both books, she said it had 'gone through the roof.' Rushton reported that the sales for *The Da Vinci Code* had gone up over the three-week trial by 54 per cent but the more amazing was that the sales of the non-fiction *The Holy Blood and the Holy Grail* had soared by 750 per cent. 'It was registering before, now it's right near the top of the charts,' she said. 'And *The Da Vinci Code* has just pushed past the four million mark here, which is huge.'[206]

When asked by Siegel how the defence had dealt with the plaintiffs during cross-examination, Rushton replied that they regarded Baigent 'as a disaster in the witness box, and either a fool, or he was deceiving the court.'

On 13 March, the BBC News site reported on Brown's testimony that day. Brown said the idea that he'd copied Baigent and Leigh's work was 'completely fanciful'. 'I would like to restate that I remain astounded by the claimants' choice to file this plagiarism suit,' Brown continued. 'For them to suggest, as I understand they do, that I have hijacked and exploited their work is simply untrue.'[207]

Brown then stated that Blythe had done most of the research because of her passion for the Sacred Feminine and that it was difficult to know exactly which sources of information they used for the novel. 'On the way, we met with historians and other academics and extended our travels from the Vatican and France to England and Scotland in order to investigate the historical underpinnings of the novel,' he said.[208]

According to the BBC News article Brown appeared to be nervous when he was on the witness stand. Instead of his normal tweed jacket and black polo neck shirts, he had gone for a suit and tie. 'But he was playful with the courtroom and at times he was laughing and even cracking mild jokes.'[209]

The same day another piece on the trial, by David Sillito, appeared on the BBC News web pages, written from the perspective of a journalist expecting dramatic revelations from Brown on the witness stand. 'This was a day of high expectations dashed by legal reality,' Sillito wrote. Court 61 was packed to the rafters and he could not get in for the first 15 minutes of testimony but as the case got bogged down in the legal reality it began to thin out.[210]

The journalists were out for a dramatic story but Brown, Sillito claimed, had been jostled by reporters on his first day in court and this time he came in via the side entrance looking 'far from the "jostled" and "harassed" author of his witness statement. Tanned, smiling and confident, he appeared just how a multi-millionaire author should,' Sillito wrote.

But once the cross-examination began it became clear that there would be little drama in the courtroom that day. 'It began with an interchange about his computers and then carried on with the details of how his wife, Blythe, would pass on information to him and how he would disagree with her over what was included in the book.'[211]

There was then a long debate over margins and how each piece of information researched by Brown appeared in *The Da Vinci Code*. While it was not the gripping courtroom drama the journalists were looking for, it was very important for the court to hear when Brown got to know about information that appeared in the book, *The Holy Blood and the Holy Grail*.

Sillito's piece called Brown's witness statement a 'masterclass for anyone who might want to write a blockbuster.' He continued by saying that Brown 'often wrote his final chapter first and that he then tries to get his characters to reach that end point within the 24 hours within which he sets his books.'

In his statement Brown explained that it was Blythe who came up with many of the ideas for the novel and passed them on to him to include in his writing. Brown then claimed that while the Baigent and Leigh book had been important for research purposes, he hadn't gotten the ideas from it. 'He said he hadn't even finished the book which he said was "hard to read",' Sillito wrote. 'However, he had acknowledged the book's importance by mentioning it in *The Da Vinci Code*.'

The following day the BBC posted another story as Brown took the stand again. The lawyer for Baigent and Leigh, Jonathan Rayner James, accused Brown of having purchased a copy of *The Holy Blood and the Holy Grail* before he stated he had in his witness statement. Brown denied this, saying that he had not included it in the biography of the synopsis for *The Da Vinci Code*. 'That is the clear piece of evidence to me that *The Holy Blood and the Holy Grail* was not around when I wrote the synopsis.' If he'd had the book when he was writing the synopsis, the author continued, he would have included it in the bibliography 'as it would have impressed his publishers.'

Rayner James countered by pointing out that Brown had listed it as 'essential reading in another book he'd written before the synopsis for *The Da Vinci Code*.'[212]

'I had everything I needed for that synopsis,' Brown replied. 'I'm looking at the big picture, not the details.'

Though Brown said the book had not been used while preparing his synopsis for the novel, he did admit he used the book while writing *The Da Vinci Code* but added that 'it was used as one of several sources and I did not use its central themes.'

'I have never been shy about saying *The Holy Blood and the Holy Grail* is part of this,' Brown continued. 'The whole Teabing section of the book – those are the sorts of snippets of information that *The Holy Blood and the Holy Grail* is very good on.'[213]

The following day, *The Washington Post* ran a lengthy story by Kevin Sullivan, who added the detail that a court clerk had approached the author while he was still in the witness box just as the court was recessing for lunch, to get him to sign her copy of *The Da Vinci Code*.[214]

'Hour after hour,' Sullivan wrote, 'Brown seemed to struggle to answer the questions of the claimants' attorney, Jonathan Rayner James, who, like the judge and the other attorneys, wore an august black robe and a white wig with Shirley Temple curls.'

Being as helpful and polite as he could, Brown told Rayner James he was having difficulty understanding his line of questioning. 'I'm not quite sure what the point is here – what I'm being asked,' Brown said. 'It is as if you have asked me to go back five years or 10 years and asked me not only what I got for Christmas, but what order I opened the presents.'

Sullivan reported that Brown seemed 'utterly stumped by one question about his research' for the novel. 'I couldn't possibly tell you the exact date I learned that Mary Magdalene was not a prostitute,' Brown said.[215]

Most of the questioning by Rayner James was based on Brown's witness statement, in which the author asserted that he'd never heard of *The Holy Blood and the Holy Grail* until he had already established the major themes of *The Da Vinci Code* from numerous other books and extensive research by himself and his wife, Blythe Brown. He added that he didn't write in books in the same way that Blythe did, and that she had frequently marked up texts for him to read.

Rayner James then asked Brown to look through some of the marked-up research books and identify which marks had been made by him and which ones had been made by Blythe. Drawing Brown's attention to a particular section where a star had been drawn, Rayner James asked the author, 'is this the kind of star your wife might make, or would she draw some other kind of star and if so, what kind of star might that be?'

Wearily, Brown replied, 'It's a star like anybody else would draw.'

For Katherine Rushton of *Bookseller* magazine, the trial's high point came when Rayner James attacked

Brown because Blythe wasn't at the court. 'She conducted a lot of the research for *The Da Vinci Code*,' Rushton commented to NPR, 'and they say – and in fact the judge agreed – she would have been a very useful witness to have in the trial.'

As the case drew to its conclusion, BBC News posted another story on 17 March 2006 quoting Mr Baldwin QC as saying that the claims against Brown were a 'travesty' and that there was no evidence to support them. In his summing up, Baldwin told the court that the ideas contained in *The Holy Blood and the Holy Grail* were not original and too general for them to be covered by copyright. He said that Brown had shown that the book, *The Holy Blood and the Holy Grail* didn't have 'anything like the importance to Mr Brown's book that the authors had claimed.'[216]

Baldwin went on to say Brown had written his synopsis before he'd read *The Holy Blood and the Holy Grail* and that the claimants' case was now in tatters. 'It is true that Mr Brown cannot recollect exactly which source or sources he used for any particular point. But since his clear evidence was that he did consult the sources he referred to and this evidence was not challenged, the court cannot conclude that he copied *The Holy Blood and the Holy Grail*.'[217]

Baldwin then told the court that even if Brown had lifted the ideas from Baigent and Leigh, they would still have lost the case because the themes and ideas were too general to be protected under copyright. 'Many of the ideas complained of were not original to *The Holy Blood and the Holy Grail*. They were merely copied from others.' The claimants, he said, had done the same thing they were accusing Brown of.

On 8 April 2006 Cahal Milmo reported in *The*

Independent that Mr Justice Peter Smith had thrown out Baigent and Leigh's claim that Brown had plagiarised *The Holy Blood and the Holy Grail*. After reading both books and the subsequent legal arguments, he had decided that there was no evidence to support these claims, and that they had pulled out 'a number of facts and ideas from the book for the purpose of the court case.'

The judge did find that Brown had copied some of the text from Baigent and Leigh's non-fiction book. Brown had 'insisted his attention had only been brought to *The Holy Blood and the Holy Grail* by his wife and researcher, Blythe, in the closing stages of writing *The Da Vinci Code*', but the judge said that his claim not to have used 'his well-thumbed copy of the book' early on in the process of writing *The Da Vinci Code* was 'untenable'. [218] But the authors of *The Holy Blood and the Holy Grail* were told that there was 'no evidence that Mr Brown had infringed their copyright, and thus dented their bank balances, by appropriating the central theme of their book for his unashamedly populist potboiler, which has sold 40 million copies worldwide.'[219]

The judge added that it wasn't for him to judge the two books' literary merit and the truth of the facts they presented. However, he supposed that in the case of *The Da Vinci Code*, '40 million buyers cannot be wrong.'

To make matters worse, Mr Justice Peter Smith savaged Baigent and Leigh in his judgement. He called Baigent a 'poor witness' stating that the evidence he brought against Brown had been completely destroyed.

Baigent and Leigh claimed afterwards that although they hadn't won the case, the moral victory was theirs. Leigh stated that the case had been about the spirit and letter of the law. They had lost on the letter but won on the spirit 'and to that extent we are vindicated.'[220]

But in the end, all that Baigent and Leigh had to show for their experience in court was a legal bill for almost £2 million. For their first payment of £350,000 both authors had to start cashing in their assets. It was a terrible time for them both.

In Kennedy's article in *The Guardian* Baigent said he'd expected other authors to rally round them and provide support but all they got was silence. Perhaps it was because people perceived them as trying to get their hands on some of Brown's millions, a claim that Baigent hotly denied. But then he would, wouldn't he? As for doing it for extra publicity, he told Kennedy that they would need to sell upwards of nine million copies of *The Holy Blood and the Holy Grail* to pay the legal fees. 'But what have writers got except the intellectual copyright in their work?' Baigent asked. 'We've done very well – not as well as Dan Brown, but very well – so we could afford to stand up to one of the biggest publishers in the world, and so we had to. I believe that the protection for all writers has been seriously weakened, in Britain at least, by this judgment.'[221]

In fact Baigent and Leigh went on to launch an appeal against the decision Justice Smith had handed down. But on 29 March 2007 the Court of Appeal threw out their case, leaving the two authors with a combined legal bill of £3 million.[222]

In an interesting footnote, during the trial the Associated Press agency ran a story on Stan Planton, the now retired head librarian at Ohio University-Chillicothe, who had helped Brown research *The Da Vinci Code*. Planton said that a mutual friend had put him in contact with the author in

1998. At that time Brown had been a struggling, unknown writer, and he had just been doing his job as a librarian helping an individual locate the information they needed. His contact had been limited to emails helping him 'on the lineage of French kings and other minor details.' He added that he hadn't saved any of his emails and that he knew that Blythe did much of the research for the book.[223]

But if Brown thought his legal troubles were over, he was mistaken. Just days after the Old Bailey trial had concluded, more bad news arrived. On 14 April 2006 BBC News reported that a Russian art historian had jumped on the 'sue Dan Brown bandwagon'. Accusing the author of plagiarism, Mikhail Anikin from St Petersburg claimed that Brown had stolen his idea that Leonardo da Vinci was also a theologian and that he had painted the Mona Lisa as an allegory to the Christian Church. Anikin demanded an apology and compensation.[224]

The basis of Anikin's claim was that he, a Da Vinci expert, had told his colleagues at a museum in Houston Texas of his ideas about Da Vinci back in 1998. Brown's book had been published in 2003. Anikin told the Agence France Presse that he had agreed only if the author in question acknowledged that the idea had come from him.

Brown's reaction to the case was reported in a piece published on the BBC News web pages on 24 April 2006, when he said that people 'should let the biblical scholars and historians battle it out.'[225]

The case was eventually dropped, so Brown was able to move on. After an arduous trial and many months of poring over the research sources he and Blythe had used, Brown had won the plagiarism case and now all of that was behind him. The controversy around *The Da Vinci Code* was dying down and at this stage he no longer needed to hit the promotion trail and do all the talk shows. Now he could get back to researching and writing his fifth novel. Destined for release in 2007, it would not be finished for another two years.

CHAPTER FOURTEEN

THE DA VINCI CODE

The mystery is: how on earth did this ever become the world's top bestseller, making Dan Brown the world's wealthiest author? This, to many, is the book's great secret.[226]

After looking at the controversy, the court cases and the anger surrounding *The Da Vinci Code*, let's consider the book itself. What is it that has made this book the most popular novel of all time?

The book has sold more than 80 million copies worldwide. It has been translated into 44 languages and, at the time of writing, is the bestselling English language novel of the 21st century. Perhaps it just comes down to the fact that it is a good story, well told.

Essentially, the book is a detective-mystery thriller following the hero, symbologist Robert Langdon and his colleague Sophie Neveu as they investigate the murder of the curator of the Louvre museum in Paris. They discover two secret societies, Opus Dei and the Priory of Sion, locked in a life-and-death struggle over the possibility that Jesus of Nazareth had been married to Mary Magdalene and they'd had a child, whose descendants are with us today.

The code of Brown's novel centres on the way the murder victim died. He is found stripped naked in the Denon Wing of the Louvre, his body posed like that of the Leonardo da Vinci drawing *The Vitruvian Man*. On the floor beside the body, scrawled in special ink that can only be seen under a black or ultraviolet light, is a cryptic code and on the victim's stomach is a pentacle drawn in his blood.

The pace moves incredibly fast. The action takes place over a 24-hour period, and the scenes cut back and forth between the antagonist and the protagonists in very short chapters that read like a film script. Maybe that's the secret of the book's success.

Film has changed the way novels are written. In its humble beginnings in silent movies, the cinema used English classics in the public domain for its first stories. But many of these novels were great long tomes that were totally unsuitable for the silent film genre. When talkies arrived Hollywood hired novelists and playwrights to write the scripts. As film makers began to understand more about editing techniques, pacing and dramatisation, they found that dialogue-heavy plays didn't quite work. So they turned to the pulp fiction magazines that offered themes that connected more with people – love stories, murder, betrayal, jealousy and so on. These magazines told short stories and serials in an easy, straightforward narrative.

As selling unsolicited manuscripts to Hollywood producers became more and more difficult writers turned to agents and the two would work together to get stories to producers. To get agents and producers on side, writers would first create a film idea of roughly 50 pages, known as a treatment or proposal, and then expand it into a novel. The key was to find agents who specialised in writers and screenwriters for the film and the publishing industries. Brown wrote a 60-page proposal for *The Da Vinci Code* which could almost be looked upon as film treatment with short, cross-cutting chapters with minimal description, use of dialogue to push the plot forward and each ending with a cliffhanger. One could argue that it looks a lot like a lengthy screenplay.

Another reason why Brown's novel is so popular could be because he has refined the standard procedural plot line that is so popular in film, television and popular fiction today. It is most prevalent in television police dramas that follow a team of investigators, as this allows cross-cutting between scenes, situations and characters – much the same way as Brown has done with *The Da Vinci Code*.

The 1970s saw the police procedural combining with the conspiracy thriller, as with Fredrick Forsyth's *Day of the Jackal*. Forsythe wrote from his own experiences and from his extensive research into secret Anglo-French organisations. It was a mix of fact and fiction that left the reader wondering how much of what they'd read was the truth.

The procedural then took a different turn with non-fiction books that investigated some of the dirtier aspects of late 20th-century history, such as Watergate, JFK and so on. This kind of investigative journalism took off after Watergate when many people no longer took the authorities on their word. It also brought forth speculative alternative histories such as Erich von Däniken's *Chariots of the Gods*, which questioned the established theories of science and religion, as did *The Holy Blood and the Holy Grail*.

Many of these books ask a big question – what if? – and the authors write them as personal journeys that take the reader on a road of discovery. Often no real proof is found at the end but the authors have used the procedural framework so the book reads more like a thriller. These books usually have a puzzle that needs to be solved, or a series of mysteries where the goal is to uncover the truth of the myth or the legend.

In his books Brown uses ancient manuscripts, paintings and other treasures to provide clues to solve mysteries long forgotten or held secret. He claims that almost all the material is real. Indeed, at the very beginning of *The Da Vinci Code*, Brown says the places and organisations described are real. By doing this he is providing the readers with authority and the inspiration to go and find out more information for themselves – a guidebook for their own treasure hunt or spiritual enlightenment.

The story of the Sacred Feminine running throughout the book has attracted women to the thriller genre. The story about the key role of Mary Magdalene as the wife of Jesus and being written out of history by a male-dominated church has resonated with women across the world. Brown's success with *The Da Vinci Code* is his ability to converge the various elements of popular writing with a central aspirational theme, culminating at the point where fact and fiction meet and blur.

The plot of *The Da Vinci Code* has all these elements. Its central character, Robert Langdon, a Harvard professor of symbology lecturing in Paris, is woken in the middle of the night by the police and taken to the Louvre museum to help them solve the murder of the curator, Jacques Saunière. Langdon had been due to meet Saunière on the evening of his murder.

From the moment Langdon arrives at the museum the action begins to heat up. He finds out, through Sophie Neveu – Saunière's granddaughter and a cryptologist for the police – that the police captain, Bezu Fache, suspects

Langdon as the killer. Langdon and Sophie embark on a trail of hidden clues as they try to sort out the bizarre code that Saunière left for Sophie to find.

At this point none of the characters know that Saunière was a Grand Master of the Priory of Sion and that he was killed by a monk called Silas, who is an assassin for a man known only as The Teacher. They're after the location of a keystone, a clue that will lead them to the Holy Grail. Sophie was very close to her grandfather when she was young until she accidentally found him involved in a pagan sex ritual on a surprise visit. This ritual she saw is hinted at throughout the book but only revealed at the end.

The cipher they find near Saunière's body leads to a second set of clues near Da Vinci's *Mona Lisa* painting. Sophie works out the clues and discovers a key hidden behind the painting. The key has the symbols of the Priory of Sion on it and an address. Sophie and Langdon, now working together, manage to escape the police and discover that the numbers in the cipher beside Saunière's body are part of a 10-digit account number to a safe deposit box at the Paris branch of the Depository Bank of Zurich.

The key opens the safe deposit box, which contains a cylindrical device called a cryptex that Brown claims was invented by Da Vinci for transporting secure messages. The only way to open it is by turning a series of rotating dials until all the symbols are aligned in the correct order. Forcing it open will result in the rupture of an enclosed vial of vinegar which will dissolve the papyrus on which the message inside is written. The cryptex is held inside a rosewood box, which has clues on it to the combination of the cryptex, which is written in backward script, similar to Da Vinci's journals.

Before Silas shot Saunière, the curator told the murderous monk a well-rehearsed lie that the keystone was buried beneath an obelisk in the Church of Saint-Suplice. The obelisk lies directly along the ancient Rose Line, which was the Prime Meridian until it was moved to Greenwich. But there is no keystone at the base of the obelisk, just a passage from the *Book of Job* (38:11a): 'Hitherto shalt thou go and no further.' Furious, Silas realises he's been tricked.

The options for Langdon and Sophie are fast running out. With the police hot on their trail, they are desperate to find some answers. Langdon decides to take the keystone to his friend Sir Leigh Teabing, an expert on the Holy Grail.

At Teabing's chateau some of the background to the cryptex is revealed. Teabing tells Sophie of the clues in Da Vinci's painting *The Last Supper* that reveal the disciple next to Jesus that looks like an effeminate boy is Mary Magdalene. However, Teabing's history lesson is interrupted when Silas arrives and tries to kill them to get the cryptex. Teabing and Langdon fight Silas off and with Sophie they flee in Teabing's private plane to London just as the police arrive to raid the house. (We later discover that there is a tracking device in the van that Langdon and Sophie had stolen from the bank.)

On the plane they have time to think and figure out how to open the cryptex. Once they do, they discover it contains a smaller cryptex and a clue to reveal the combination to open it for the message inside. This code tells them to seek an orb on the tomb of 'a knight a pope interred'. This refers to Sir Isaac Newton, who was buried at Westminster Abbey, where the eulogy was delivered by Alexander Pope. [227]

As the plot unfolds we discover that Teabing is The Teacher and that he had sent Silas to kill the leaders of the Priory of

Sion, Saunière being the last one. Teabing has contacted – while concealing his true identity – the US head of Opus Dei, Bishop Aringarosa, and tricked him into financing the quest to find the Grail. Teabing has played on the resolve of Opus Dei to find the Grail but he has no intention of handing it over. He wants to reveal the documents on the Grail to the world, because he believes the Priory of Sion failed to reveal the Grail's secret when they were supposed to. Teabing hopes his revelation will bring down the Church, which is his ultimate goal. In the meantime Teabing had informed Silas that Langdon and Sophie were taking refuge in his house and when the monk arrived Teabing fought him to ensure suspicion didn't fall on him.

At this point Langdon and Sophie still trust Teabing, who leads them to the Temple Church in London where they have a showdown. Teabing kills his own assistant Rémy and tells the police that Silas is hiding in the Opus Dei headquarters in London.

The action swiftly shifts to Westminster Abbey where Langdon manages to open the cryptex and remove the message without Teabing seeing what he is doing. He then destroys the cryptex in front of Teabing. The police arrive and Teabing is arrested. As he is taken away he shouts over his shoulder to Langdon, asking him what the second message said, what the location of the Holy Grail is, but Langdon says nothing.

Langdon and Sophie are cleared after Bishop Aringarosa contacts Bezu Fache and tells him the whole story, but then the Bishop is mistakenly shot by Silas outside the Opus Dei house as the monk tries to escape from the police. Realising his error, Silas bends over the stricken Bishop and is shot by officers of the Metropolitan Police.

Sophie and Langdon now head for Rosslyn Chapel in Scotland. The Grail was 'indeed once buried there, below the Star of David on the floor (the two interlocking triangles are the blade and chalice, i.e. male and female symbols).'[228]

At Rosslyn Sophie discovers the docent is her brother, whom she thought had been killed with her parents in a car crash when she was a child. He survived the crash, as did her grandmother, Saunière's wife, Marie Chauvel, who is now the guardian of Rosslyn Chapel – and the woman with whom her grandfather had been involved with in the sex ritual Sophie had stumbled upon many years ago. At this point we discover that Sophie is a descendant of Jesus Christ and Mary Magdalene and that her true identity had been kept a secret by the Priory of Sion to protect her life.

Looked at coldly, the plot seems highly implausible. But there is something in Brown's telling of the tale that makes *The Da Vinci Code* extra special. The book's short, cliffhanger style chapters, cross-cutting between scene and characters, minimal description and crisp dialogue give it that filmic feel, and are testament to how the thriller genre has been changed by film. Literary critics may have lambasted it, but more than 80 million people have bought and read it.

How does it stack up against the Curzon Group's five elements of good thriller writing? As regards whether it entertains, consider these statistics from the Wikipedia entry on *The Da Vinci Code*. The book was outsold only by *Harry Potter and the Order of the Phoenix* when it came out in 2004. That same year it won the Book Sense 2004 Book of the Year Award for the Adult Fiction category. Dozens of non-fiction books have come out explaining its references to art and religion, as well as debunking the claims in the novel. *The Washington Post*, *The New York Times* and *People* magazine gave it rave reviews. Other authors have been inspired by it to write novels along similar lines, including Steve Berry (*The Templar Legacy*) and Raymond Khoury (*The Last Templar*). In Australia *The Da Vinci Code* came fourth in a survey of 15,000 people on the best books ever written.

The hundreds of reader reviews posted on Amazon tell an interesting story. Here is one:

'I read *The Da Vinci Code* before it became a bestseller, and I must say I did find it five-star entertainment. You just couldn't second guess the next chapter, never mind the end. It goes at a cracking pace throughout.'[229]

Or this from another reviewer:

'I have to say I avoided reading this for a number of reasons until my wife picked up the paperback copy a few weeks ago. She read it in three days and handed it over to me with a hugely positive recommendation. Reluctantly I began to read and would you believe it I too read it in three days. Why? Because it's one of those books you just cannot put down once you begin reading. I love books which have a factual basis and although *The Da Vinci Code*'s facts are very controversial and debatable, it's exactly this that grabs the reader and certainly leaves you thinking at the end as to how much you may have learned and the seeds which have been implanted in your mind.'[230]

Both these reviewers gave the book five stars. Others have given it a big thumbs up as well, such as…

'A work of pure genius, excellent story, brilliant and beautiful photos, and Dan Brown has this uncanny way of making you want to keep on turning the pages. I was literally reading this book late into the night and I had to force myself to put it down. A fantastic read and I personally would recommend it to anyone with a sense of adventure and an interest in historic and beautiful places.'[231]

The following glowing review of the book also shows its entertainment value:

'Of course it's flawed, but this was only ever an airport thriller; perfect for killing a few hours before, during and after a flight. Like all of Dan Brown's pulp novels it is hard to put down and pretty easy to read in a couple of hours. Don't take it seriously, just read it, enjoy it, and pass it on.'[232]

Elsewhere, *People* magazine called it a 'pulse-quickening, brain teasing adventure,' while *The New York Times* said, 'Not since the advent of Harry Potter has an author so flagrantly delighted in leading readers on a breathless chase.'

More accolades came from other sources. *The Review of Books* said that an author of a thriller novel 'must provide a protagonist whose skin we can comfortably inhabit, a mystery that challenges our intelligence, and enough believable twists and turns to keep the reader turning the pages. *The Da Vinci Code* by Dan Brown does all this just right. This is how a mystery thriller should be written.'[233]

This review, by W.R. Greer, also said 'the chapters in *The Da Vinci Code* are short, usually not more than a couple of pages. Most of them end with a cliffhanger that immediately catapults you into the next chapter. So grab this book, sit back, and prepare to be entertained and educated. It's well-written, it's intelligent and best of all, it's fun.'

Bookreporter.com said, 'Brown has given us a controversial subject wrapped in thriller clothing that will provoke debate in the circles of religious and secret societies

– and among readers. Curl up on the couch and dive into a title filled with speculation, action and intrigue.'[234]

But not everybody thought the book was dynamite. Many critics loathed it for its literary value and portrayal of history. *The New Yorker* wrote a scathing review about its writing and historical accuracy, Anthony Lane calling it 'unmitigated junk'. Linguist Geoffrey Pullum and others posted entries critical of Brown's writing at *Language Log,* calling him one of the 'worst prose stylists in the history of literature' and saying his writing was 'not just bad; it is staggeringly, clumsily, thoughtlessly, almost ingeniously bad.'[235] Other authors joined in: Salman Rushdie said the book 'gave bad novels a bad name.' Stephen Fry called it 'arse gravy of the worst kind' and Stephen King likened it to a macaroni-and-cheese ready meal.

There are also bad reader reviews of the book on Amazon, with people calling it 'turgid pap', 'an awful book' and 'inaccurate, insubstantial and preposterous'.

'As a piece of literature it fails on every count. The characters are emotionless automata which could be bested by any high school English assignment. The plot and background are preposterous and inaccurate from start to finish. The alleged historical significance is the biggest fiction in the book, right after Robert Langdon's so-called "expertise". The overall result is a piece of insubstantial and preposterous fluff barely worth using to prop up the leg of a wobbly table.'[236]

But the positive comments far outweigh the bad reviews. Indeed, with millions of readers worldwide, the book certainly meets the mark for entertainment value.

To see how well it reflects the world around it, we need to look at how Dan Brown researched it and created the world in which Robert Langdon lives, one that is familiar to all of us and yet strangely different.

In January 2001, when Heidi Lange had taken on Brown and they were in the process of negotiating with Pocket Books, Lange suggested to Brown that he put together several book proposals so they could negotiate a multiple book deal. Brown put together a 56-page synopsis for *The Da Vinci Code*. 'I remember trying hard to make the synopsis exciting and cinematic,' Brown said. 'I had already written a similar synopsis of *Angels & Demons* in hopes of selling the novel to Hollywood, but that had never happened.'[237]

The synopsis included a partial bibliography that would give the novel authority and allow Brown to create the world that Robert Langdon inhabits. The bibliography listed seven books, including *The Templar Revelation*, *The Hiram Key* and *The Woman with the Alabaster Jar*. 'Much of the research for the novel came from conversations, research trips, online sources and essentially sources that are hard to cite,' Brown said in his witness statement.

While Brown has said that he tries to blend fact with fiction, he also tries to anchor his books in a realistic and recognisable world. 'In the final version of *The Da Vinci Code* I used *The Vitruvian Man* as a model for the opening murder scene (placing a dead character on the Louvre floor in the same body position as Leonardo da Vinci's *The Vitruvian Man*),' he said, referring to the drawing most people would probably know by sight if not by name. 'The murder is still set in the Louvre, but I was having problems making this work, and I thought *The Vitruvian Man* would be a far better murder victim.'

Brown peppers his stories with academic lectures by

the protagonist, in order to provide information for the reader as well as a grounding in reality. Brown tells us these lectures require 'a firm grasp of specifics. Invariably, when I am preparing to write one of these academic lectures, I ask Blythe to collect and compile as much information as possible on the lecture topic. *The Da Vinci Code* includes lots of lectures – some long, some short – on topics such as Opus Dei, the *Mona Lisa*, goddess worship and suppression of the feminine, symbology, Fibonacci, hidden meanings in paintings and other art, and Rosslyn.'[238]

Three chapters in *The Da Vinci Code* provide the reader with academic lectures on the Templars, the Priory and the Holy Grail. 'Chapter 55 deals with Christianity, Constantine and the Bible,' said Brown in his witness statement. 'Chapter 58 deals with lost history, Jesus' marriage and the Grail as bloodline.'

The sources for these lectures, which Langdon gives in the book, come from the many books that Brown used to research his novel, such as *The Hiram Key* and *The Templar Revelation*. Chapter 58 sees Langdon telling Sophie about his ideas on the origins of Christianity, Constantine and the Bible. 'I was already familiar with much of this information, particularly that about Constantine, the Council of Nicea, and the surrounding politics,' said Brown. 'In general terms I have been aware of Constantine's role in the origin of the Bible as we know it for many years. In addition, I researched the topic while preparing the content of *Angels & Demons*. But I read a lot more about the topic while writing *The Da Vinci Code*.'[239]

Blythe helped her husband research his novels and *The Da Vinci Code* in particular. Part of that was the Constantine document that she prepared for him. The chapter about Constantine is crucial to the book and talks about how Constantine had copies of the Bible made that did not include the Gospels of Mary or of Philip 'which both allude to Mary Magdalene's relationship with Jesus and her important role in his Church. The Gospels of Philip and Mary both come from the Gnostic Gospels and I recall seeing them in many sources,' Brown explained, citing sources such as *The Templar Revelation, The Goddess in the Gospels* and *The Gnostic Gospels.*

Blythe's document came from a variety of different sources and texts. Brown needed support for the hypothesis he was trying to create, which would provide that sense of realism and reflect the world in which Langdon lived. 'I would usually take a document like this, read it, consider it, and blend it in my mind with all the other material that I had read on the topic,' Brown explained. He would cross-reference other notes and source material before writing a draft that would eventually become a chapter or section of the book. He would go through several drafts before he felt the section was complete and would quite likely refer to the source material again before final completion.

Chapter 58 sees Langdon and Teabing showing Sophie the bloodline theory and the secret imagery in Da Vinci's painting of *The Last Supper*. 'I prepared the lecture parts of these chapters in the same general way as I prepared the lecture in Chapter 55,' Brown explained. 'A document that I would very likely have looked at while writing such chapters is entitled *Langdon Reveals to Sophie*. The first part of the document deals with the history of the Knights Templar and it goes on to give an explanation for what they were looking for under the Temple of Solomon. A lot of this information (including some of the text), I believe, had come from *The Hiram Key*. The document then goes on to look at the Priory of Sion, San Graal, and marriage of Jesus and Mary Magdalene.

'All of the research books are different pieces of history in theory. Often the books reach the same conclusions – just in a different way. Blythe likes to mark or underline where she finds common links, as it helps her piece the big picture together. Our studies into the origins of the Christian movement and the ancient mysteries continue to this day. Our research and Blythe's note-taking is a continual process.'[240]

While research is crucial for Brown to provide the fact and authenticity he seeks, the other key to creating a realistic feel to the book is ensuring his locations are accurate. One could say that this is Brown's biggest trademark. Many readers used *Angels & Demons* as a guidebook to the locations in the Vatican and across Rome for walking in the footsteps of the characters. The same is also true of *The Da Vinci Code* – location is key.

Some of the detail of the locations came from online sources or guidebooks and photos, but there is no substitute for going to that location and experiencing it. 'In the case of *The Da Vinci Code*, Blythe and I spent a year or so travelling and conducting research during the writing of *The Da Vinci Code*.'

Indeed, Brown states that the locations are often as important to him as the symbols, codes and art in telling the story. 'Locations not only make the read more enjoyable (in my opinion), they add to the credibility of the ideas put forward. They also give the character of Robert Langdon a further opportunity to "teach" readers. Most people are unaware of the pagan origins of the Pantheon, for example, or the existence of demons' holes in some churches.'

The Louvre in Paris figures heavily in *The Da Vinci Code* and that's because Brown wanted to pay homage to the museum building as a work of art in its own right. He spent a lot of time researching I.M. Pei, the man who designed the famous Louvre Pyramid. Brown's research on this architect was done online at *greatbuildings.com*. Here he was able to download the Computer Assisted Drawings of the Louvre pyramid and other famous buildings. 'I became very frustrated that my inexpensive computer was too weak to fully display these spatial models without crashing. Nonetheless, I could scroll through the rendered frames slowly, and I became very excited about the internet as a tool for researching the architecture of the buildings that I would be writing about.'

Other sites that Brown featured in his novel include St Sulpice, Notre Dame and Westminster Abbey which, 'I either visited myself, researched on the internet or used guidebooks,' he said. 'One useful research source was *Fodor's Guide to Paris 2001*, which particularly has information on the Louvre, St Sulpice, and Notre Dame.'

One of the key locations in the book is Rosslyn Chapel in Scotland. The chapel is famous for its links to the Templars and for its symbols, so it was a must for Brown to include. It is where Sophie discovers her history and heritage, as well as being reunited with her grandmother and brother. Brown's major sources of information on Rosslyn were the book *The Hiram Key* and the Rosslyn Chapel's website. [241]

At the very end of the novel Brown brings the reader full circle to the final resting place of the Grail. 'It seemed more appropriate to me that Mary Magdalene would be returned by the Priory to France. The symbolism of the inverted angel at the Louvre – a chalice – appealed to me, so I returned the focus to the Louvre, where the thriller began.'

Another key element that Brown uses to provide a veil of reality in his novel is information on Leonardo da Vinci. 'An artist, inventor, mathematician, alchemist, he was a man centuries ahead of his time. Perhaps the greatest scientist the world had ever seen,' Brown said in his witness statement. 'Da Vinci faced the challenge of being a modem man of reason born into an age of religious fervour; an era when science was synonymous with heresy.'

Crucial to Brown's story is the idea that Da Vinci saw proof of a divine Creator in all of nature's miracles. 'The ratio PHl is a perfect example of this. Leonardo da Vinci employed this "Golden Ratio" in much of his religious artwork,' explained Brown. 'His philosophy was one in which science and religion lived in harmony. As I have said, I have a fascination with the interplay between science and religion, and I think that's one of the reasons I became so quickly engrossed in Leonardo da Vinci as a topic. He is perhaps the perfect subject for me, given my love of codes, science, religion, art and secrecy.'[242]

Art also features very heavily in the book, helping to give the story authenticity and a basis in reality. 'From the moment I started conceiving *The Da Vinci Code*, it was a certainty that art would feature significantly,' Brown wrote in his witness statement. 'Langdon is not merely a symbologist, he is an art historian.'

But *The Da Vinci Code* remains a novel, a work of fiction and should be taken as such. 'While the book's characters and their actions are obviously not real, the artwork, architecture, documents, and secret rituals depicted in this novel all exist (for example, Leonardo da Vinci's paintings, the Gnostic Gospels, Hieros Gamos, etc.),' Brown wrote in his witness statement. 'These real elements are interpreted and debated by fictional characters.

'If you read the "Fact" page at the beginning of the novel, you will see it clearly states that the descriptions of artwork, architecture, documents and secret rituals in the novel are accurate. The "Fact" page makes no statement whatsoever about any of the ancient theories discussed by fictional characters. Interpreting those ideas is left to the reader. My hope in writing this novel was that the story would serve as a catalyst and a springboard for people to discuss the important topics of faith, religion, and history.'[243]

The Da Vinci Code easily meets the first two principles of good thriller writing but falls down on the third: the idea of it not having to be written to a formula to be good. Indeed, Brown admits in his witness statement that *The Da Vinci Code* is written to a formula without actually using the word. 'As with my earlier books, there is a lot in *The Da Vinci Code* that is familiar – a murder, a chase through foreign locations, the action taking place all in 24 hours, a code, a ticking clock, strong male and female characters and a love interest.'

Explaining this in his witness statement he goes on to say that the 'book also builds on what I saw as the great leaps forward I made in *Angels & Demons*. Again, it is thriller as academic lecture, there is plenty of hidden information, symbology, codes and treasure hunts. And even more so than in *Angels & Demons,* the reader is accelerated through the book – I used short chapters, ideally with some form of cliffhanger at the end of each one.'

This brings us to the next principle: is it an adventure? From the reader comments in this chapter we can see that it is. Phrases like 'breathless chase' or 'for someone with a sense of adventure' prove that it is an adventure. Indeed, the story moves at the high-octane pace that is the hallmark of such great thriller writers as Alistair MacLean, Dick Francis, Robert Ludlum and Fredrick Forsyth. Brown has learned his craft well.

The final Curzon Group principle says that thrillers should be written in a stylish and witty way. The comments and reviews included in this chapter are only a smattering of what's out there on *The Da Vinci Code*. But whether the book is stylish and witty is up to the reader.

By 2007 there was no sign of Brown's much anticipated fifth book. A few hints had been dropped. It was to be called *The Solomon Key* and Brown was going to take on the Freemasons. The book was to be set in Washington DC. Initially, Brown had doubts about setting the book there, as he felt the American capital might lack the grandeur of Rome or Paris. 'In fact, the more I researched about Washington's architecture and its history, the more I'm starting to think it may surpass Rome in its secret history.'[244]

CHAPTER FIFTEEN

THE WAIT IS OVER

I wanted to write a thrilling book set in a city that I love that has a lot secrets and great architecture.

DAN BROWN

The pressure to produce a success that came even close to that of *The Da Vinci Code* was intense. Brown wanted to make it as perfect as possible and while it took him a long time to understand and digest the facts he was researching, he was nervous about how well the book would be received. 'There is a moment in everyone's life when they've had some success when they realise what I am doing now is no longer on the small stage,' Brown said. 'This is the big deal and you become self-aware and before when you just wrote for yourself and thought, "This sounds good," now you write a word and think, "Wow, millions of people around the world are going to read this."'[245]

'I always think of novels [as] they come together like galaxies, like giant clouds of dust and planet and start to form and we are sort of in the dustcloud at the moment,' he said to Matt Lauer during an interview on the *Today Show*. 'Nature abhors a vacuum and sadly if you are looking to take a vacation and you are a writer it doesn't happen, the voices are there.'

Brown decided he would crack on and write a book that he – and others who shared his tastes – would want to read. But the pressure was still there and still as intense.

On 15 September 2009, six years after *The Da Vinci Code*, Brown's fifth novel hit the streets. The book was called *The Lost Symbol* and was set in and around Washington DC. This time Robert Langdon found himself embroiled with the Freemasons and he didn't have to leave the country.

By one minute past midnight the book had sold more than half a million copies in the UK alone, making it the fastest-selling adult fiction book ever, according to *The Guardian*. In its first two days the book did sell more than a million copies in the UK, Canada and the US, breaking every first-day sales record for adult books. In the UK the Waterstone's chain reported it was their fastest-selling eBook and hardback of all time, and their highest-selling audio book ever. And that's for 17 hours of listening! Only J.K. Rowling's final Harry Potter book has sold more (over two million) in the adult and children's markets combined within its first 24 hours. Harry Potter may remain unbeatable, but no one can get close to Dan Brown in adult fiction sales. [246]

A lot of this success was down to the publishers, Doubleday, who launched the book simultaneously worldwide. So confident were they of success that their UK imprint Transworld alone printed a million copies. Tight security surrounded the release, with only four people in the UK having a copy, and they were sworn to silence.

But Brown and his publishers went much further than just secrecy for the launch – they created a remarkable campaign of disinformation around the book. In April 2009 the publication date was announced as 15 September. Prior to this virtually nothing had been given out by Brown or by the publishers as to what the novel was all about. Over the next five months, intense and hysterical speculation would flood the internet as clues and hints were given out about the new book.

The title was to be *The Solomon Key*. 'This was an interesting title, hinting at a medieval book on magic, *The Key of Solomon*, supposedly written around the 14th century in Renaissance Italy,' wrote Simon Cox – a respected historian of 'obscure and hidden subjects' in *Decoding The Lost Symbol*. [247] This man is also author of *Cracking The Da Vinci Code*, *Illuminating Angels & Demons*, and *The Dan Brown Companion*.

The years between 2003 and April 2009 had been filled with rumours about *The Solomon Key*. Some believed Brown had scrapped the book or that the court case brought by Baigent and Leigh had taken such a toll on the author that he'd decided to take a long break from writing. 'It was even claimed that the movie *National Treasure* had stolen so much of the new book's thunder that a complete rewrite was called for,' said Cox.

'A lot of people were trying to figure out what I was writing about,' Brown said. 'There were all sorts of people posturing as to what this book was about. I couldn't very easily walk in and ask all the key questions I needed to know and have somebody send an email "This is what he's writing about."'[248]

The publication date was announced at the London Book Fair. Doubleday (Transworld in the UK) sent out press releases saying that the new Dan Brown book would now be called *The Lost Symbol*, sparking even more speculation and rumour. Shortly after this announcement Brown's publishers set up a website, *thelostsymbol.com*, that had links to Twitter and Facebook pages for Dan Brown. 'Excitement grew to a fever pitch as overnight thousands of people became Facebook and Twitter followers of Brown.'[249]

Clues and hints flooded from the Twitter and Facebook pages, some actually providing co-ordinates to specific places. Cox set to work to puzzle out the answers to these clues, one of which was the co-ordinates to Bimini Road. 'This unusual underwater structure off the island of Bimini in the Bahamas is believed by some to be a man-made edifice and a remnant of Atlantis,' he said.

More clues were given out, some pointing to the Great Pyramid of Giza while others indicated Newgrange, the rite-of-passage tomb in Ireland known for its alignment to the rising sun on the winter solstice. 'Possible adversaries and secret societies were hinted at,' Cox said. Hundreds of internet sites were examining in great detail the places, people and groups being mentioned on the Twitter and Facebook pages. 'It was an internet feeding frenzy.'

Suddenly Cox realised that the publishers were playing a game. He remembered that one of the characters in *The Da Vinci Code* was Bishop Aringarosa and he realised that *aringa* was Italian for herring and *rosa* in Italian meant red, so the clues on the Twitter and Facebook pages were probably red herrings.

He also spotted that the publication date was a clue – 15 September 2009 or 15/09/09, which together added up to 33, the highest numbered rank of the Scottish Rite Freemasons. 'The Freemasons would be a central theme of the book – something that had been hinted at on the dust jacket of *The Da Vinci Code* all those years ago.'[250]

Once the book had been published, Cox soon discovered that most of the clues had indeed been red herrings. 'There was no Morgan affair, no Aaron Burr, no William Wirrt (and the strange story of his skull), no Knights of the Golden Circle, no substantial mention of Albert Pike, no Benedict Arnold, no Confederate gold, no Babington Plot.' The Sons of Liberty, Checkpoint Charlie in Berlin and other people and places that Cox had noted on the Twitter and Facebook pages were also absent. Neither was there any mention of Bimini Road or Newgrange, nor anything about the ancient book, *The Key of Solomon*. The Great Pyramid was mentioned, but in a completely different context.

Brown and Doubleday had pulled off a hugely effective campaign of misinformation, pushing interest away from the real plot while stimulating massive interest and intrigue so people would rush to the shops to buy the book when it came out. 'This was something of a coup,' Cox said. 'They successfully kept the plot of *The Lost Symbol* pretty well hidden until the day of publication.'

The secrecy surrounding the novel had been so complete that virtually no leaks appeared on any internet sites about the real nature of the novel's plot. Instead, Brown and Doubleday managed to get people focused on subjects 'that at best were only on the fringes of the novel. It was an incredible undertaking that guaranteed a huge amount of media and public attention on launch day.'[251]

More than five million copies had been printed, which was a massive gamble. Packing crates of *The Lost Symbol* had been wrapped in protective and legal seals to ensure that no one opened them before the allotted release time.

E-books and audio books were also readied at the same time and under a strict veil of secrecy. 'It was all to safeguard a marketing campaign which some believe could come close to achieving sales on a par with Rowling's last Harry Potter book, which sold 3.5m copies in its first eight days.'[252]

On publication day the mayhem began. In the UK, Tesco, the UK supermarket giant was selling 19 copies a minute of *The Lost Symbol* while Asda had sold 18,000 copies by 4pm, taking it from just another publishing activity to an event of phenomenal proportions. Then a price war started with Asda and Tesco dropping the price of the hardback edition to £5 per copy. Waterstone's followed up by slashing the price of the book in half and other booksellers did the same. Tim Godfray, chief executive of the Booksellers Association, said that a huge price war always comes after the release of a massive-selling title, *The Guardian* reported. The result of this price war is that 'the trade as a whole makes very little money on its most valued assets.'[253]

In an article by Richard Booth, writing in *The Guardian*, it was stated that the first announced title of the book was *The Solomon Key*, and the biblical story of the building of King Solomon's Temple in 1000 BC is central to Freemasonry's ritual ceremonies and mythical origins.

While some of Freemasons may be unhappy with Brown's novel, it did not generate the widespread condemnation that *The Da Vinci Code* did. Indeed, the Freemasons' reaction was largely one of nervousness 'that I might focus on the macabre side of their rituals,' Brown said. 'There is some very potent philosophical material and some amazing science that I am hoping will spark debate.'[254]

Debate was exactly what happened across the internet, with some people seeing the Freemasons as the antagonists.

'This is not the case,' said Cox. 'Brown makes a good case for Freemasonry being a tolerant and enlightened movement with some interesting and forward-thinking ideas.'[255]

Does he? Since the publication of *The Lost Symbol*, the Masons have had to respond to some of the book's claims by creating a website to address them. 'For three centuries, almost immediately after its modern formation in 1717 in London, the fraternity of Freemasonry has been the subject of wild accusations and disinformation,' the website states. It goes on to say that the site has been created 'in cooperation with the Masonic Service Association of North America, and the George Washington Masonic Memorial as an ongoing project to address the subjects concerning Freemasonry that are found in Brown's *The Lost Symbol*, as well as to explain its references to the history, practices, ceremonies, philosophy and symbolism of Masonry.'[256]

Brown's great gift is his ability to blend fact and fiction, and he has gone on record to say that the science, societies and organisations in his books are real. In both *The Da Vinci Code* and *The Lost Symbol* he has put in a Fact page at the beginning. 'While groups like the 18th-century Bavarian Illuminati and the modern Catholic organisation Opus Dei have indeed existed in fact, they bear little resemblance to Brown's fictional universe,' the Masonic website states. 'Unfortunately, readers are not always aware of the difference between fact and fiction.'

The Masonic Society's web pages devoted to Brown's novel state that he has treated Freemasonry in 'an overwhelmingly positive' light. However, 'he does engage in some dramatic licence for the sake of his plot.' The ritual of drinking from a skull is one of those areas. The skull has appeared in Masonic rituals over the centuries but it is not unique to

Freemasonry. It represents mortality and can be found in many other organisations, 'The Latin term, *memento mori*, means "remember, you will die" and is often accompanied by a depiction of a skull as a reminder of the end of physical life. Such specific images have appeared as early as Pompeii in the first century AD.'

The Masons' web pages say that the ceremony in the beginning of the book, where the initiate drinks blood red wine from a hollow skull, is an adaptation from a 'sensationalised exposé, *Scotch Rite Masonry Illustrated*, published in 1887 by the Reverend John Blanchard. Blanchard's description of the 33rd degree has been repeated by many anti-Masonic authors over the years, even though it is not accurate.'

Brown also includes a pyramid that Langdon carries around with him as he searches for clues that will free his friend Peter Solomon. While the pyramid is central to the book, it is not a Masonic symbol, according to the website. 'The pyramid does not appear in the symbolism of regular, accepted Freemasonry or its appendant groups, the Scottish Rite or the York Rite. This is a longstanding myth,' it states. 'Neither is the "unfinished pyramid" topped by the "all-seeing eye" – found in the Great Seal of the United States as seen on the reverse of the dollar bill – a Masonic symbol.'

The website goes on to say that the all-seeing eye inside a triangle first appeared in the 1500s in the Catholic Renaissance art, where the eye represented God and the triangle represented the trinity. The symbol is not exclusive to one organisation but has been used by many over the centuries to represent God.

One thing that is very Masonic, however, is secrecy. 'It is one of the most misunderstood aspects of the fraternity,' the website states. 'Freemasonry teaches its philosophy to its members through symbolism, and secrecy is actually a symbol of honour.'

The website explains this by saying that the original medieval stonemasons kept their skills and practices secret so that their livelihood would be protected and no Tom, Dick or Harry could set themselves up as a stonemason without being a member of the fraternity. This was to ensure only qualified men were employed. 'Likewise, passwords and secret signs were developed so members of the guild in different parts of the country could recognise each other, even if they had never met.'

Today's Freemasonry has kept this tradition of secrecy. According to the website, 'If a person can't be trusted to keep a simple secret like a password or a handshake, his word isn't really trustworthy. He is not an honourable person.'

Besides testing to see if someone is a Freemason or if they are trustworthy, the Masons have other secrets concerning the ceremonies and rituals of initiation into the brotherhood. 'Others are more personal and different for each Freemason,' the website suggests. 'Like all initiatic experiences in the world, the real secrets of Freemasonry are the effects its teachings and ceremonies have on the individual, and how he applies them to his life.'[257]

The initiate's journey, like all such journeys, had begun at the first degree. On that night, in a ritual similar to this one, the Worshipful Master had blindfolded him with a velvet hoodwink and pressed a ceremonial dagger to his bare chest, demanding: 'Do you seriously declare on your honour, uninfluenced by mercenary or any other unworthy motive, that you freely and voluntarily offer yourself as a candidate for the mysteries and privileges of this brotherhood?'

'I do,' the initiate had lied.

'Then let this be a sting to your consciousness,' the master had warned him, 'as well as instant death should you ever betray the secrets to be imparted to you.'

At the time, the initiate had felt no fear. They will never know my true purpose here.

THE LOST SYMBOL

In the book Brown alleges that many high-ranking government officials are Freemasons and the website tells us that 14 US presidents have been Masons, Gerald Ford being the most recent. 'Ronald Reagan was made an honorary 33rd degree Scottish Rite Mason, which has no real Masonic standing,' the website states. 'Bill Clinton was a member of the Masonic youth group, the Order of DeMolay, as a teenager, but never became a Mason; neither George H.W. Bush, nor George W. Bush are Freemasons; Barack Obama is not a Freemason.'

Brown hopes that readers will use his novel as a stepping stone for finding out about some of the ideas and themes he's included in the book. 'My hope is that readers will be so fascinated with the plot line that they can't possibly stop and they read the entire novel,' Brown said. 'Then they go back and say, "In this scene, could this possibly be true? Could this ritual look like this?" and then go and do their own research.' [258]

As with his other books Brown reveals information – mostly symbols and codes that might hitherto only have been known to scholars – to the masses in an entertaining way. One of those pieces of information is the circumpunct, more commonly known as a circle with a dot in the middle. Brown says it is quite possibly the oldest symbol we have today and it is the most universal symbol. 'Everything from the singularity to the all-seeing eye has come from there.'

'In the idiom of symbology, there was one symbol that reigned supreme above all others. The oldest and most universal, this symbol fused all the ancient traditions in a single solitary image that represented the illumination of the Egyptian sun god, the triumph of alchemical gold, the wisdom of the Philosopher's Stone, the purity of the Rosicrucian Rose, the moment of Creation, the All, the dominance of the astrological sun, and even the omniscient all-seeing eye that hovered atop the unfinished pyramid. The circumpunct. The symbol of the Source. The origin of all things.'

THE LOST SYMBOL

Already there are a lot of conspiracy theorist-style internet pages dedicated to providing their own unique take on the circumpunct. The reality is that it can be used to symbolise many different things, from a road sign denoting a city centre in Europe to the alchemists' symbol for gold. The most common use is as a symbol of the sun and most scholars and historians connect this to ancient Egypt, when it was used to represent Ra, the Sun God.

However, in the book the tattooed villain, Mal'akh, is not hunting for the lost symbol but the lost word, which he believes will give him immortality. Brown neatly ties the circumpunct to the Freemasons when Langdon explains that the ancient Egyptians who built the pyramids were the ancestors of the modern stonemasons and within Masonic symbolism the pyramid and other Egyptian themes are very common.

In the book, the circumpunct's meanings are sometimes varied and often they are spiritual in nature. A circle with a point, for example, is now a common symbol for the sun, just as it is an ancient symbol for gold, considered to be the perfect metal, because a sphere is perfectly shaped and this perfect shape stands for unity and wholeness.

Is this true or is this another one of the facts that Brown has misinterpreted as he did with the Priory of Sion? The point or dot within the circle is known in the Hindu religion as a 'bindu', which is said to 'signify the spark of male life, the point at which creation begins within the cosmic womb and one becomes many.' [259]

Something else that Brown brought to light in *The Lost Symbol* is noetic science, the starting point for the novel's big idea. Noetic science is the study of how thought can affect matter. There is an old expression 'mind over matter' and this is the literal study of that idea. But it also covers a wider area, such as the study of how mind energy and consciousness relate to life.

'I'd studied some particle physics and knew that there was this world of noetic science that was kind of out there,' Brown said, referring to his research on *Angels & Demons*. 'I knew I wanted to come back to it. And in the 10 years between *Angels & Demons* and now, that field has exploded, and I became very, very interested with it. So that really is this idea of a science that's tied to these ancient mysteries, the old and the new I love to tie together, and the codes, they really just – they serve a plot line.'[260]

This science is one of the book's central themes and Brown claims that it is on the cusp of becoming a worldwide phenomenon, but the reality is different. Though he claims the science is real, the research being done in this field through the Institute of Noetic Sciences is considerably different from that in the book. The Institute is pursuing research into areas such as extended human capacity through meditation, psi studies, global medicine, placebo affects and bio-fields.

The Lost Symbol took Brown almost six years to write. One reason was the chaos surrounding The *Da Vinci Code* distracted him but, Brown said, 'The real reason *The Lost Symbol* took so long is that the subject matter behind it – the science behind it, the philosophy behind it – is so complicated and really so mind-blowing that I needed a lot of time to process it and understand it to a point where I could use it in a thriller.'

Like his character Robert Langdon, Brown remained a sceptic while he was writing the book. 'It took me a long time to get to the point where I could look at the science and look at the philosophy and really begin to believe it,' he said. 'I had a lot of people saying, "You go after someone and you attack them." That's not true. Whatever I found in the Masons I was going to write about and it just happened to find a group of people I was really impressed by.'

When it came to gaining access to the secret world of the Freemasons, the notoriety he had gained with *The Da Vinci Code* proved a double-edged sword. On the one hand his fame opened doors to places that he would never have had access to before, but it also hampered some of his research into specific places. For example, when he went to the Masonic House of The Temple to research the location, he did so as anonymously as possible, in a baseball hat and sunglasses. [261]

A lot of action in the book takes place in the House of the Temple and Brown needed the details to be accurate. 'Researching a room like the room in the House of the Temple might be three separate trips,' he said. 'I may go in as a tourist and [think], "Can I set a scene here? What's here?" Then I decide I can set a scene here and go back.' Brown had a Masonic guide the second time he went to the House of the Temple and on this trip he 'took a lot of notes, a lot of pictures and then I would write the section and go back a third time and, say, I focused on the altar or whatever it was that interested me and take more notes.'

In an interview with Steve Bertrand of Barnes & Noble, Brown explained how he hoped the Freemasons would react to his novel. 'My hope is that they love it and see it for what it is: a reverential look at their organisation mixed with the one thing they may not like is that a lot of their rituals are laid bare and you see a lot of things about their organisation.'

Brown said in that interview that it was the spiritual underpinnings of the Freemasons in the early period of America that provided them with political power. He claimed that many of the Founding Fathers were deists rather than theists. 'The difference being that deism believes in a God that does not intervene in world affairs,' Brown explained. 'Theism believes in a God that does intervene. If you pray to God he will fix things for you or arrange things for you.'

At the core of the Masonic philosophy is the notion that everyone is responsible for their own actions – that no God takes responsibility – and that ultimately we must treat our fellow man with the same respect and dignity we would expect to be treated ourselves. 'We as human beings have to do that and that really was a message I wanted to get across in the novel.'[262]

American Freemasonry has its origins in Europe and according to Brown, Washington D.C. is the capital of Freemasonry in the US. But Washington itself is not a modern city. 'It has underground tunnels, it has cathedrals it has crypts and obelisks and a lot of the grand architecture of Rome,' Brown said. Indeed, he tells us it was founded to be the new Rome. He finds it fascinating that Washington with its modern power base is 'framed in this classical architecture, classical art and a lot of classic ideals.'[263]

Brown believes that Washington has everything that London, Paris and Rome have in the way of art, architecture and so on. 'Washington has ... a great shadow world that we don't see,' he said. 'And one of the luxuries of having written *The Da Vinci Code* is that I had access to all sorts of specialists in Washington who were very, very generous to open up the doors of some of these monuments and museums and great structures and give me behind-the-scenes tours. That was very exciting.'

For Brown the philosophy of the Freemasons is fascinating. 'Here you have a global organisation that is spiritual and will bring Moslems, Jews, Christians and even people confused about religion together and agree that we all believe in some big thing out there but we're not going to put a label on it, and let's worship together.'

According to Cox, Freemasonry can be described as a secretive organisation but it is not a secret society. 'Membership is easy to research, and most members are not shy about letting you know that they are within the craft.' He states that since its inception and its 'heyday in the 1700s Freemasonry has attracted men of a certain social standing.' [264]

Today it is more welcoming but Brown describes the membership of Freemasonry as being important folk who tend to be thinkers and well connected people. 'The Masons are an organisation for both of those people thinkers and well-connected thinkers.'[265] But it is still a very traditional society and does not have any women members. The rituals it clings to are also traditional and arcane.

According to Brown there are Masonic lodges in most American towns. 'We drive by them and we think, "Well, that's a bunch of men who dress up in what – I'm not sure what it is,"' he said. 'What they do is fascinating and that is the topic of the book.'

Brown's claim that much of the book is real can be seen at the very beginning when he puts in a Fact page as he did with *The Da Vinci Code* – even though since that book was published, reams of books, websites and articles have claimed that the facts he put in it were wrong. 'The reality in this book [*The Lost Symbol*] is that all the science is real, all the locations are real,' Brown explained. 'The Masonic history is real. There is no Peter Solomon, there is no Zachary Solomon and there is no Robert Langdon, so these characters and their back stories are all fiction. There really is a museum support centre that has a giant squid. You can go and see it.'[266]

One of the things Brown found fascinating when he was researching *The Lost Symbol* was *The Apotheosis* in Washington. 'This idea that in the very centre of America, the top of the Capitol building, is a painting that shows George Washington ascending as a god to me was absolutely shocking and was part of the genesis of this novel.'

Brown admits he is a very sceptical person and that he has to understand and believe in what he is writing about for it to be believable to his readers. That understanding and belief is the framework for the structure of the novel.

Even so Brown once again blended fact with fiction to a point where some might find it hard to tell the difference. That, of course is his skill or genius, but just how real is it?

CHAPTER SIXTEEN

THE LOST SYMBOL

One thing I love to do is to get people to see things through a slightly different lens.

DAN BROWN

In the middle of what most people think of as a modern city stands an eerie, strange temple with a huge entrance guarded by massive stone sphinxes. Inside, the walls are adorned with strange symbols, mystical numbers and ancient inscriptions that date back to the ancient Egyptians and before. This all leads into a room shaped like a pyramid, with a large altar in its centre and an eye that points up to the heavens. Powerful and influential men are gathered in this room, adorned in ceremonial costume. They are overseeing the initiation of a new member, enacting an ancient ritual where the new member drinks blood-red wine out of a human skull.

This ritual takes place in the opening chapter of *The Lost Symbol* and Dan Brown claims it is real. It takes place in the Masonic House of the Temple, only a few blocks from Capitol Hill in Washington D.C.[267]

In this book Brown raises many questions about the power

of the human mind – for example, about the rituals and philosophy of the Freemasons, about George Washington and about people becoming gods. These are provocative questions. 'It doesn't matter to me if someone agrees or disagrees with what I say,' Brown said. 'But I'd like them to at least think about it.'

That no backlash materialised as it did with *The Da Vinci Code* may be because the Masons opened up to some public scrutiny. As we saw in the previous chapter, the language of their website about *The Lost Symbol* is calm, matter-of-fact and certainly not hysterical in the way that the Catholic Church responded to Brown's fourth novel.

Strip away all the philosophy and weird New Age science and what you have is a chase through the streets and famous landmarks of Washington DC. In this race against time Langdon has to work his way through puzzles and secret codes, and move from landmark to landmark to uncover clues as he delves into the dark corners of history. On the way, we discover that George Washington was a Mason and that Benjamin Franklin used his own printing press to publish a book on Freemasonry. It turns out also that the Declaration of Independence was signed by nine Freemasons, including John Hancock, who has the biggest signature on that document.

Because of Masons' secrecy, conspiracy theorists have seen shadows in every corner of Freemasonry. The brotherhood have been accused of secretly controlling the American government, of murder, even of Devil worship and much more. On the Great Seal on the back of the US dollar, a five-pointed Star of David can be drawn, with one of the points touching the all-seeing eye. Look at the other points of the star and you can see there are five letters which spell out M.A.S.O.N.

This could just be a coincidence but Brown doesn't believe

in coincidences, or does he? Perhaps, that's the enigma of the man. He has this persona of being an average guy but secret organisations, no matter who they are, will always be fascinating to him. 'Any time you have powerful people who aren't telling you what they're doing – you're going to assume the worst,' he said.[268]

Yet Brown did not treat the Freemasons badly in the book, as some have claimed he did or feared he would. 'There's a point in the book where Langdon makes the point that misinterpreting people's symbols is often the root of prejudice, and part of what I hoped to do with this book is shed some light, from my perspective, on Masonic symbolism and Masonic ritual.'

Brown believes that Freemasonry provides us with a perfect framework for 'universal spirituality' because it is an organisation that embraces people from different religions to worship with them. The only caveat is that every member or initiate that comes into the brotherhood believes in a god. 'They'll all stand in the same room and proclaim their reverence for a god,' Brown said during an interview with Matt Lauer.

But Brown has always said that he is a sceptic when it comes to the more alternative views of science and religion. His leading character is a sceptic as well. In *Angels & Demons* it took Langdon a long time to accept the idea of the Illuminati and antimatter, and in *The Da Vinci Code* it took him even longer to accept the theories being promoted by Teabing. In *The Lost Symbol* he takes some time to accept noetic sciences. 'I think one of the reasons these books have found a mass appeal is that he's diving into these conspiracy theories from the standpoint of somebody who doesn't believe them.'[269]

Brown also wants to take his readers on a journey of discovery along with Langdon. 'You can be an intelligent reader and say, "Well, I'm sort of interested in this, but I really doubt it's real." And at every point Langdon is right there with you, doubting it's real.'[270]

When you go through the plot line or a synopsis of a Brown novel, it will often sound preposterous, unreal and completely implausible. But when you start reading the book you are propelled into the world of Robert Langdon, following him on a race against time, on an adventure where failure means death. You get too lost in the action, in the chase and in the hunt to think about the implausibility of the plot.

'What no one could guess, despite all advance hints about setting and subject matter, was whether Mr Brown could recapture his love of the game,' said Janet Maslin of the *New York Times*. 'Could he still tell a breathless treasure-hunt story? Could he lard it with weirdly illuminating minutiae? Could he turn some form of profound wisdom into a pretext for escapist fun? By now his own formula has been damaged by so much copycatting that it's all but impossible for anyone to get it right.'[271]

In fact, *The Lost Symbol* is the first of Dan Brown's books to have a single villain. There is no criminal mastermind controlling a killer or killers – this time the mastermind and the killer are one. Mal'akh has infiltrated the Freemasons because he believes they have the key to a great secret that will make him a god and enable him to carry out his evil plan. Mal'akh is covered from head to toe with tattoos of occult symbols. For example, on his chest he has a large double-headed phoenix. Mal'akh is searching for the last piece of the puzzle known as the lost word.

While Mal'akh searches for this word to turn himself into a demon, he also has a twisted belief that by showing the American public that many of its top-ranking officials are Freemasons practising strange rituals, he can bring down the government. Would being a Freemason in real life bring down a president? One has to wonder if anyone would really care. Still, it's part of the motivation in Mal'akh's twisted mind and Langdon must stop it from happening to save the life of his old friend and mentor, Peter Solomon, who comes from an extremely wealthy but philanthropic family. He has to find the lost word or symbol before Mal'akh does.

After the opening ritual, the actual story of *The Lost Symbol* begins with Langdon heading for Washington, ostensibly to give an address to several of Peter Solomon's colleagues and friends, many of who are Masons, as is Peter. At the same time Brown introduces us to his younger sister Katherine Solomon, who has a connection to Mal'akh that helps to push the story forward. It is also in these opening chapters that Brown brings in noetic science, of which Katherine is one of the leading lights.

Langdon is drawn into Mal'akh's web through the discovery of the severed and bloody right hand of Peter Solomon, which is tattooed with mystical symbols. Solomon has been kidnapped by Mal'akh so that Langdon will do his bidding, to find the answer he searches for that will make him god-like.

Solomon is a 33rd degree Mason of the Scottish Rite and much of the action takes place in the headquarters of the Scottish Rite Freemasons in Washington. The 33rd degree is an honorary office for Scottish Rite Masons who have made a significant contribution to society or to Masonry in general. (However, 33rd degree Mason is not considered to be a high-ranking Mason simply by virtue of his degree number.)[272]

Solomon is also head of the Smithsonian Institute. The summons that Langdon gets he believes comes from Solomon, but it turns out to be a fake. Standing in the Rotunda, staring down at the severed hand, Langdon's cellphone suddenly goes off and he learns the sickening truth. The call is from Solomon's private cellphone and is from Solomon's executive assistant but during the call the voice changes to an eerie whisper telling Langdon that he has been chosen.

Somewhere, Solomon hovers between life and death while the man who holds his life in the balance, Mal'akh, is charging Langdon to find the Mason's Pyramid. It is hidden somewhere in one of the many underground tunnels and rooms in Washington DC, but this is not the only task that Mal'akh charges Langdon with. He must also find the Lost Word and if he doesn't do these things, Solomon will die.[273]

At the Rotunda, the Capitol police and the CIA arrive, brought there by Mal'akh. On security TV the chief of the Capitol police, Trent Anderson, sees a bald-headed man leave the building and goes rushing after him only to find him gone, directed down a corridor by a blond man who turns out to be Mal'akh in disguise.

Anderson heads back to the security centre and is surprised to find the elusive Inoue Sato, the head of the CIA's Office of Security, taking over the investigation. For her, this is all about national security, although she won't say why, believing that she is dealing with people so far beneath her that they have no reason to know anything.

Sato wants to know what Langdon knows but he doesn't know what she's talking about. But he does tell them about the tattoos on the severed hand. They find a clue that leads them into the Capitol's sub-basement, where they discover a small pyramid in Solomon's altar room. But the pyramid isn't complete – it's missing a capstone – but it does have an inscription carved into it.

When Langdon first came into the Capitol building he put his bag through X-rays as he went through security. In that bag he was carrying – in response to the kidnapper's demands – is a package that Solomon had entrusted to him many years ago, but Langdon has no idea what is in it. Sato does and confronts him with an X-ray of the bag showing a smaller pyramid in the package.

Langdon tries to explain his innocence but Sato doesn't believe him and tries to have him taken into custody. Her arrest goes awry when she and Anderson are attacked by the Architect of the Capitol, Warren Bellamy, who is also a Freemason. He and Langdon manage to get clear of the authorities and once again, Langdon finds himself running from the police.

While Langdon flees the scene, Mal'akh is at the lab where Katherine Solomon has been conducting her noetic science research. Her lab has been sponsored by the Smithsonian – indeed her older brother helped her set it up – but now Mal'akh destroys it. Before he does he kills her assistant Trish by throwing her into a massive tank that has a dead squid in it. She drowns in the poisonous embalming liquid.

Langdon and Katherine are captured by Mal'akh, who seriously injures Katherine. It's at this point that we find out what Mal'akh wanted Langdon for. Mal'akh places Langdon into a tank that slowly fills with water and threatens to drown Langdon if he doesn't unlock the code at the base of the pyramid. Langdon does unlock it and gives it to Mal'akh who takes the ailing Peter Solomon to the Temple Room of the Scottish Rite's House of the Temple, leaving Langdon and Katherine to drown in the tank.

They are rescued by CIA personnel led by Sato and they race to the House of the Temple. Langdon arrives ahead of Sato and discovers that Mal'akh is still holding Solomon hostage. He tells Langdon that he is going to release a heavily edited video showing government officials carrying out bizarre, secret Masonic rituals that will bring down the government. We discover that Mal'akh is Peter Solomon's son, Zachary, who everyone thought was long dead.

Mal'akh forces his father to tell him the Word and this he tattoos on the last remaining patch of bare skin, on top of his head. He then orders his father to sacrifice him, because it is the only way that he will become a demon and lead the forces of darkness. But just as he is forcing Solomon to do this, the Temple's overhead glass panel is smashed as Sato arrives in a helicopter. Shards of glass thunder down and Mal'akh is fatally impaled, but the video release has been put in motion and the CIA rush to stop it from being broadcast to the nation.

Solomon now tells Langdon that the Lost Word that Zachary tattooed on his head is not the real Word. He takes Langdon to a room on top of the Washington Monument where the true secret of the Word lies. In the Monument's cornerstone Langdon sees the symbols that spell out the words *Laus Deo* which means 'Praise God'. These same words are carved on the capstone at the top of the Monument that is the true Masonic Pyramid.

So how does The Lost Symbol fare when compared to The Curzon Group's five principles of thriller writing?

Does *The Lost Symbol* entertain the reader? The answer

lies in the quotes from reviewers and from the readers that are listed below. They will also give us the answers to how well *The Lost Symbol* stacks up against the rest of the thriller-writing criteria.

In its review of *The Lost Symbol*, the *New York Times* praised the book, saying that one had to read it from cover to cover in one sitting. Brown, reviewer Janet Maslin said, 'enlivens his story with amazing imagery. Some particular hot spots: the unusually suspense-generating setup for Katherine's laboratory, the innards of the Library of Congress, the huge tank of the architeuthis (giant squid) and two highly familiar tourist stops, both rendered newly breathtaking by Mr Brown's clever shifting of perspective.' [274]

However, not everything was to Maslin's liking. She noted Brown's habit of using too many italics to emphasise a character's thoughts. Indeed, the book is filled with them. She also asked what would happen if suddenly phrases such as 'What the hell?' 'Who the hell?' and 'Why the hell?' no longer existed because he uses these phrases so often, Maslin wonders how Brown would cope if they weren't there. Even so, she concluded that Brown had sexed up a genre that had all but withered away.

Maslin also had some reservations about plausibility – 'Mal'akh's story is best not dissected beyond the facts that he is bad, self-tattooed, self-castrated and not Langdon's friend' – but in the end it didn't matter. 'Within this book's hermetically sealed universe, characters' motivations don't really have to make sense; they just have to generate the non-stop momentum that makes *The Lost Symbol* impossible to put down.'[275]

On the other side of the country the *Los Angeles Times*

published a review that was largely positive but said that while Brown's narrative moved like an express train, it often got bogged down in 'the moments when people sound like encyclopaedias.'

The review ended with the speculation that people are not likely to be standing up and debating freemasonry in Washington after reading Brown's novel 'the way people did Brown's radical vision of Jesus and Mary Magdalene in *Code*. That book hit a deep cultural nerve for obvious reasons; *The Lost Symbol* is more like the experience on any roller coaster – thrilling, entertaining and then it's over.'[276]

Newsweek called the book contrived. 'You have to swallow a lot of coincidences. You have to believe that a man will board a private jet and fly from Boston to Washington DC on a moment's notice without once speaking to the man who asks him to make the flight. You have to buy into the idea that fathers do not recognise sons. You have to accept that people do not talk as they do in life but instead converse in whole paragraphs in which they exchange large clumps of abstruse information.'

Indeed the review also said Brown doesn't care much about the normal conventions of fiction. 'He doesn't care about things that occupy most novelists – realistic dialogue, characterisation and apparently neither do his legions of readers.' Complaining about this is the same as complaining that BMW isn't a good car manufacturer. It's not important. Brown, according to the review, 'is a maze-maker who builds a puzzle then walks you through it. His genius lies in uncovering odd facts and suppressed history, stirring them together into a complicated stew and then saying, *what if?*'

Ultimately the review also praises the novel as being a fun

read. 'Brown may not be much as a conventional novelist, but he knows how to make you keep turning pages.'[277]

The opinion in *The National Post* was not enthusiastic. The reviewer, Robert Wiersema, believed it was wrong to stack Brown's books up against other novelists: 'any new work from Dan Brown needs to be evaluated on its own terms, and in the context of his other works.' Evaluating it in this way, Wiersema found *The Lost Symbol* to be 'a staggering disappointment'.

Wiersema felt that the new book lacked what was unique about his previous work. 'Mal'akh, for example, is a psychotic villain straight out of B-movie central casting, always implausibly one step ahead of Langdon and his cohorts. He also bears an uncomfortably close similarity to Francis Dolarhyde, the tattooed, Blake-obsessed, apotheosis-seeking killer in Thomas Harris' *Red Dragon*.'

The plotting and direction, Wiersema felt, were considered to be clumsy, and the trademark twists and turns that Brown had used so well in previous novels were not in evidence in *The Lost Symbol*. 'An effective approach in his previous books, here the metronomic regularity of leading declaratives ("If Langdon had not yet grasped his role here tonight, soon he would" and "...Robert Langdon might suffer a similar fate" etc.) is almost insulting in its clumsy manipulativeness.'

Wiersema went on to state that Brown had insulted the reader when using his usual procedure of keeping information back to build tension while the real identity of Mal'akh was 'so thuddingly obvious I would be stunned if a single reader hadn't figured it out less than a hundred pages in. This makes the next 350 pages, and the big "reveal" an exercise in frustration. I was distracted from the narrative as

I tried to convince myself that Brown couldn't possibly be so obvious, couldn't possibly stoop so clumsily. Unfortunately, he was. And he did.'

The review ended by calling *The Lost Symbol* a 'heavy-handed, clumsy thriller'. The disappointment, it said, came from knowing that Brown can do better. 'If it didn't have Brown's name on the cover, it would disappear without a ripple. Sure, it sucks the reader in, but, ultimately, it plays them for suckers.'[278]

In the UK *The Daily Telegraph* also gave *The Lost Symbol* a rough ride, saying that although it wasn't 'quite the literary train wreck expected, there is less distraction from the familiar hokum which, precisely because it is so familiar, looks ever-less like ingenious puzzle-spinning and ever-more like a wearisome party trick.'

The reviewer, Jeremy Jehu, suggested that as *The Da Vinci Code* had divided families, perhaps *The Lost Symbol* might bring them back into the fold because 'they could all find it simply bland.' Jehu certainly didn't hold back. He called the narrative 'lumpen, witless, adjectivally promiscuous and addicted to using italics to convey excitement where more adept thriller writers generally prefer to use words.' If the book had a saving grace, he said, it is the setting, which gave Brown much more opportunity to get his locations right because it was set in America, 'not Europe, a culture whose manners and mechanics Dan Brown utterly and hilariously failed to comprehend in *The Da Vinci Code* and *Angels & Demons*.'[279] Harsh words.

Countering that point of view was *Time*, which said that the story was fun, if not a little bruising. Even though there were a lot of things the *Time* reviewer did not like about the book, there were some fundamental things that were right.

'It would be irresponsible not to point out that the general feel, if not all the specifics, of Brown's cultural history is entirely correct,' wrote Lev Grossman. 'He loves showing us places where our carefully tended cultural boundaries – between Christian and pagan, sacred and secular, ancient and modern – are actually extraordinarily messy.'

For example, Langdon points out that the Capitol building was created as a shrine to the Temple of Vesta, 'one of Rome's most venerated mystical shrines,' and that the Temple features a painting that shows George Washington looking like Zeus. 'Power is power, and it flows from religious vessels to political ones with disturbing ease. This may or not be obvious, but it is true, and deeply weird, and not at all trivial.'

Grossman also said that in Brown's world there are no such things as coincidences 'and things are not just things: they mean something. Brown's hero, Robert Langdon, is after all a symbologist (following a branch of human intellectual inquiry that – it cannot be stated enough times – doesn't exist, at Harvard or anywhere else).' [280]

Another area where Grossman provided positive feedback was in talking about Langdon's 'inexhaustive sense of wonderment'. According to the review, Langdon's inner struggle lies between his healthy scepticism that is firmly routed in academia and 'the ever mounting evidence that the world contains something miraculous that said scepticism can't account for.'

Grossman concluded that in *The Lost Symbol* Brown was trying to illustrate the fact that Washington DC is one of the world's great capitals, with its own share of secrets, mystery and intrigue, 'one that can hold its own with Paris or London or Rome.' Brown, Grossman says, was trying to reclaim Washington's richness, 'its darkness, and its weirdness. It's probably a quixotic effort, but it is nevertheless touchingly valiant.'

So we know what the reviewers thought of *The Lost Symbol* but what about the readers? At the time of writing more than 700 people had written a review for *The Lost Symbol* on Amazon UK, with the book getting an average three-star rating (193 people had given it five stars and 167 one star).

One reviewer who gave the book five stars called it 'excellent,' and said, 'You couldn't ask for anything better from Dan Brown.' But the one general thread running through the comments was that *The Lost Symbol* was disappointing compared to *The Da Vinci Code*.

'Don't get me wrong – the book is certainly a page turner and in the style of Dan Brown always leaves you on a cliffhanger wanting to know what happens in the next chapter – but I felt the story line was a little disappointing and seemed to lack depth and fizzle away towards the end. I expect more from this author now and am interested to see how (or if) the character develops in the future.'[281] That said, the reviewer still gave the book a four-star rating, even though he said Langdon's actions had become 'a bit boring'.

Another four-star review said the book was entertaining and 'like all of Brown's books it is hard to put down with cliffhangers at the end of each of the short chapters. I enjoyed the book and I guess the best conclusion is that this, like his other works, is pure escapism, as they are very far-fetched and the plots do stretch the imagination.'[282]

At the lower end of the spectrum, one two-star review opined that the 'plot didn't flow as it was broken up by too many "facts" and I couldn't personally understand the links that the characters were making to move the plot forward. For this reason, I found myself scanning certain pages and wishing I could hurry up and finish it.'[283]

Another reviewer said, 'You do not sympathise with any of the characters whatsoever. In fact you are more likely to wish that the villain would come out on top. At least that would make things interesting. Dan Brown has concentrated far too much on facts and figures that end up becoming awfully tedious, and you end up feeling that you would have been better off reading an encyclopaedia. I suspect that, as can sometimes happen after an author becomes successful, Dan Brown has been a little lazy with this novel. I hate to be so negative, as I really do enjoy most books I read, but this book was really bad.'[284]

And finally, one of the many one-star reviews intoned, 'This is a complete load of rubbish, based clearly on a formula which may have worked once or even twice but clearly it is short on ideas and relying very much on reputation to carry it through.'[285]

Another urged readers to save their money, while one ended by saying, 'Face it, Dan Brown, your basic story wore out with *The Da Vinci Code*, time to try a different approach.'

So we can say from the above that first, the book is entertaining for some readers but not for all, and secondly that it reflects the world around us through the facts, realistic locations and culture that Brown has gone to great lengths to include in the book. The locations are certainly real and described accurately.

However, it is formula writing. Brown hit on his formula with *Angels & Demons* and has simply substituted locations and science, but the characters are very similar. Langdon's female companions are almost identical, the villains are very similar as are the plot lines. On that principle, Brown falls down with *The Lost Symbol*.

Is it an adventure? Those readers who gave it four or five stars think it is. Many said it was a page-turner and very hard to put down because of Brown's trademark cliffhanger chapter endings. So we can say that most people think it is an adventure.

Is it written in a witty stylish way? The answer to this is probably not, because there isn't any indication from the reviews or comments from readers about this book being witty or even having any humour or charm at all. Most of the reviewers agree that the writing is not good or is heavy-handed, which makes the idea of it being written in a stylish way a little difficult to accept. Still, it is up to the reader to decide if Brown's fifth novel meets the five principles or not.

This brings us to the facts and the science. 'Our history is as sick and weird as anybody's!' Lev Grossman wrote in his *Time* review. 'There's signal in the noise, order in the chaos! It just takes a degree from a nonexistent Harvard department to see it.'[286] Brown says it's almost all real. He puts a Fact page right at the beginning of this book and expects us to embrace his version of the truth. But is it fact or is it all smoke and mirrors?

CHAPTER SEVENTEEN

SMOKE AND MIRRORS

Now we've come full circle in the Dan Brown story, there is one question that only Brown can answer.

In both *The Da Vinci Code* and in *The Lost Symbol* Brown started each book with a Fact page. In the case of *The Lost Symbol* that page says that all the rituals, science, artwork, organisations and monuments in the novel are real. The book opens with a ritual where the new initiate to the Freemasons drinks red wine out of a human skull that represents the decay of the flesh while the wine represents blood. This is said to be part of the 33rd Degree ritual and it is performed at night in the Scottish Rite House of The Temple in Washington DC. According to Brown, 'The ceremony is described accurately. The fiction comes in as to whether or not it still happens at this moment in history in this room.'[287]

However, this claim was refuted on NBC's *Today* programme in October 2009 by the Grand Archivist of the Scottish Rite of the Freemasons, Arturo de Hoyos, who is also a 33rd degree Mason. He said that there were errors on the first page of the book. 'We don't perform the 33rd Degree in this building. We don't confer it at night. The candidates to the members are dressed wrong. And the ceremony's wrong.'

But in the same programme Lodge 198 in Colorado opened its doors to the cameras. The Senior Warden in this lodge said he was sick and tired of people saying that Freemasons had no secrets. 'Nothing could be further from the truth.'

This lodge practices alchemy, which in the old days tried to turn base metals into gold but now represents personal transformation, taking men who are already good and turning them into something special. Initiates into the brotherhood are taken through an intense ritual that begins when the initiate's vision is taken away by a 'hoodwink' which is placed over his head. Dressed as the Grim Reaper, a Master Mason warns the initiate that he will be enlightened, overcome darkness and be purified, but if he is afraid he is not to continue.

The initiate then goes into a chamber of reflection where the 'hoodwink' is removed 'and you're presented with what is a very interesting image. And Dan Brown described it pretty well in his book.'[288]

Brown's hope with this book is that 'it starts to pull people in the direction of the ancient mysteries, to look at the world through a different lens. This idea of the power of the human mind and the ability of thought to actually transform the world in which we live,' he explained.

Perhaps one of the most telling revelations by Brown is that the symbols and ancient mysteries come from a book called *The Secret Teachings of All Ages*. 'That really is a core book for a lot of what I research and a lot of what I believe,' Brown said.

Written by Manly P. Hall in the 1920s, the book studies

the wisdom of the ancients. Hall founded the Philosophical Research Society in Los Angeles to take these studies further, to look at how a person can become more fully human through reaching a higher level of consciousness. 'The ancient mysteries deal in the concept of the power of the human mind,' explained Brown. 'The Masons celebrate mankind and the power of the human mind. In fact, in the Second Degree ritual there's actually a line where they say, "Here you will learn the mysteries of human science."' [289]

This human science is noetic science, which Brown said was the reason it took him so long to write *The Lost Symbol*. 'I'm a sceptic and I hear about these experiments that are being done that categorically and scientifically prove that the human mind has power over matter.'

Marilyn Schlitz, Director of the California Institute of Noetic Sciences, told the *Today* programme that the Institute's researchers are running experiments where people through thought alone can affect how ice crystals are formed. Researchers in this field have put machines called random generators in many countries. 'These are essentially electronic coin flippers. So if you imagine flipping a coin 100 times, you would expect based on a normal probability distribution, that you'd get an equal number of heads and tails.'[290]

But perhaps there's another way to find out more about Dan Brown and his version of the truth. TV presenter Tony Robinson of *Time Team* fame followed in Langdon's and Brown's footsteps to decode the mysteries of *The Lost Symbol* for Channel 4. At the beginning of his quest Robinson asked if there are 'ancient secrets that turn men into gods and can you really move objects through the power of thought alone?'[291]

Robinson's impression on reading the book was that Dan Brown 'absolutely loves Masons. He says they are the most trustworthy people in the world.' They should be, because according to Brown they are the keepers of secret knowledge that could be incredibly dangerous if it fell into the wrong hands. 'According to Brown, this secret ancient knowledge can unlock godlike powers that lie dormant within us but only a handful of people can do this, those who are deemed worthy,' Robinson explained.

First Robinson visited the United Grand Lodge in England. The first surprise was that the doors to the lodge were not locked, as one would expect if the Freemasons did really hold such powerful ancient knowledge. He also discovered that there is no Chamber of Reflection in this lodge. Could it be that the English Masons don't use these chambers but others do?

Robinson next found out that initiates are blindfolded at first because the ceremony of initiation is meant to represent rebirth. He also finds out that on the first ceremony the masons roll up a trouser leg, which in the old days was done 'to show the state of your leg, if you were diseased or weak. Then you wouldn't have the strength to work in the quarry.'

Of course Masons don't have their trouser legs rolled up all the time, just in this ceremony. 'Stone masonry is the source of the symbols rituals and language of freemasonry today. It is also the source of its secrecy,' Robinson explained. 'Once builders of fabulous castles and cathedrals, stone masons were considered to be masters of a magical art. They were important members of society answerable to kings and bishops. The skills they passed onto their apprentices were jealously guarded. In a period of mass illiteracy it's likely that elaborate secret handshakes and passwords identified members of the stone mason fraternity.'[292]

Robinson was next taken into a room adorned with ancient symbols and icons, and where the ceiling was covered with symbols and images from the ancient world. But he discovered, at this lodge at least, the Freemasons are not the guardians of secret ancient mysteries.

As he couldn't find what he was looking for in England, Robinson continued his quest overseas, in Washington DC. 'The men who created Washington were political idealists. Revolutionary and democratic ideas were common to the enlightened 18th century and to Freemasons, whose core values included fraternity, equality and liberty,' Robinson explained.

To find out if the Founding Fathers of America had a Masonic agenda, Robinson went to the Pennsylvania Statehouse in Philadelphia, where in the summer of 1776 the United States came into being when the Declaration of Independence was signed. Many of the Founding Fathers were Masons and Robinson stated in the programme that their Masonic influence should be seen in the Declaration of Independence.

Meeting up with a high-ranking Mason, Akram Enlias, Robinson asked him if he thought the creation of America was a Masonic experiment. The second line in the Declaration of Independence – 'the law of nature and of nature is God' – is at the heart of Masonic philosophy, Robinson was told. 'The Founding Fathers believed in the natural order of the universe and if you look at the rituals of Freemasonry, this part of the teachings in the Second Degree, which says it is part of the endeavour, is to imitate the divine plan which manifests itself in nature,' Enlias told him.

Next stop on his epic quest was the Library of Congress in Washington DC. 'Thomas Jefferson, the principal author of the Declaration of Independence, and his idealistic words are deeply woven into the fabric of the US. If America was anyone's vision it was his,' Robinson told the viewing audience. 'The progressive values that Jefferson championed – liberty, equality and progressive democracy – were in tune with Freemasonry, as were his calls for universal education. This ideal was set in stone in the Library of Congress, which grew out of his collection of books.'

In *The Lost Symbol*, Langdon takes refuge in the reading room of the Library of Congress and marvels at its architecture. The Founding Fathers created the building because they realised that members of Congress would need information on virtually any subject. Robinson asked the curator if the building was Masonic because of its ornate symbols and architecture. The answer was disappointing. It isn't a Masonic building, despite the fact that it shares some images. 'Dan Brown says it is the most beautiful room in the world and it's hard to argue with that.'

Robinson learned that the Masons did not hold a monopoly on enlightened ideas. Thomas Jefferson promoted similar values. 'He shared many of the same ideas as the Masons – liberty, equality, justice for all and that sort of thing – but he saw them as commonsense values,' explained Robinson. 'So while a handful of Founding Fathers were Masons, America wasn't their creation. There was no Masonic masterplan.'

Robinson next claimed that Brown explored ideas in his novel that 'George Washington and his friends adorned their capital city with Masonic symbolism, architecture and art. So what's the reality?'

George Washington hired French-born architect Pierre L'Enfant to design the new capital city as one that would rival the great European capitals. Brown, Robinson said, claims that L'Enfant was a Mason. Part of L'Enfant's design included an elaborate street plan. 'The original plan was designed in a grid shape. There are lots of stars exploding all over it,' Robinson said. 'In addition there are all these diagonal lines crisscrossing the grid as well. And if you look at it very closely shapes start to emerge out of it. Above the White House is a pentagram – Masonic. Between the White House and the Capitol a set square – really Masonic. Apex from the Capitol – super-Masonic. Some people say it is a deliberate attempt to imprint Masonic symbols onto the city.'

Robinson next went to a top Washington architect to discuss the street plan and discovered that there is no hidden Masonic design at all. 'Dan Brown got it wrong,' Robinson said. 'L'Enfant wasn't a Mason and his plan for the city didn't hide any Masonic secrets.'

Robinson then turned his attention to the Washington Monument, the world's tallest stone structure and supposedly a very potent Masonic symbol. 'It harks back to ancient Egypt, as do so many Masonic rituals and myths.' The architect of the Monument was a Mason, Robert Mills. The number five figures prominently in the obelisk and that is a very important Masonic number, Robinson told his viewers. The obelisk is 550 feet high with a base that is 55 feet by 55 feet.

In the book Langdon and Katherine are in a cab tearing through the streets of Washington when Katherine shows Langdon the dollar bill 'which is absolutely riddled with Masonic symbols. This unfinished pyramid is a massive

Masonic symbol and above it an all-seeing eye that was such a big Masonic symbol that George Washington had one of these on his Masonic apron,' Robinson continued. Brown, he said, claims the image of the pyramid is probably the most famous in the world. 'The pyramid is one half of the Great Seal, America's national emblem.' The other side of the dollar shows an eagle that has 13 olive branches in its talons behind 13 stars and stripes.

But when he went looking for answers Robinson was disappointed again. The 13, for example, stood for the 13 states of the time rather than being a Masonic symbol. The images on the dollar bill are not specifically Masonic but common images that could have been used by anyone. 'While there is no doubt that DC was founded by a Freemason, most of the symbols in the city are nothing of the sort,' said Robinson.

The next stop on his quest was to investigate the claim by Brown that everyone has god-like powers but they are all dormant within us. In the book, Brown has the severed hand pointing up to a mural on the ceiling of the Rotunda. Known as *The Apotheosis*, it depicts a mythical moment when George Washington is transformed from man to god. 'This could simply be veneration for the father of a new nation but Dan Brown thinks it's much, much bigger,' says Robinson.

According to Robinson, Brown thinks the ancient mysteries can unlock vast untapped powers in the human mind. 'This is the theme he returns to again and again,' Robinson said. But this ancient knowledge, passed down through the generations, was lodged with a group of 17th-century British scientists such as Isaac Newton and Robert Boyle. Brown claims the knowledge was so dangerous that these men were forced to create an underground society they called The Invisible College. So Robinson went from DC to the Oxford Museum of Physical Science, where the men of the Invisible College met.

What Robinson discovered was that these highly intelligent, highly educated and high profile men were discussing medicine, astronomy, engineering, chemistry, microscopy and meteorology. 'There was no occult tradition in them.'

The more Robinson dug, the more he discovered that the Invisible College were not discussing the ancient mysteries or keeping ancient secrets, and that what Brown was offering was 'a trainload of fantasy and a thimble full of fact'.

Disappointed but in search of evidence of the power of thought, Robinson continued by looking at noetic science. 'Dan Brown says that people can move solid objects just through their mind alone. Brown says that a focused thought can affect anything – the direction that fish swim round in a bowl, the manner cells split up in a Petri dish, the way a plant grows – but is this true or a little far-fetched?'

To find out Robinson visited a research institute studying parapsychology. Brown claims in his book that this science is on the verge of a breakthrough, but Robinson found this science is only just scratching the surface.

The institute has one random event generator and Robinson tested his mental abilities by pushing a needle into a green zone on the computer screen using just the power of his mind. The generator creates random numbers that move the needle in the direction of the number. Without using the computer, Robinson had to try to push the needle to the highest number using his mind, to try to override the computer. He is connected to the computer with diodes but the computer generates the numbers which Robinson has to change. He is told he will have to try this many times, probably more than a hundred.

Sure enough he did have to do it more than a hundred times and his results were average. But Robinson knew that there have been some remarkable results in this area but nobody can explain why. 'At the moment, they are just in the foothills and not about to come up with something world-shattering like Einstein, Newton or Galileo did,' Robinson said. 'That is the exact opposite of the way Dan Brown describes this science in his book. His noetic science just doesn't stack up.'

Next up was a trip back to Washington DC to investigate Brown's claim that the laboratories of the Smithsonian Institute Support Centre, where Katherine Solomon did her work, are real. Brown claims in his book that the Support Centre is the cutting edge of noetic research, that it is a complex that houses the museum's overspill collection and is located on the outskirts of Washington DC.

Brown portrays Katherine Solomon as working in a sterile hangar known as Pod 5, which is 'full of amazing machines like random event generators that help her to understand the incredibly powerful forces that lie latent in the human mind,' Robinson said. 'While Katherine is about to make some important scientific announcements that will change the course of human history, the baddie is outside trying to get in, determined to destroy her work at any cost.'

What's the reality? Robinson discovered that there is a Pod 5 and that inside there is a canoe, just as Brown mentions, and that the collection has a giant squid, but it is in another Pod. In the book Mal'akh attacks Katherine's assistant, Trish, and throws her alive into a giant tank full of ethanol where the squid is. But the real tank in Pod 5 has an octopus, and the Pod is completely full, housing 25 million specimens.

When Robinson asked the curator where the cube was that Katherine did her work in, he was told that there is no cube in Pod 5 and to make matters worse, the curator also tells him they do not do any research on noetic science. 'This is a disaster,' said Robinson. 'It would seem that almost none of the things in Dan Brown's book that we've investigated are not quite as factual as he makes out.'

The final leg of his quest was to investigate Brown's claim that the Masonic ranks are filled with powerful and influential men, and that if it was revealed that they take part in bizarre, secret rituals it would bring down the US government. To get an answer Robinson went to the House of the Temple and asked one of the highest-ranking Masons in the US, Brent Morris, how powerful the Masons really are.

To Robinson's dismay, Morris said that while they are very proud of the 14 Presidents who have been members, today 'nearly all the Masons are from the middle class.' Hundreds of years ago, Morris said, Freemasonry was feared by the church because the Masons promoted the ideas of 'representative democracy, freedom of speech and universal education. Today we are the epitome of middle class.' They are not part of a global plot.

So Robinson found that at the end of his quest he was no wiser than when he'd started. 'I've been frustrated at just about every turn,' he said. 'So what do I learn from the world's fastest-selling novel of all time? Well, the monuments and the organisations may be real but as for the rituals and the science, I think he's taking more than just a little bit of artistic licence there. I cannot find just one hint of ancient knowledge anywhere.'[293]

So Robinson's quest to confirm that the claims that Brown makes in his novel are real turned out to be a failure. Was it because Robinson didn't do the research that Brown did or didn't talk to the right people? Or is it possible that Brown is playing games with us all? Is he that kind of person?

We know that his education at Phillips Exeter Academy shaped his view of the world. His education has instilled in him a need to succeed, to achieve, to always be curious, which he has bestowed on Langdon. The treasure hunts run by his parents every Christmas influenced him so much that each of his novels contain elements of treasure hunts and chases. There is always a goal that must be achieved. In Langdon's world, as in Brown's, there is no room for failure.

Look at his musical career. He put everything he had into his music but at the end of the day it just wasn't right for the time. Whether it was good or bad isn't important. It just didn't catch on – it didn't have that spark, the X-factor if you will. Lesser men would have crawled away but Brown persevered because his education and upbringing gave him the grounding to always strive for better, to put everything into life, to be as successful as possible, to achieve.

He only left the music scene after a contract for *187 Men to Avoid* had been secured. But he was still teaching and writing at the same time. He could have walked away after publication of *Deception Point* after he saw how bad the sales were for all three of his earlier books. But he didn't. As he stared at his blank screen realising his fourth novel had to be the breakthrough book – had to be the one that would enable him to write full time and make a living at it – he didn't pack up and walk away.

Instead, he began to write. Slowly at first, the letters and words coming in dribs and drabs onto the screen as he typed; as he and Blythe scoured the hundreds of research books, documents and files they'd amassed; as he looked at the hundreds of photographs they'd taken on their trips to Paris, London and Edinburgh. And when he'd finished writing, he'd turned out one of the most successful novels of all time.

The question then is: if Dan Brown spends years researching his novels, how can he get the facts so wrong – or is the Fact page at the beginning of *The Da Vinci Code* and *The Lost Symbol* part of his fiction? By now he must know that by putting a Fact page at the beginning of his novels he is inviting people to pick holes in his research and show him up to be mistaken, as Robinson's quest showed. Only Brown can answer this.

However, if we look at the Fact page in his books as being part of the story, part of the fiction, then perhaps we can see that Brown is playing a little joke on all of us. Whatever the answer, Dan Brown is an industry now. He is bigger than just about any author out there and there are dozens of people writing books and making a living off the novels he's written.

Maybe part of Brown's genius – and enigma – is that the Fact page in his books was never meant to be taken literally. Maybe it is all a code or a puzzle that no one has figured out yet. If we look at it from that perspective, then Brown doesn't need to get his facts right if they are fiction. Because it's hard to believe that Brown would spend so much time researching each book to get the facts he claims are real so wrong.

Or is it all just smoke and mirrors? 'If I have a big beef with Dan Brown it is this,' Tony Robinson said in the conclusion to his quest. 'He was lazy. Why did he choose the Masons as a basis for a modern conspiracy thriller? Why didn't he do what novelists are supposed to do, make up a story and then tell it to us instead of pretending it's all real?'[294]

THE CHARACTERS

DIGITAL FORTRESS

Susan Fletcher: The protagonist, she is the National Security Agency's Head Cryptographer and is engaged to be married to David Becker. She is slender, tall with dark hair, very intelligent and perceptive. She finds herself at the centre of a conspiracy that threatens to bring down the government.

David Becker: Engaged to Susan Fletcher, Becker is a linguistic expert and is the youngest professor of languages at the university. In the past he's worked for the NSA and has been asked to again, unknown to Susan. He is walking into a trap.

Ensei Tankado: A brilliant former NSA employee who creates the unbreakable code called Digital Fortress. The plot of the novel revolves around his design of the code and the attempts that NSA makes to try to break it. He chose to create the code because of moral and ethical grounds but is killed by the hired assassin to get the code-breaker key.

Commander Trevor Strathmore: He is the Deputy Director of Operations for the NSA and is the main antagonist. Susan Fletcher sees him as a father figure but he is deeply in love with her and he sends Becker to Spain to get him out of the way, so he can have Susan. He is the most complex character of the novel, because he is doing these evil things yet he believes that he is doing them for the right reasons.

Phil Chartrukian: A technician who works for Systems Security (Sys-Sec) division of the NSA that monitors the computer systems, he is the first one who realizes that something is wrong, but is killed by Strathmore.

Greg Hale: Another NSA Cryptographer, he has a shady past but is brilliant at his work. He believes that something is wrong but is also a minor antagonist to Susan.

Leland Fontaine: As Director of NSA Fontaine is the only person that Strathmore answers to and he is the person who ultimately picks up the pieces.

Hulohot: This character is an assassin hired by Strathmore to kill Becker in Spain and to retrieve the killcode from Tankado and then from Becker after Tankado's death.

Midge Milken: A mature and experienced woman she is Fontaine's internal security analyst and has a friendly sparring relationship with Fontaine's personal assistant, Chad Brinkerhoff.

Chad Brinkerhoff: A young thrusting personal assistant to Fontaine who also has an attraction to Milken. He is reluctant to believe that things are not as they seem but soon gets on the bandwagon when Milken provides him with proof.

Jabba: The large, rotund man, nicknamed 'Jabba the Hutt' because of his resemblance to the fictional character in Star Wars, he is the NSA's senior Systems Security Officer and Chartrukian's boss.

Soshi Kuta: She is Jabba's assistant.

ANGELS & DEMONS

Robert Langdon: The main protagonist of the book and a professor of symbology at Harvard University. He is a broad dark-haired man and usually wears chino pants, turtleneck (sweater with a turnover collar) and tweed jacket. His name is Brown's tribute to ambigram artist John Langdon. He is described as being inquisitive, curious and passionate about puzzles, codes and ancient mysteries to the point of putting himself in danger, but he is overall a sceptic.

Leonardo Vetra: Vetra is a priest and a scientist working at CERN in Switzerland, researching antimatter. He dreams of merging science and religion together. When he was invited to work at CERN he adopted Vittoria and they moved to Geneva, both becoming physicists. Together they created antimatter which they kept in canisters under tight security that used retina scanners for their identification.

Vittoria Vetra: In the book, Vittoria is the adopted daughter of Leonardo Vetra and they both work at CERN. Leonardo and Vittoria formed an attachment at the orphanage, with Vetra teaching her while she added warmth and laughter to his life. He adopted her as his daughter and they went to CERN to work. It was her idea to create antimatter. She's fluent in English, French, Italian and Latin. She is tall, slender, has black hair, large expressive eyes, very athletic with the classic Mediterranean look and in the book is Langdon's love interest.

She helps him locate the kidnapped cardinals by working out the clues. The Hassassin (see below) kidnaps her and he takes her to his hideout – the Castle Saint' Angelo. Langdon finds her bound to a divan and gagged with the Hassassin about to rape her. During the struggle between the Hassassin and Langdon Vittoria frees herself and they push the Hassassin over the balcony to his death. At the end of the book it is implied that Langdon and Vittoria form a sexual relationship while in *The Da Vinci Code* we learn they were to meet up every six months, but never do. Her father Leonardo and their relationship together are not in the film. She is not kidnapped in the film nor does she have a romantic relationship with Langdon.

Camerlengo Carlo Ventresca: Ventresca is the Papal Chamberlain or the Camerlengo during the papal conclave. He is the main antagonist and uses the codename 'Janus' to deal with the Hassassin. In the film his name is Patrick McKenna and not Ventresca; this alteration was done to accommodate Scottish actor Ewan McGregor, and the film character McKenna is from Northern Ireland, as opposed to Italy, where the book's Ventresca is from.

Raised a devout Catholic by his mother, Maria, he never knew his father because his mother always said he had died before Carlo was born. His mother dies too in an attack by Red Brigade terrorist group on a church in Sicily that he and his mother were visiting. In the film version, the attack takes place in Northern Ireland by the Ulster Volunteer Force (UVF). Sole survivor of the blast he is taken into a monastery by a Bishop from Palermo where he lived with the monks but when he reached sixteen he was conscripted into the Italian Army. However, he refused to fire a weapon and so they taught him to fly a helicopter and to use a parachute. After the army Carlo entered a seminary but his life changed when the bishop from Palermo was elected Pope and Carlo became his Camerlengo.

Carlo's motivation for carrying out his evil deeds stem from when the Pope sent him to CERN to investigate Vetra's claims that he'd made a discovery of deep religious significance. Ethically disturbed by the discovery Carlo reported his findings to the Pope, who saw it as positive. Shocked by this response Carlo thinks he receives a message from God telling him to kill the Pope, which he does.

As Janus, Carlo hires the Hassassin to kill the four Cardinals and steal the antimatter. He dies after he is exposed as Janus and learns the Pope was his father. He is overcome with guilt and burns himself alive on the balcony of St Peter's Basilica.

Cardinal Saverio Mortati: The most senior cardinal in the conclave, and the current Dean of the College of Cardinals. He was the Devil's Advocate for the late pope.

Commander Olivetti: The commander of the Swiss Guard in Vatican City, he is responsible for protecting the Cardinals during the papal conclave and he discovers that a security camera has gone missing, but when Langdon and Vittoria arrive explaining the real danger, he refuses to believe it. Four cardinals are also missing and the commander is searching for them. Even when The Hassassin contacts them Olivetti has a difficult time trusting Langdon, but he eventually does.

He is killed by the Hassassin helping Langdon find the third cardinal. However, in the film, Olivetti is much more sympathetic to Langdon and Vittoria and believes them straight away. He fights The Hassassin at the scene of the third cardinal's death and has his throat cut.

Captain Rocher: The second in command of the Vatican Swiss Guard after Commander Olivetti, in charge of the search for the antimatter canister. Brown describes him as being barrel-chested with 'putty-like features' and a little flamboyant due to the red beret he wears with his uniform. Rocher only searches the public access areas because he firmly believes that the Swiss Guard are incorruptible.

When the Swiss Guard break into the Camerlengo's office after hearing him scream they discover the Camerlengo has been branded with the Illuminati logo. He accuses Rocher of being 'Illuminatus' and Lieutenant Chartrand shoots Rocher; in the film, Rocher has been changed to Father Simeon, who is shot after the Camerlengo calls him 'Illuminatus' along with Commander Richter.

Hassassin: A killer of Middle-Eastern origin hired by 'Janus' to carry out his plans against the Vatican. Throughout the novel the killer has a sadistic lust for women. He kills Leonardo Vetra to steal the antimatter canister in the underground vault of Vetra's lab. He cuts out Vetra's left eye, brands his body with the Illuminati symbol and uses the eye to get past the retina scanners and steal the canister.

The Hassassin contacts Langdon, Vittoria and the Camerlengo in Vatican City, telling them that a cardinal will be killed every four hours and they will be branded Earth, Air, Fire and Water in four churches across Rome. He tells the BBC crew this as well.

After killing the fourth cardinal the Hassassin heads back to his hideout and fights Langdon and Vittoria who together push the Hassassin over the balcony where he falls to his death.

In the film he dies when the getaway car that has been set up for him by Janus explodes when he starts the car.

Maximilian Kohler: The director of CERN, he is paralysed from a childhood illness and gets around in a high-tech wheelchair containing a computer, telephone, pager, video camera, and a gun. Kohler blames religion for his paralysis because his religious parents denied him treatment when he was a child, believing his illness was a sign from God but he survived when he was treated by a doctor without his parents' knowledge, accounting for his hatred of religion and love of science. In the film his character becomes Commander Maximilian Richter and shares many of Kohler's characteristics.

Gunther Glick and Chinita Macri: Respectively a reporter and camerawoman who work for the British Broadcasting Corporation (BBC). They are in the Vatican to cover the papal election that forms the backdrop of the novel. Glick is slim with a thin face and Brown describes him as looking odd while he describes Macri as being of African/American descent, a little overweight, but of a very sunny disposition. Of the two, Macri is the conscience while Glick is more of a sensationalist and conspiracy theorist. For most of the novel they hinder the protagonists and are only useful at the end.

The Hassassin contacts Glick to give him a scoop on the murders of the four cardinals as well as telling them about an impending bombing of the Vatican. These two provide live updates on the action to the rest of the world through the BBC, capturing the final actions at the end of the novel and finish by announcing the new pope, Cardinal Saverio Mortati.

Lieutenant Chartrand: A young Swiss Guard. He, together with Commander Olivetti and Captain Rocher, search desperately for the antimatter hidden somewhere in the Vatican. He shoots and kills Captain Rocher after he is mistaken as an 'Illuminatus'. Near the end of the novel, he is sent by the new pope to give the Illuminati Diamond as an indefinite loan to Langdon.

Cardinal Ebner: One of the four cardinals who dies in the book. He is originally from Frankfurt, Germany. The Hassassin asphyxiates him by putting dirt and soil in his mouth. The killer brands him 'Earth'.

Cardinal Lamassé: Another of the four cardinals killed in the book. He is from Paris and is killed when the Hassassin punctures his lungs which fill with blood. He is branded 'Air' by the Hassassin.

Cardinal Guidera: The third of the cardinals to die and he is from Barcelona in Spain. The Hassassin burns him alive. He is branded 'Fire' and his death is the most horrific of them all.

Cardinal Baggia: From Milan, Italy, he is the fourth cardinal to be killed in the book, though he is nearly saved by Langdon. His chest has been branded with the 'Water' sign by the killer and he is drowned by the Hassassin. He is the favourite to be elected as the new Pope.

DECEPTION POINT

Rachel Sexton: She is one of the main protagonists in the novel and is very similar to Susan Fletcher. She is highly intelligent, lithe, dark-haired and slender. She works for the National Reconnaissance Office (NRO) in Washington and is the chief Intelligence Analyst to the White House. She is also Senator Sexton's estranged daughter. She blames him for her mother's death, which she still feels very deeply.

Michael Tolland: He is the second protagonist and becomes Rachel's love interest as the novel progresses. He is a famous television celebrity-scientist and an oceanographer and has his own research vessel, the *Goya*. He is deeply affected by the loss of his wife.

President Zachary Herney: The embattled President of the United States, currently involved in a bitter re-election campaign which is going very badly as the book opens. He supports NASA despite their many setbacks, and hopes the find in the Arctic will vindicate his campaign.

Senator Sedgewick Sexton: He is one of the antagonists and Rachel's estranged father. A deeply selfish man he treated his ex-wife, Rachel's mother, very badly and Rachel blames her death on him. The Senator is running an anti-NASA campaign which is doing very well, his main platform being the privatization of the space agency. Everything he does is for political gain.

Corky Marlinson: Brown has this character as a world-renowned astrophysicist called in by the President to authenticate the NASA find in the Arctic. He has no social skills and does not know how to engage with people.

William Pickering: Director of the NRO, Pickering is the main antagonist and has hired Delta Force to monitor the find and kill anyone who tries to expose the hoax. His motivation is complex. Rachel sees him as a father figure and is shocked when he turns out to be her enemy.

Gabrïelle Ashe: Senator Sexton's beautiful aide, who had a sexual liaison with him but as the story unfolds she begins to see the Senator for what he is and also decides that she must do the right thing.

Norah Mangor: She is a glaciologist and one of four scientists called in to authenticate the Arctic find by NASA. She is killed by Delta Force.

Dr Wailee Ming: A paleontologist, he is one of the four scientists the President brings in to authenticate NASA's discovery along with Tolland, Marlinson and Mangor. He is one of the first to realize something is wrong, and dies as a result.

Charles Brophy: Brophy is in the opening of the book and is forced by Delta Force agents to send a bogus message. He is a Canadian geologist and is pushed out of an aircraft to his death after he sends the message.

Chris Harper: He is the mission director of the Polar Orbiting Density Scanner (POLADS) that, it transpires, does not work.

Yolanda Cole: Gabrielle Ashe's friend and employee at the Washington news branch of ABC TV, covering the election campaign. She encourages Gabrielle to expose Senator Sexton for what he is.

Katherine Wentworth Sexton: Rachel Sexton's deceased mother and Senator Sexton's wife.

Celia Birch: Michael Tolland's deceased first wife.

Marjorie Tench: Senior Advisor to the President she appears to be an antagonist suspicious of Rachel. She is described as being an ugly woman, a chain smoker but extremely intelligent and perceptive.

Lawrence Ekstrom: He is the embattled NASA Administrator.

Diana Pickering: William Pickering's deceased daughter.

Xavia: She is a marine geologist and a colleague of Tolland, working on his research ship the *Goya*. She helps Tolland and Rachel when they land on the ship.

The Controller: he is the head of the Delta Force team but turns out to be William Pickering in disguise.

THE DA VINCI CODE

Bishop Aringarosa: Head of Opus Dei he is the patron of the albino monk Silas. Before the story begins he learns that the Pope will be withdrawing his support for Opus Dei, which he believes is keeping the Catholic Church from being corrupted by the modern era. He is contacted by 'The Teacher' who tells him he can help ensure Opus Dei retains the Vatican's support by providing him with clues leading to the Holy Grail. The Bishop accepts readily. The Teacher tells the Bishop he can't communicate with Silas. The Bishop later learns from police captain, Bezu Fache, that the albino monk has killed Sister Sandrine Bieil. He tells Fache what has gone on and heads to London to track down Silas. At the London Opus Dei Centre, Silas accidentally shoots the Bishop, who recovers in hospital.

Sister Sandrine Bieil: The Sister works and lives at Saint Sulpice and is a member of the Priory of Sion, there to warn the members of the Priory if the false keystone is ever found beneath the Roseline. When Silas comes to the church in search of the keystone she tries to warn the four guardians but, unable to reach any of them and before she can raise the alarm, Silas kills her.

Jérôme Collet: A lieutenant in France's Direction Central Police Judiciaire (DCPJ) he is Captain Bezu Fache's second-in-command. He brings Langdon to the Louvre where

Jacques Saunière has been murdered and manages to slip a tracking device into Langdon's pocket. Collet manages to track down Langdon and Sophie to Leigh Teabing's villa and after hesitating to wait for Fache he finds that everyone has fled. At the end Collet credits Fache on TV for the arrest of Teabing, while also stating that the pursuit of Langdon and Sophie was a ruse to bring out the real killer.

Bezu Fache: Captain in the DCPJ, he is shrewd, tough and persistent as he investigates the murder of Jacques Saunière. Convinced that Langdon is the killer by the clues left by the dead man, he relentlessly goes after Langdon and Sophie. But after he is contacted by Bishop Aringarosa about the murder of Sister Sandrine Bieil, he realizes Langdon is not the killer but Silas is. Fache follows Sophie and Langdon to London, where Teabing is arrested.

Robert Langdon: He is the main protagonist and a highly respected and intelligent professor at Harvard University. Together with Sophie, he unravels the mysteries of the Jesus bloodline.

Rémy Legaludec: He is Teabing's butler and has a shady past. He is the only one who knows Teabing's secret identity as The Teacher. He flees along with Langdon, Sophie and Teabing to London in Teabing's private jet with Silas, who they captured at Teabing's house and tied him up.

Jacques Saunière Saint-Claire: Curator of the Louvre, he is also Head of Priory of Sion and Sophie's grandfather. Before Silas murders him in the museum he gives the monk false information about the keystone. Saunière uses the last minutes of his life to leave clues for Sophie to de-code. The woman and her grandfather are estranged because when she was young she witnessed Saunière perform a sex ritual named Hieros Gamos, which she misunderstood. His character, while small, sets the whole story in motion.

Sophie Neveu Saint-Claire: A French National police cryptographer she is also Saunière's granddaughter, as stated above. When she was young her parents were killed in a car crash and she was raised by her grandfather but, as explained above, became estranged from him when seeing him perform a ritual sexual act with his own wife whom she believed to be dead. She misunderstood the meaning of this ritual, and as a result became estranged from him, then later saw the truth. He trained her to solve complex puzzles which help her in decoding her grandfather's clues. At the end of the book she discovers that she is a descendant of the Merovingians and subsequently of Jesus. She agrees to spend a week in Florence with Langdon.

Silas: An albino monk who practices severe corporal mortification. When he was seven his father killed his mother, so Silas killed his father. He ended up living on the streets in Marseille and in Toulon where he killed a sailor and was sent to prison. He was befriended by the Spanish priest named Manuel Aringarosa who later becomes Bishop and head of Opus Dei. It was Aringarosa who named him Silas.

Believing that he is saving the Catholic Church Silas kills Jacques Saunière and the other heads of the Priory of Sion under orders from The Teacher, (Leigh Teabing) who later tells him to go to the London Opus Dei Centre, where he ends up getting shot by policemen and accidentally shooting Aringarosa. He dies in Kensington Gardens.

Sir Leigh Teabing KBE: The main antagonist, Teabing is also The Teacher. He is a Royal Historian, a Knight of the Realm and Grail scholar as well as Langdon's friend. Teabing's wealth comes from the fact that he is a descendent of the Duke of Lancaster and he lives at Château Villette with his butler Rémy Legaludec. He is crippled from polio and uses crutches. Fanatical about the Holy Grail he blames the Catholic Church for not revealing the truth so he schemes to find the documents that show Jesus and Mary were married and had a child whose descendents are still alive. As The Teacher he instructs Silas to carry out the killings.

Teabing pretends to help Sophie and Langdon when he realises he needs them both to unlock the keystone. But after they arrive in London he confronts them at Westminster Abbey threatening to kill them if they don't join him. He is arrested and taken away without ever knowing what was in the keystone.

André Vernet: President of the Paris branch of the Depository Bank of Zurich he is told that Langdon and Sophie are wanted by the police so when they arrive at the bank he wants no adverse publicity and wants them gone as quickly as possible. He helps them escape in one of the bank's trucks but turns against them. Langdon and Sophie steal the truck and head for Teabing's place.

THE LOST SYMBOL

Robert Langdon: A professor of symbology at Harvard University and the main protagonist of the novel.

Mal'akh (also known as Dr. Christopher Abaddon/Andros Dareios): The antagonist, he is a Mason and his body is covered in tattoos. He is revealed by the end of the story to be Zachary Solomon, the estranged son of Peter Solomon, long believed to be dead, whose appearance was made unrecognizable to his family, in part due to the use of steroids. He is quite insane, believing that the Masons hold the key to him becoming a demon, to rule the world.

Peter Solomon: He is Langdon's closest friend and mentor. Also he is a billionaire philanthropist, Smithsonian secretary, Freemason and father of Zachary Solomon.

Katherine Solomon: A noetic scientist she is Solomon's younger sister, being in her forties and becomes the love interest for Langdon. Beautiful and intelligent, her lab is in Pod Five of the Smithsonian spill-over complex.

Isabel Solomon: She is the mother of Peter and Katherine Solomon, and grandmother of Zachary Solomon.

Trish Dunne: Peter and Katherine Solomon's lab assistant, she is killed by Mal'akh who dumps her in a vat with a giant squid, where she drowns.

Mark Zoubianis: A computer hacker, he is a friend of Trish.

Warren Bellamy: A fellow Freemason, like Peter Solomon, he is also the Architect of the Capitol.

Inoue Sato: Director of CIA's Office of Security, she is a tiny, dangerous, withered Japanese lady with no sense of humour, but is highly intelligent and very suspicious.

Nola Kaye: CIA analyst.

Rick Parrish: CIA security specialist.

Turner Simkins: CIA field operations leader.

Reverend Colin Galloway: A Freemason like Peter Solomon and Warren Bellamy, he is also the Dean of Washington National Cathedral.

Trent Anderson: Capitol police chief, he is very rugged, determined and straight.

Alfonso Nuñez: Capitol security guard, he is level-headed and very perceptive.

Jonas Faukman: This name is an anagram of Brown's real-life editor, Jason Kaufman and plays an editor of a New York newspaper.

Officer Paige Montgomery: She is a private security company officer.

THE FILMS

The following information can be found on a variety of websites across the internet, including the Wikipedia web pages for each film and imdb.com.

THE DA VINCI CODE

Production
Director:Ron Howard
Producers:Ron Howard, Brian Grazer and John Calley
Screenplay:Akiva Goldsman, based on Brown's *The Da Vinci Code* novel
Original Score:Hans Zimmer
Cinematography:Salvatore Totino
Editing:Daniel P. Hanley, Mike Hill
Studio:Columbia Pictures, Imagine Entertainment
Distribution:Columbia Pictures
US Release:19 May, 2006
Running time:149 minutes
Languages:English, French, Spanish and Latin
Country of Origin:United States

Budget:$125 million
Gross revenue:$758,239,851

Cast
Professor Robert Langdon:Tom Hanks
Sophie Neveu:Audrey Tautou
Sir Leigh Teabing:Sir Ian McKellen
Silas:Paul Bettany
Bezu Fache:Jean Reno
Bishop Aringarosa:Alfred Molina
Mary Magdalene:Charlotte Graham
André Vernet:Jürgen Prochnow
Lt. Jérôme Collet:Etienne Chicot
Remy Jean (Rémy Legaludec in the novel):Jean-Yves
    Berteloot
Jacques Saunière:Jean-Pierre Marielle
Young Silas:Hugh Mitchell
Michael the Cleric:Seth Gabel
Sister Sandrine: Marie-Françoise Audollent

Description
The film was released in the US on 19 May 2006 through
Columbia Pictures entering major release in many other
countries the day before. On 17 May 2006 it was previewed
at the Cannes Film Festival opening night.

As with Brown's book the movie generated a lot of
controversy from the Catholic Church. Indeed, many
churches called for its members to boycott the film.
Protestors appeared at some early screenings and some
early reviews were very negative but this had little impact
on audience numbers. In fact, the film grossed more than
$230 million the first weekend, making it the third most

profitable film opening weekend ever while worldwide, *The Da Vinci Code* earned more than £758,239,851 as of 2 November 2006, proving it to be the second highest-grossing film of that year.

Ron Howard and Tom Hanks had both worked together on two other Howard films, *Splash* in 1984 and *Apollo 13* in 1995. They also worked on the prequel film version of Dan Brown's second novel and first Robert Langdon book, *Angels & Demons* along with the third Robert Langdon novel, *The Lost Symbol*.

Composer Hans Zimmer was nominated for the 2007 Golden Globe Award for Best Original Score.

Film Notes

Dan Brown sold the film rights for *The Da Vinci Code* for $6,000,000 with the filming scheduled for a May 2005 start but delays caused the filming to start on 30 June 2005.

For locations, the film producers procured permission to film in the Louvre but were not allowed to shine any light on the *Mona Lisa* so they used a replica and used the *Mona Lisa*'s chamber as a storage room during filming. For the scenes set in Westminster Abbey the crew were able to use Lincoln and Winchester cathedrals to substitute for Westminster Abbey and Saint-Sulpice.

The Saint-Sulpice location was recreated by *Rainmaker U.K.* a post-production company. The fee for the use of Lincoln Cathedral was £100,000 and filming there took place between the 15 and 19 August 2005. Winchester Cathedral was heavily criticised for allowing its premises to be used for the film and so answered these jibes by funding an exhibition and lecture series debunking the book. Other UK locations included Belvoir Castle in Leicestershire for

Castel Gandolfo and Shoreham Airport in West Sussex for Le Bourget Airport, along with Fairfield Halls, the Temple Church in London, Burghley House in Lincolnshire, and Rosslyn Chapel in Scotland. Other locations were shot in France and Germany.

Pinewood Studios was used for many of the interior scenes including the opening sequences, where a replica of the interior of the Louvre was created. Also shot at Pinewood were the underwater sequences at the new state-of-the-art Underwater Stage at Pinewood.

Reactions to the Film

Before the film was released Archbishop Angelo Amato, on behalf of the Vatican, called for a boycott of the film at a conference on 28 April 2006 while Opus Dei, the organisation figuring prominently in the book, issued a statement on 14 February 2006 asking for references that could offend Catholics be removed from the film. The same organisation later issued another statement on 16 April asking the film makers to include a disclaimer as a sign of respect to the history of the Church, religious beliefs of viewers and to Jesus Christ.

In America, the *United States Conference of Catholic Bishops' Office for Film and Broadcasting* rated the film as morally offensive because of the errors and theories in it. Catholic groups and churches across the world denounced the film with church leaders urging their members not to see it. In China, the production did very well, grossing over $13 million before the government quickly pulled it for no reason.

Other countries followed, especially in the Philippines where the *Philippine Alliance Against Pornography* demanded the president of the country pull the film, saying it was pornographic. It was eventually rated as 18 Restricted without interference from President Malacañang. In Lebanon the film was banned outright. In India influential Christian groups demanded the film be banned and in some states such as the Punjab it has been. But where it was released it was given an 'Adults Only' rating along with a disclaimer saying the film is a work of fiction.

Tom Hanks, who plays Robert Langdon, said during an interview with the *Evening Standard* that the film was merely a fun scavenger hunt and should be taken at face value.

Critical Response

Overall the response from the critics is poor and it was poorly received at the Cannes Film Festival where it debuted. The reviews were not all bad; some praised the film as being a production that assumes the audience have the intelligence to understand the many twists and turns in the plot.

Box Office

Even so, the film grossed more than $29 million on its opening day in the US and more than $224 million around the world on its opening weekend. It stands as third for opening weekends behind *Pirates of the Caribbean: Dead Man's Chest* and *X-Men: The Last Stand* while being in second place in the highest grossing opening weekend worldwide behind *Star Wars Episode III: Revenge of the Sith*. In its first week it was Number 1 at the US Box Office, grossing more than $111 million and in 2006 was the fifth highest gross of that year. Less than a month after its release in the US it passed the $200 million mark.

On DVD

Three editions of the film were released on 14 November 2006, a three disc release in widescreen and full screen along with a *History Channel* documentary, a two-disc set and a special edition set including a Robert Langdon replica journal and working cryptex along with the two-disc set. Each edition includes director Ron Howard's introduction and other bonus material. An extended version with an additional 25 minutes of film was released in Australia, New Zealand and Latin America. Both Hong Kong and Korea got the extended version on a two-disc set along with the special edition featuring the working cryptex and journal which was also released in France and Spain. On 28 April 2009 the extended version was released in North American on blue-ray.

ANGELS & DEMONS

Production

Director:Ron Howard

Executive Producers: Dan Brown, Todd Hallowell, Marco Valerio Pugini (Italy)

Producers:Ron Howard, Brian Grazer and John Calley

Associate Producers:William M. Connor, Anna Culp, Kathleen McGill and Louisa Velis

Screenplay:Akiva Goldsman and David Koepp

Cinematography:Salvatore Totino

Original Score:Hans Zimmer

Editing:Dan Hanley

Casting:Janet Hirschenson, Jane Jenkins and Michelle Lewitt

Production Design:Allan Cameron
Art Direction:Alex Cameron
Set Decoration:Robert Gould
Costume Design:Daniel Orlandi
Makeup Department:David Abbott
Studio:Columbia Pictures, Imagine Entertainment
Distribution:Columbia Pictures
US Release:15 May 2009
UK Release:14 May 2009
Running time:138 minutes, 146 minutes extended edition
Languages:English, French, Spanish and Latin
Country of Origin:United States
Budget:$150 million
Box Office Gross:$133,375,846 (USA) 2 August 2009,
    $352,600,000 internationally, and $485,975,846
    worldwide according to *The Numbers* web site at http://
    www.the-numbers.com/movies/2009/ANDEM.php

Cast
Robert Langdon:Tom Hanks
Camerlengo McKenna:Ewan McGregor (Carlo Ventresca
    in the book)
Vittoria Vetra:Ayelet Zurer
Commander Maximilian Richter: Stellan Skarsgård
    (Combination of Kohler and Rocher in the book)
Inspector Ernest Olivetti:Pierfrancesco Favino
The Assassin:Nikolaj Lie Kaas
Claudio Vincenzi:David Pasquesi Vatican police officer
Cardinal Strauss:Armin Mueller-Stahl (Mortati in the book)
Lieutenant Chartrand:Thure Lindhardt
Cardinal Petrov:Elya Baskin

RAI reporter:Pasquale Cassalia
Swiss Guardsman:Auguste Fredrik
CERN Scientist:Endre Hules

Description

The film rights to this book were acquired in 2003 by Sony along with the rights to *The Da Vinci Code*. Akiva Goldsman was brought in to adapt the novel *Angels & Demons* for the screen. But the filming, due to start in February 2008 was halted by the 2007-2008 Writers Guild of America strike. Instead of a release date in December 2008 the strike pushed the release date to 15 May 2009 and David Koepp was brought in to finish the script.

With *The Da Vinci Code*, director Ron Howard had taken a reverential approach because of the popularity of the book but with *Angels & Demons* he wanted to be more liberal with the adaptation of the story. He wanted a much faster paced action tale rather than the more ponderous story that the earlier film had been.

Differences between novel and film

One key difference was that of the Camerlengo, who was changed from being Italian to Northern Irish, largely to accommodate actor Ewan McGregor.

The character of Leonardo Vetra, Vittoria's father, is omitted from the film while Cardinal Baggia, the one tipped to be the next Pope, doesn't die in the film and it is he who shows Langdon the hiding place of the Illuminati. Baggia is elected Pope while in the novel Cardinal Mortati, the Dean of the College, is elected and Baggia dies. The assassin doesn't die at the hands of Langdon and Vittoria and no relationship develops after Langdon rescues Vittoria in the film whereas it does in the book. The brand that is indefinitely loaned to Langdon for his help at the end of the book which is an ambigram of a combination of the four elements is replaced by Galileo's Diagramma della Veritatis in the film.

Film Notes

Three weeks of shooting took place in Rome starting on 4 June 2008 under the working title *Obelisk*. The rest of the film was shot at Sony Studios in Culver City California, due to an impending Screen Actors Guild strike and Roman Catholic Church officials in Rome refusing the film makers to shoot any scenes in their churches. This forced them to use different locations such as the *Caserta Palace* for the inside of the Vatican and the *Bibliotheca Angelica* for the Vatican Library.

While the Writers Guild strike had forced Howard to shoot quickly it gave him greater opportunity to use handheld cameras, injecting more energy into the film and giving it a documentary feel.

To replicate the interior of St Peter's Basilica the area around the crypt beneath St Peter's baldachin, along with the bottom parts of St Peter's Statue and the columns, were reproduced on the soundstage and the rest of the structure created digitally in post production.

Allan Cameron, the Production Designer, sent twenty people to the Sistine Chapel to sketch, photograph and enlarge paintings and mosaics for the digital recreations. The Chapel was created to full size in the sound stages but the Sala Regia was built to smaller scale to fit in the soundstage with its 80-foot high ceilings.

273

Music

Hans Zimmer wrote the original score for *Angels & Demons*, which was released on 22 May 2009 on the Columbia Pictures Industries Inc label. Zimmer developed the track at the end of *The Da Vinci Code* known as 'Chevaliers de Sangreal' as Langdon's main theme in the new film.

Reception

Though the Catholic Church has not been as vocal in condemning *Angels & Demons* one Italian priest in Santa Susanna stated they did not want scenes of murder to be associated with the Church. The President of the *Catholic League*, William A. Donohue, said that Catholics should let other Catholics know about the anti-Catholic sentiments in the film. Howard responded by saying that the film wasn't anti-Catholic because Langdon supported and protected the Church as well as its depiction of the priests who support scientific advances.

However, the film received a positive review from the official Vatican newspaper *L'Osservatore Romano*, that stated the Church was on the side of good in the film which contradicted its earlier stance that it would not approve it.

Critical reception

Overall critics gave the film mixed reviews. *Rotten Tomatoes* website said that out of 237 critics only 36% gave it a positive review. The general feeling was that it was an improvement on *The Da Vinci Code*. However, despite this the site said the story didn't translate well to the big screen.

Box office

After its release in May 2009 the film's overseas position remained at number one for the second weekend ahead of *Night at the Museum: Battle of the Smithsonian*. Domestically, the film met Columbia Pictures opening predictions of $40-50 million while *The Da Vinci Code* opened to $77.1 million. The difference was put down to the film's material not being as popular as *The Da Vinci Code*.

However, worldwide the film grossed $478,869,160 within more than a month, making it the largest grossing film of 2009 until *Transformers: Revenge of the Fallen* surpassed it. Interestingly, of this total amount only 27 per cent were domestic takings, the rest being from worldwide totals. For example, in the UK it grossed over $30 million, in Spain it was $21 million, with $13 million in Brazil and in Russia, Japan grossed $34 million and Germany saw earnings of $47 million. At the time of writing *Angels & Demons* stands at the ninth highest grossing film of 2009 worldwide.

DVD

On 24 November 2009 a two-disc set DVD was released in Region 1 that was an extended edition running six minutes longer, while in Region 2 a single disc DVD was released a month earlier on 4 October 2009.

THE LOST SYMBOL

This film is, at the time of writing, still in pre-production.

Production:
Director:Ron Howard (not yet confirmed)
Producers:Ron Howard, Brian Grazer and John Calley
Screenplay:Steven Knight and Dan Brown
Original Score:Hans Zimmer
Release Date:2012
Distribution:Imagine Entertainment and Columbia Pictures
Country of Origin:United States
Language:English
Robert Langdon:Tom Hanks

DAN BROWN US/UK BIBLIOGRAPHY

BY CRAIG CABELL

What follows is a guide to collecting the first editions of Dan Brown in both the UK and US. As there are not many titles, special signed and illustrated editions are also included for clarity. Interesting paperbacks are also included, but not every paperback, as these are not as collectable as hardback books; only paperbacks that pre-date hardback issues are listed.

Special note regarding first hardback editions: If you are seriously collecting first edition hardbacks, either US or UK, ensure that the number line – if the book has one – on the copyright page has a '1' in it, which denotes first edition, or has 'First Edition' clearly written on it. A good example are the Harry Potter books in first edition, where the first three books in the series has '10 9 8 7 6 5 4 3 2 1' on copyright page, while books four, five, six and seven have 'First Edition'. A number line that reads (10 9 8 7 6 5 4 3) denotes a third edition.

To my mind the most important aspects of collecting first editions are:

• A price being on the dust jacket.

- The correct publisher noted on the spine of dust jacket and on the title page of the book.
- Correct number line or first edition state on copyright page.

Books that have GP, Guild Press, BCA, Ted Smart or World Book as publisher are normally listed as Book Club Editions and therefore worthless. Books that do not have a price on the dust jacket are normally passed off as Export Editions when in fact they are more often than not reserved for Book Club or libraries.

US EDITIONS

187 Men to Avoid: A Guide for the Romantically Frustrated Woman (Berkley Publishing Group, 1995). This was a paperback written under the pseudonym 'Danielle Brown.' The book's author profile reads, 'Danielle Brown currently lives in New England: teaching school, writing books, and avoiding men.' The copyright is attributed to Dan Brown.

187 Men to Avoid: A Guide for the Romantically Frustrated Woman (Berkley, 2006): Paperback re-issue.

The Bald Book by Blythe Brown (1998) (although Dan Brown apparently did much work on it).

Digital Fortress (St Martin's Press, 1998) (Press release version with press notes written by Brown's wife Blythe): Hardback in dust jacket.

Digital Fortress (St Martin's Press, 1998): Hardback in dust jacket.

Digital Fortress (Thomas Dunne Books, St Martin's Griffin, 1998): Reissue hardback.

Angels & Demons (Pocket Books, 2000): Hardback in dust jacket.

Angels & Demons and *The Da Vinci Code* (Doubleday and Atria): X2 US hardback books in slipcase. First thus.

Angels & Demons Illustrated Edition (Atria, 2003): First hardback reissue in different wrapper to first US Edition.

Angels & Demons Illustrated Edition (Atria, 2005): Reissue hardback in yet a different dust jacket to anything previously issued.

Deception Point (Pocket Books, 2001): First US edition in dust jacket.

The Da Vinci Code (Doubleday, 2003): First US edition in dust jacket.

The Lost Symbol (Random House, 2009): Signed book plate edition limited to 700 copies only.

The Lost Symbol (Random House, 2009): US hardback variant limited to 1,000 copies in dust jacket and slip case.

The Lost Symbol Illustrated edition (Random House, 2009).

UK EDITIONS

Digital Fortress (Bantam Press, 2005): First UK hardback in dust jacket.

Deception Point (Corgi Books, 2002): First UK paperback, pre-dates UK hardback releases.

Deception Point (Bantam Press, 2003): First UK hardback edition in dust jacket.

Angels & Demons (Corgi, 2001): UK paperback proof copy.

Angels & Demons (Corgi, 2001): UK paperback edition, pre-dates UK hardback releases.

Angels & Demons Illustrated Edition (Bantam Press, 2005): UK hardback in dust jacket.

Angels & Demons and the Da Vinci Code Omnibus Edition (Bantam Press, 2005): First UK Edition in dust jacket.

The Da Vinci Code (Bantam Press, 2003): First UK edition in dust jacket.

The Da Vinci Code Special Illustrated Collector's Edition (Bantam Press, 2004): First UK hardback in dust jacket.

The Lost Symbol (Transworld, 2009): Standard UK hardback in dust jacket.

The Lost Symbol Limited signed edition (Transworld, 2009). The first 150 copies of the UK first edition had a colour pictorial key bookplate signed by Brown and were available from Waterstone's, Piccadilly on the morning of release. These books were sold at face value and the most collectable today are those sold with 'Signed by the Author at Waterstone's' sticker to front cover, till receipt, Waterstone's carrier bag, Da Vinci Code Travel Journal and a free paperback in the Dan Brown style.

The Lost Symbol Illustrated Edition (Transworld, 2010): First UK edition in dust jacket.

The Lost Symbol (Transworld, 2010) first UK paperback edition: Unread copy with press release.

ENDNOTES

CHAPTER TWO

[1]   Dan Brown did an interview with Steve Bertrand in the Barnes & Noble Studio in March 2003, which can be found on their web pages and from which this quote was taken

[2]   *Life After The Da Vinci Code*, by James Kaplan, published on Parade.com on 09/13/2009

[3]   *Life After The Da Vinci Code*, by James Kaplan, published on Parade.com on 09/13/2009

[4]   *The Dan Brown Revelations*, by David Shugarts, published in *Secrets of the Code*, edited by Dan Burstein, CDS Books, 2006 p 363

[5]   *The Witness Statement*, by Dan Brown, published in the High Court of Justice Chancery Division, Intellectual Property between authors Michael Baigent and Richard Leigh and Brown's publisher Random House, 21/12/2005

CHAPTER THREE

[6]   *The Man Behind The Da Vinci Code: An Unauthorized Biography*, by Lisa Rogak, published by Robson Books, 2005 p 18

[7]   This description of the people in his apartment building comes from *The Witness Statement*, by Dan Brown, published in the High Court of Justice Chancery Division, Intellectual Property, 21/12/2005

[8]   See Lisa Rogak's book, *The Man Behind The Da Vinci Code: An Unauthorized Biography*, published by Robson Books in 2005 p 20

[9]   IBID

[10] See Lisa Rogak's book for more details p 23

[11] Lisa Rogak states that the larger issue for the couple was probably the age gap rather than possible misuse of her position and there may have been some 'raised eyebrows' despite the laissez-faire attitude of the L.A. music business.

[12] IBID

[13] See Rogak's book where she cites an interview Brown did in *The Calendar* published in 1992

CHAPTER FOUR

[14] See Dan Brown's *Witness Statement* in the section entitled *187 Men to Avoid*.

[15] This information comes from page 34 of Lisa Rogak's book *The Man Behind The Da Vinci Code: An Unauthorized Biography*

[16] See the interview in March 2003 with Bookbrowse.com

[17] *Life After 'The Da Vinci Code'*, by James Kaplan, published on Parade.com on 09/13/2009

CHAPTER FIVE

[18] The quotes from this paragraph and the preceding one are from *British Thriller Writers Mount Challenge to US 'Production Line'* which appeared in *The Guardian* Newspaper on 20 April 2009, guardian.co.uk © Guardian News and Media Limited 2010

[19] See Brown's *Witness Statement,* the *Digital Fortress* section

[20] Information and quotes in this paragraph and the preceding one come from *The Witness Statement* Brown made in 2005

[21] See Kaplan, *Life After 'The Da Vinci Code'*, published on Parade.com on 09/13/2009

[22] This quote and the entire piece by Fleming was published on the blog ifthisisablogthenwhatschristmas.blogspot.com on 17 June 2010

[23] This quote, the quotes in the previous paragraphs and the paragraph below are from the Fleming piece

[24] See the Barnes & Noble interview from March 2003

[25] This information on Brown's writing technique comes from his *Witness Statement,* paragraphs 6 & 7 dated 21 December 2005

[26] See the Barnes & Noble interview conducted by Steve Bertrand with Brown

[27] From the Wikipedia entry on Dan Brown, published on Wikipedia the Free Encyclopedia internet site and updated 22 July 2010

[28] This quote comes from the Barnes & Noble interview with Brown that took place in March 2003

[29] The two quotes in this paragraph are from the *Bookbrowse* interview

[30] This information comes from a radio interview Brown did on *National Public Radio* in 2009

[31] The quote in this paragraph and in the preceding one are from the James Kaplan interview with Brown published as *Life After 'The Da Vinci Code'*

[32] *An Evening With Dan Brown*, a talk Brown gave in support of the New Hampshire Writer's Project, The Capitol Center for the Performing Arts, Concord, New Hampshire, 18 May 2004

[33] See the Barnes & Noble interview

[34] From the talk Brown gave at the Capitol Centre for the Arts in support of the New Hampshire Writers' Project

[35] Brown said this to Steve Bertrand during the interview for Barnes & Noble back in March 2003

CHAPTER SIX

[36] This quote comes from an article, *How Dan Brown's wife unlocked the code to bestseller success*, by Joanna Walters and Alice O'Keeffe, published in the *Observer*, 12 March 2006

[37] IBID

[38] Walters cites a quote from David Shugarts, author of *The Dan Brown Revelations* published in *The Secretes of the Code* edited by Dan Burstein, a book aimed at explaining some of the mysteries in *The Da Vinci Code*. Walters quotes Shugarts as saying that 'Blythe paints and sculpts and Dan always put out an image of her engrossed in marble dust and the smell of oils in their house, but I do not know a single soul who has seen her art,' from an article, *How Dan Brown's wife unlocked the code to bestseller success*, by Joanna Walters and Alice O'Keeffe, published in the *Observer*, 12 March 2006. Could this be Dan Brown stretching the facts to portray a more enhanced truth for the media?

[39] From Lisa Rogak's book

[40] *The Witness Statement*, the *Digital Fortress* section

[41] This quote comes from an article, *How Dan Brown's wife unlocked the code to bestseller success*, by Joanna Walters and Alice O'Keeffe, published in the *Observer*, 12 March 2006

[42] Lisa Rogak states in her book, *The Man Behind The Da Vinci Code: An Unauthorized Biography*

[43] The quote is found in Brown's *Witness Statement* paragraphs 66-68

[44] According to Brown's *Witness Statement*, he and Blythe spent a lot of time criss-crossing the country in their car trying to sell copies of *Angels & Demons*

[45]   Rogak quoting Brown from an interview he did with Craig MacDonald

[46]   See *The Witness Statement* by Dan Brown, this quote and the preceding few come from the section on researching *The Da Vinci Code*

[47]   This quote and the one before it come from *The Witness Statement,* paragraphs 108 and 111 respectively

[48]   See *The Witness Statement*, the section on Researching The Da Vinci Code

[49]   Paragraphs 113-114 of *The Witness Statement*

[50]   *Life After 'The Da Vinci Code'*, by James Kaplan, published on Parade.com on 09/13/2009

[51]   *The Dan Brown Revelations*, by David Shugarts, published in *Secrets of the Code*, edited by Dan Burstein, CDS Books, 2006 p 363

[52]   *The Witness Statement*, paragraph 154 on how Brown and Blythe work well together

[53]   IBID

CHAPTER SEVEN

[54]   The opening quote and the subsequent quotes in this paragraph are from *The Witness Statement* Brown made for the plagiarism trial that took place in the Old Bailey

[55]   Interview with Dan Brown, by Claire E. White, posted on the *Internet Writing Journal*, www.internetwritingjournal.com, published by Writers Write Inc. 1997-2010

[56]   *Digital Fortress* Review, by Tony Bradley, posted on the web pages of About.Com/Internet Security on Sunday 15 August 2004

[57]   *Digital Fortress Review*, by Claire E. White, published in the May 1998 edition of *The Internet Writing Journal*

[58]   Reviewed by Rashmi Srinivas for *Curled Up With A Good Book*, published in 2004

[59]   See the interview of Dan Brown by Claire E. White

[60]   This review was posted on the *Indiareads* website on 22 June 2010 and can be found at indiareads.com

[61]   See the review in it's entirety on the politics and current affairs forum at www.politicsandcurrentaffairs.co.uk

[62]   These figures were posted on January 7 2005 on *The Times Literary Supplement* web pages, Timesonline by J.C.

[63]   This quote and the subsequent quote by Brown comes from the interview with Claire E. White published on the *Internet Writing Journal*

[64] These quotes are from the book, *Digital Fortress.*

[65] Brown said this in the interview with Claire E. White

[66] *The Man Behind The Da Vinci Code: An Unauthorized Biography*, by Lisa Rogak published by Robson Books, 2005, pp45

[67] This and the preceding quote come from Brown's *Witness Statement*

[68] *A Collision of Indiana Jones and Joseph Campbell*, by Craig McDonald, published in *Secrets of the Code*, edited by Dan Burstein, CDS Books, 2006 pp 334

[69] See the Review of *Digital Fortress* by Rashmi Srinivas for *Curled Up With a Good Book*

[70] This is part of a review by A. Edge, on the *Amazon* UK website published August 2007

[71] *Digital Fortress Review*, by Magda Healey, published to the *Bookbag* web pages, July 2004

[72] Brown said this in the Claire White interview on *Internet Writing Journal*

[73] IBID

[74] IBID

[75] *The Witness Statement*, *Digital Fortress* section, paragraphs 20 to 30

CHAPTER EIGHT

[76] The quotes on pages 69, 70 and this quote all come from the *Angels & Demons* section of Brown's *Witness Statement*

[77] Brown discussed this during his interview in late spring 2003 with Craig McDonald which appears in McDonald's book *Art in The Blood*, published by J T Lindroos for Wildside Press, 2006 pp 129-138

[78] IBID

[79] *The Witness Statement*, *Angels & Demons* section, paragraph 63

[80] IBID

[81] From an interview conducted online at *Bookbrowse*, published in 2001, at www.bookbrowse.com

[82] This information comes from the *Bookbrowse* 2001 interview about *Angels& Demons* with Brown

[83] See the 2001 interview with Brown on *Bookbrowse* web pages

[84] IBID

[85] See the *Angels & Demons* section of Brown's *Witness Statement*

[86] This quote comes from Lisa Rogak's unauthorised biography of Dan Brown

[87] See the 2001 *Bookbrowse* interview with Brown

[88]   From the *Bookbrowse* interview on *Angels & Demons*

[89]   IBID

[90]   IBID

[91]   The quotes from the preceding two paragraphs and from this one are from the *Angels & Demons* section of Brown's *Witness Statement*, paragraphs 55 -57

[92]   The plot summary list here is based on the synopsis for the *Angels & Demons* entry published on Wikipedia, 02 October 2010

[93]   Review of *Angels & Demons,* by Kelly Flynn, published on *Amazon,* under the Editorial Review section of this listing of *Angels & Demons*

[94]   *Angels & Demons* review by Douglas Richardson, published on *Amazon,* 23 July 2005

[95]   *Amazing. Angels & Demons* review, published on *Amazon* on 11 October 2010

[96]   *Oh Dear Me... Angels & Demons* review, by S. Glover, published on *Amazon* on 25 October 2005

[97]   *Demonically awful...Angels & Demons* review, by J. Macdonald, published on *Amazon,* 22 March 2010

[98]   *Awesome Book, Angels & Demons,* four-star review, by J. Djumpah, published on *Amazon* 12 August 2010

[99]   These inaccuracies are mentioned in the Wikipedia entry for *Angels & Demons*

[100]   *The Witness Statement, Angels & Demons* section

[101]   IBID

CHAPTER NINE

[102]   *Ice Station Zebra,* by Alistair MacLean, published by William Collins Sons & Co. Ltd., 1963 quote from the opening paragraph of the book

[103]   *The Witness Statement, Deception Point* section, paragraph 71. Note that this section on his third novel is the shortest of all the sections.

[104]   This quote, the one from the preceding paragraph and the one in the following paragraph are from Brown's *Witness Statement,* the *Deception Point* section describing how he came up with the ideas and wrote the book

[105]   *Deception Point* Review, by Joe Hartlaub, published on *Bookreporter.com*

[106]   *Deception Point* Review, published on the *Bookbrowser.com* web pages, 2002

[107]   *Deception Point* Review, published on the Barnes & Noble web pages, 2006

[108] *Deception Point* Review, by Joseph L. Carlson, Allan Hancock, published by the *Library Journal* and placed on the Barnes & Noble website 2006

[109] *Deceived? Yes Indeed.., Deception Point* Review, by G. Battle published on *Amazon*, 11 April 2006

[110] *Deceptive To A Point, Deception Point Review*, published on *Ciao.co.uk* web pages, 30 March 2005 and while it appears to be a review from an amateur reviewer it is insightful and very comprehensive and worth taking into account here.

[111] This quote and the following information are from the *Deception Point* section of Brown's comprehensive *Witness Statement*

[112] IBID

CHAPTER TEN

[113] Interview with Dan Brown, published on *Bookreporter.com* 20 March 2007

[114] See Lisa Rogak's book, *The Man Behind The Da Vinci Code: An Unauthorized Biography* p 83

[115] *The Witness Statement, The Da Vinci Code* section

[116] From Lisa Rogak's book p 78

[117] The facts in this paragraph are detailed in Lisa Rogak's book, p 78

[118] IBID pp80-81

[119] *An Evening With Dan Brown*, New Hampshire Writers' Project, The Capitol Center for the Performing Arts, Concord, New Hampshire, 18 May 2004

[120] The quotes and information in this paragraph and the three paragraphs before it all come from the interview published on *Bookreporter.com* on 20 March 2003

[121] *Good Morning America*, Brown did an interview with Matt Lauer for the NBC morning programme in March 2004

[122] Brown said this during his talk to the New Hampshire Writers' Project at Concord New Hampshire

[123] *The Witness Statement*, paragraph 156

[124] See the interview published in *Bookreporter.com* on 20 March 2003

[125] See James Kaplan's *Life After 'The Da Vinci Code'* which can be found at www.parade.com

[126] See Lisa Rogak's *The Man Behind The Da Vinci Code: An Unauthorized Biography*, p 87

[127] This information about his research comes from another online interview he did that appeared on *Beliefnet*.com that can be found in the entertainment and movies section of their website at www.beliefnet.com

[128] See Lisa Rogak's book, pp 90-91

[129] See Brown's detailed *Witness Statement* for the High Court, The Da Vinci Code section

[130] Taken from the High Court *Witness Statement* paragraph 82

[131] The information in this paragraph regarding the codes and the accuracy of the locations, paintings and so on is taken from Brown's High Court *Witness Statement.*

[132] *Good Morning America*, NBC TV interview Brown did with Matt Lauer, March 2004

[133] The quote and the information in this paragraph and the preceding one come from *Table Talk, An Interview With Dan Brown*, by Bill Ewing, published in the *Exeter Phillips Journal*

[134] IBID

[135] Dan Brown, *The Man Behind The Da Vinci Code: An Unauthorized Biography*, by Lisa Rogak, pp 95-96

[136] *The Witness Statement, The Da Vinci Code* section, paragraph 125

[137] *New Statesman Man Of The Year* – Dan Brown, by Jason Cowley, published to the *New Statesman* web pages on 13 December 2004

[138] IBID

CHAPTER ELEVEN

[139] NBC *Today* Programme with Matt Lauer, published on the *Transworld* website under *Dan Brown* at booksattransworld.co.uk

[140] The facts here are from Lisa Rogak's *The Man Behind The Da Vinci Code: An Unauthorized Biography*, pp 98-99

[141] *Entertainment Weekly*, Dan Brown interview by George Kirschling, published to the EW website on 24 March 2006

[142] See Lisa Rogak's book, pp 99-100

[143] Matt Lauer Interviews with Dan Brown, published to the *Today Show* web pages, 15 September 2009

[144] *Entertainment Weekly* Interview with Dan Brown by George Kirschling

[145] *Good Morning America*, ABC TV, hosted by Charles Gibson with Dan Brown, aired November 2003 and Rogak says the contest was set up between *Good Morning America* and Doubleday

[146] The *Today Show*, The Matt Lauer Interviews with Dan Brown

[147] IBID

[148] The information in this paragraph is from Lisa Rogak's book, p 102

[149] *Dan Brown: Indiana Jones meets Joseph Campbell*, by Craig McDonald, *Art in The Blood*, published by Wildside Press, 2006, p 131

[150] See the *Entertainment Weekly* online interview with Dan Brown

[151] This quote and the preceding one are from the *Entertainment Weekly* online interview

[152] See Craig McDonald's interview, *Dan Brown, Indiana Jones meets Joseph Campbell* p 105

[153] IBID p 137

[154] This quote and the preceding one comes from the Craig McDonald interview with Brown

[155]   See Craig McDonald's interview with Dan Brown p 131

[156] *Secrets of the Code, The Case Of The Purloined Plot*, An Interview with Lewis Perdue, by Dan Burstein, published by CDS Books, 2006 p 443

[157] IBID

[158] This quote and the preceding quotes are from the *Secrets of the Code, The Case of The Purloined Plot*

[159]   IBID

[160] IBID p 448

[161] The Matt Lauer Interviews, with Dan Brown

CHAPTER TWELVE

[162] *Secrets Of The Code, The Dan Brown Revelations*, by David A. Shugarts, edited by Dan Burstein, p 382

[163] *Secrets Of The Code, The Vatican Code*, by Maureen Dowd, edited by Dan Burstein, p 416

[164] See the *Secrets Of The Code, The Cardinal and The Code*, by Dan Burstein, p 425

[165] IBID p 427

[166] See David A. Shugarts piece, *The Dan Brown Revelations in Secrets Of The Code* edited by Dan Burstein, p 382

[167] See Burstein's *Secrets Of The Code, The Cardinal and The Code*, p428

[168] IBID p 429

[169] See Dowd's *The Vatican Code*, in *Secrets Of The Code, The Vatican Code* p 417

[170] This quote comes from the Wikipedia entry on *The Da Vinci Code*, October 2010, and while it is generally understood that the Wikipedia entries may not be reliable the entries for Brown and his books are backed up by many, many references and so must be taken seriously.

[171] Monsignor Francis J. Maniscalco, of the United States Conference of Catholic Bishops, wrote this in his Introduction on the *Jesus Decoded* web site

[172] See David A. Shugarts, *The Dan Brown Revelations*, published in *Secrets Of The Code*, p 381

[173] See the introduction by Monsignor Francis J Maniscalco on the *Jesus Decoded* web pages

[174] IBID

[175] *History vs The Da Vinci Code*, by Tim O'Neil, published to the internet in 2006 at historyversusthedavincicode.com

[176] *Cracking The Da Vinci Code*, published by *Catholic Answers*, to catholic.com 2004

[177] *The Dan Brown Companion*, by Simon Cox, published by Mainstream Publishing, 2006 p 48

[178] See *The Dan Brown Companion* by Simon Cox, pp 48

[179] *The Priory of Sion* in *The Da Vinci Code*, published in the *Priory of Sion* entry on Wikipedia

[180] This quote and the information and quotes in the preceding paragraph are from the Wikipedia entry on *The Priory of Sion* in *The Da Vinci Code*.

[181] See Brown's *Witness Statement*, paragraph 206

[182] See *Cracking The Da Vinci Code*, published by *Catholic Answers*, 2004, http://www.catholic.com/library/cracking_da_vinci_code.asp

[183] This quote and the preceding one are in the Wikipedia entry, *The Priory of Sion* in *The Da Vinci Code*

[184] See *The Da Vinci Code* Wikipedia entry on the inaccuracies in the novel

[185] A response to *The Da Vinci Code* from the *Prelature of Opus Dei in the United States,* 16 November 2006

[186] Paragraphs 117 and 118 of Brown's *Witness Statement*

[187] Page 134 of *The Da Vinci Code*

[188] Tim O'Neil provides excellent information on Constantine's bible on his site, *History vs. The Da Vinci Code,*

[189] This entire passage was taken from Brown's talk at the Capitol Centre, for the New Hampshire Writer's Project , on the 18 May 2004

CHAPTER THIRTEEN

[190] See *The Witness Statement*, paragraphs 204-205

[191] See paragraph 209 of Brown's *Witness Statement,* in *The Da Vinci Code* section

[192] In paragraph 211 of *The Witness Statement* Brown says he used these three books, *The*

Templar Revelation (Picknett & Prince) (Chapter 53); *The Woman with the Alabaster Jar* (Starbird) (Chapter 59); and *The Goddess in the Gospels* (Starbird) (Chapter 58)

[193] It must be remembered that Brown wrote his witness statement based on what he could remember were his reasons for using *The Holy Blood, The Holy Grail*, some two years earlier when he was writing *The Da Vinci Code*. Despite he and Blythe spending several months refreshing their memories before the court case Brown qualifies many passages in the statement as being what he could remember

[194] *Da Vinci Publisher in Court Case*, BBC News, published 21 October 2005

[195] IBID

[196] *Date Set For Da Vinci Court Case*, BBC News web pages, published 27 October 2005

[197] *Authors Claim Brown 'Stole Da Vinci Code Plot'*, by Richard Alleyne, published in the *Daily Telegraph*, 28 February 2006

[198] See Alleyne's article, *Authors Claim Brown 'Stole Da Vinci Code Plot'*

[199] *Da Vinci Code Case Increases Book Sales*, published on the *Mail Online*, 09 March 2006

[200] IBID

[201] *A Test Of Faith*, by Maev Kennedy, published in the G2 section of *The Guardian*, 17 May 2006 and to *The Guardian* website, guardian.co.uk the same day

[202] IBID

[203] *Da Vinci Code Challenger Copies*, BBC News, published 10 March 2006 to the BBC News web pages

[204] *All Things Considered*, broadcast on National Public Radio®. in America. The information is from a transcript of the show in 2006 hosted by Robert Siegel who interviewed *Bookseller* reporter Katherine Rushton covering the trial in London

[205] IBID

[206] Rushton reported these sales figures during the plagiarism trial to Robert Siegel, hosting the National Public Radio® show, *All Things Considered*, broadcast around March - April 2006

[207] Both quotes come from *Da Vinci Code Author Scorns Copy Claim*, published by BBC News, 13 March 2006

[208] IBID

[209] See *All Things Considered*, broadcast on National Public Radio®. in America. The information is from a transcript of the show in 2006 hosted by Robert Siegel who interviewed *Bookseller* reporter Katherine Rushton covering the trial in London

[210] *Expectations Dashed By Legal Reality*, by David Sillito, published to BBC News web pages on 13 March 2006

[211] IBID

[212] *I Did Not Lie, Says Code Author*, published by BBC News web pages, 14 March 2006

[213] This conversation comes from the BBC News online article, *I Did Not Lie, Says Code Author*, published to the web on 14 March 2006

[214] *Brown Duels In Court*, by Kevin Sullivan, published in the *Washington Post* and on the web pages of the newspaper on Wednesday 15 March 2006

[215] See Sullivan's article, *Brown Duels In Court*, published to the *Washington Post* web pages, 15 March 2006

[216] *Da Vinci Copy Claim In Tatters*, published by BBC News, 17 March 2006

[217] IBID

[218] IBID

[219] *Brown Wins Da Vinci Code Plagiarism Battle*, by Cahal Milmo, published in the *Independent*, 8 April 2006

[220] IBID

[221] IBID

[222] *Dan Brown Wins The Da Vinci Code Copyright Case*, published to the *Mirror* Celeb News pages on 29 March 2007

[223] *Librarian Comments on Da Vinci Lawsuit*, published by the *Associated Press* in 2006

[224] *Da Vinci In New Plagiarism Claim*, published on the BBC News web pages on 14 April 2006

[225] *Brown Plays Down Code Controversy*, published on BBC News online pages, 24 April 2006

CHAPTER FOURTEEN

[226] *The Da Vinci Formula, The Da Vinci Code formula for success*, published February 2006 at storyline-features.co.uk

[227] See the Wikipedia entry, *The Da Vinci Code*, 21 October 2010, at wikipedia.org

[228] IBID

[229] *5 Star Entertainment, Review of The Da Vinci Code: The Illustrated Edition*, by 'janlaws', published to *Amazon* 15 February 2005

[230] *A Thriller Which Actually Thrills!*, by Bukhtawar Dhadda, published to *Amazon* on 28 November 2004

[231] This glowing review, *The Da Vinci Code*, by Miss Andrea P Keyte, was published to *Amazon* on 27 June 2005

[232] This review comes from, *Leonardo's Last Laugh*, by Captain Pugwash 'Lidders', published to *Amazon* on 9 May 2009

[233] *The Da Vinci Code is Intelligent and Fun*, by W.R. Greer, published to the *Review of Books. com* in 2003,

[234] This quote is an excerpt of the review by Roz Shea, *The Da Vinci Code*, published to the *Bookreporter.com* in March 2003

[235] The article published on Wikipedia entry for the book sites the Salman Rushdie quote as coming from *LJworld.com,* while the Stephen Fry remark it says was originally mentioned on *QI*, Stephen King's remarks were made during an address at the University of Maine and the final comments of the quote came from the *Language Log* web pages, from a piece entitled *The Dan Brown Code*

[236] This quote comes from a review, *Inaccurate, Insubstantial and Preposterous*, by R Bain, published to the *Amazon* web pages, 1 June 2005

[237] See *The Witness Statement*, paragraph 163

[238] These references to his lectures can be found in *The Witness Statement*, paragraphs 172 to 176

[239] This information comes from paragraphs 178 and 179 of *The Witness Statement*

[240] These quotes from Brown are from *The Witness Statement*, paragraphs 192-3 and paragraph 196

[241] The information from the preceding paragraphs and the quotes by Brown come from paragraphs 138 to 143 of *The Witness Statement* and the information on the Rosslyn Chapel can be found at (www.rosslynchapel.org,uk).

[242] See paragraphs 99-100 of *The Witness Statement*

[243] This quote from Brown comes from his lengthy, detailed *Witness Statement,* paragraph 217

[244] See Lisa Rogak's book, *The Man Behind The Da Vinci Code: An Unauthorized Biography*, page 118 citing the broadcast of the National Public Radio, Weekend Edition, 26 April 2003

CHAPTER FIFTEEN

[245] The Matt Lauer Interviews, the *Today Show*, 15 September 2009

[246] The facts in this paragraph come from *Dan Brown's The Lost Symbol breaks records for first week sales*, by Michelle Pauli, published on *The Guardian* web pages 22 September

[247] This quote and the facts in the following sections come from *Decoding The Lost Symbol*, by Simon Cox, published in late 2009 by Mainstream Publishing, p13

[248] This is taken from the Barnes & Noble interview with Dan Brown, published on the Barnes & Noble website barnesandnoble.com

[249] See *Decoding The Lost Symbol*, by Simon Cox p 14

[250] The quote and information in the preceding paragraph referring to the internet feeding frenzy and the information in this paragraph come from *Decoding The Lost Symbol*, by Simon Cox, p 15

[251] See *Decoding The Lost Symbol*, page 16

[252] *The Lost Symbol Sweeps The Stores*, by Robert Booth, published on *The Guardian* web pages, 15 September 2009

[253] See Booth's article, *The Lost Symbol Sweeps the Stores*, published on *The Guardian* web pages

[254] The *Today Show*, *The Secrets Of The Lost Symbol*, Matt Lauer interviewing Dan Brown, aired Friday 16 October 2009

[255] See *Decoding The Lost Symbol* page 17

[256] This quote is taken from the Masonic website, *The Lost Symbol and Freemasonry,* Published by the Masonic Society on 14 July 2010 at freemasonlostsymbol.com

[257] This whole section comes from the Masonic Society website, *The Lost Symbol and Freemasonry*, published on 14 July 2010 to answer some of the claims in Brown's novel

[258] The *Today Show*, *The Secrets Of The Lost Symbol*

[259] The information in the preceding paragraphs on the circumpunct comes from the web pages *The Heritage Key, Dan Brown's Lost Symbol - Circumpunct, Ra, or Circle With a Dot in the Middle?*, by Gen Swart,, published on 28 September 2009. If one does a Google search on the word circumpunct roughly 1400 responses come up and the word doesn't appear in many dictionaries either. The few web pages where the circumpunct is discussed can be found in the *Wikimedia Commons* on the origins and the authenticity of the word. Some people believe the term was first coined in the 1990 by followers of the short-lived religion and teachings of 'Brian the Cyber Prophet.'

[260] See the Barnes & Noble interview with Dan Brown, hosted by Steve Bertrand

[261] The facts in this paragraph and the quotes/facts in the preceding ones come from the *Today Show, The Secrets of The Lost Symbol*, interview Brown did with Matt Lauer

[262] See the Barnes & Noble interview with Dan Brown, by Steve Bertrand

[263] IBID

[264] See *Decoding The Lost Symbol*, by Simon Cox, page 17

[265] See the interview Brown did with Steve Bertrand in the Barnes & Noble studios, now published to the Barnes & Noble web pages

[266] The information in this paragraph and quotes, along with the quotes and facts in the preceding one can be found in the Barnes & Noble interview

CHAPTER SIXTEEN

[267] See the NBC *Today Show*, *Secrets of The Lost Symbol*, originally aired on 15 October 2009

[268] All of the information in the preceding paragraphs and in this one are from the NBC *Today Show*, *Secrets of The Lost Symbol*, hosted by Matt Lauer

[269] This quote comes from a National Public Radio (NPR) broadcast, *All Things Considered*, aired 15 September 2009

[270] IBID

[271] The *New York Times* review of *The Lost Symbol*, *Fasten Your Seat Belts, There's Code to Crack*, by Janet Maslin, published to the *NY Times* web pages, 13 September 2009 two days before the official release

[272] This quote is taken from the Masonic website, *The Lost Symbol and Freemasonry*, Published by the Masonic Society on 14 July 2010

[273] The facts around the plot come from the Wikipedia entry, *The Lost Symbol,* published to *wikipedia.org*

[274] See Janet Maslin's excellent review of *The Lost Symbol*. Her reviews of Brown's previous books have been of great benefit to the author.

[275] Maslin's quotes are from her review of *The Lost Symbol*

[276] Book Review *The Lost Symbol*, by Nick Owchar, published by the *LA Times*, 14 September 2009, in both this paragraph and the preceding one

[277] Book Review, *Dan Brown's The Lost Symbol*, by Malcolm Jones published in *Newsweek* on 15 September 2009

[278] The whole section with quotes from the *National Post* review comes from *Dan Brown's The Lost Symbol*, by Robert Wiersema, published in the *National Post* online pages, 17 September 2009

[279] The passage about *The Daily Telegraph* review is from *Dan Brown's The Lost Symbol*, by Jeremy Jehu, who gave it a two-star rating in *The Daily Telegraph* on 15 September 2009

[280] *How Good Is Dan Brown's The Lost Symbol*, by Lev Grossman, appeared on *Time's* web pages on 15 September 2009

[281] *A bit boring ...*, The Lost Symbol (paperback), by BG posted to *Amazon* on 24 Nov 2010

[282] *Amazon Book Review, Dan Brown*, by J. Hollingsworth, posted to *Amazon* on 26 October 2009

[283] *Book Review, Not Great...*, by rmf85, published to *Amazon* on 28 August 2010 who added that there was no explosive ending as there had been in Brown's previous novels.

[284] *Book Review, So Dull...*, by DP was posted on to *Amazon* on 11 March 2010 that also said the book was 'extremely dull and a chore to finish'

[285] *Disappointed from Bath...*, review of The Lost Symbol, posted to *Amazon* on 04 October 2010 which also suggested that Brown had lost his way

[286] See the Lev Grossman review, *How Good is Dan Brown's The Lost Symbol*, published to *Time's* web pages on 15 September 2009

CHAPTER SEVENTEEN

[287] *Secrets of The Lost Symbol*, NBC *Today* programme, hosted by Matt Lauer featuring a tour with Dan Brown through some of the locations in his book as well as interviews with key Masonic experts providing their points of view originally aired on 15 October 2009

[288] The facts, quotes and information in this paragraph and the preceding ones all come from the *Today* programme, *Secrets of The Lost Symbol*

[289] See the *Secrets of The Lost Symbol*, NBC *Today* programme, with Dan Brown, hosted by Matt Lauer

[290] This quote is from the NBC *Today* programme, aired on 15 October 2009 and is attributed to Marilyn Schlitz the director of the California Institute of Noetic Sciences, who was a guest on that show

[291] *Decoded: The Lost Symbol*, hosted by Tony Robinson, available to view at the time of writing on Channel 4 web pages, *channel4.com*

[292] See the Channel 4 programme, *Decoded: The Lost Symbol*, hosted by Tony Robinson

[293] This entire section on Robinson's quest to find truth in Brown's claims comes from *Decoded: The Lost Symbol*, published on *channel4.com*

[294] Tony Robinson summing up his quest for the truth on *Decoded: The Lost Symbol*, available on *channel4.com*.

INDEX